DISCOVER EASTERN EUROPE

PUBLISHED BY THE READER'S DIGEST ASSOCIATION LIMITED

LONDON   NEW YORK   SYDNEY   MONTREAL

DISCOVER EASTERN EUROPE

Translated and edited by Toucan Books Limited, London
for Reader's Digest, London

Translated and adapted from the French
by John Man

For Reader's Digest
Series Editor: Christine Noble
Editorial Assistant: Lucy Murray
Prepress Accounts Manager: Penny Grose

Reader's Digest General Books
Editorial Director: Cortina Butler
Art Director: Nick Clark

First English language edition Copyright © 2002
The Reader's Digest Association Limited
11 Westferry Circus, Canary Wharf, London E14 4HE
www.readersdigest.co.uk

Reprinted 2003

Copyright © 2002
Reader's Digest Association Far East Limited
Philippines copyright © 2002
Reader's Digest Association Far East Limited
All rights reserved

ISBN 0 276 42519 7

Discover the World: EASTERN EUROPE
was created and produced by
ML ÉDITIONS, Paris for Selection Reader's Digest S.A., Paris,
and first published
in 2001 as *Regards sur le Monde: L'EUROPE DE L'EST*

©2001 Selection Reader's Digest, S.A.
212 boulevard Saint-Germain, 75007, Paris

CONTENTS

POLAND

BELARUS

CZECH
REPUBLIC

UKRAINE

SLOVAKIA

HUNGARY

MOLDOVA

ROMANIA

BULGARIA

Introducing Eastern Europe

In the early 1990s, a political hurricane tore down the Iron Curtain that divided Europe. Western nations suddenly had to reacquaint themselves with the 'other Europeans', who had been hidden behind the curtain for two generations. From the Baltic coastal plains across the Carpathian Mountains to the Black Sea, the countries of Poland, the Czech Republic, Slovakia, Hungary, Belarus, Ukraine, Romania, Bulgaria and Moldova sought to restate their independent identities.

Old and new nations

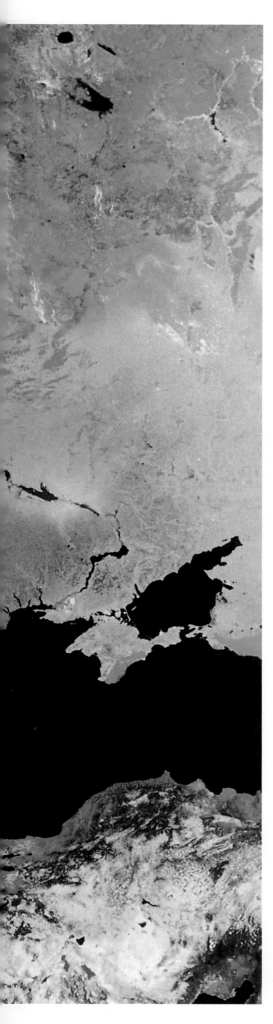

For the greater part of the 20th century, the words 'Eastern Europe' suggested a definable region beyond the Iron Curtain that included the satellite states of the Soviet Union. But with the breakup of the USSR in 1991 that definition was no longer applicable.

The quest to understand Eastern Europe as it is today goes beyond politics. Geography and climate combine to make the region a transition zone linking the maritime countries of Western Europe to the huge expanse of Eurasia. Far from the moderating influence of the Atlantic Ocean, Eastern Europe has hot summers and severe winters – but it tends not to be as cold as in some parts of Russia.

The nine countries featured in this book – Poland, the Czech Republic, Slovakia, Hungary, Romania, Bulgaria, Belarus, Moldova and Ukraine – cover an area similar in size to Western Europe. Their political borders have been redrawn over the centuries, but it is possible to cut through political and historical complexities and see the region in terms of four different areas. To the north is the Baltic seaboard, with its outward-looking ports. To the east, forest and well-farmed plains sweep towards Russia. Across the centre runs the spine of the Carpathian Mountains, giving way to the valley of the Danube. To the south-east, the nations touching the shores of the Black Sea butt against the Balkans, with their melee of cultures, languages and religions.

A constant ebb and flow of peoples has swept this region first closer to Western influences, then farther from them, and back again. The land between the Baltic and the Carpathians provided a passable route to the west for tribes in search of a better life. Many settled here rather than continue on their journeys, and gave the region its rich mixture of national and local identities.

From the late 18th century, emergent nation-states sought to carve ethnic units out of multicultural empires. But in a region in which overlapping groups have found it impossible to agree on frontiers, nationalism often led to conflict. In the second half of the 20th century, however, nationalist feeling was kept on ice by the socialist philosophy and the political influence of the Soviet Union.

The fall of the Berlin Wall and the collapse of Soviet control revived old enmities and ambitions. East Germany, once firmly part of Soviet Eastern Europe, reunited with its western sibling, the Federal Republic. Three Soviet republics – Ukraine, Belarus and Moldova – emerged as independent states.

At one time such changes would have sparked wars. Instead, the Eastern European nations opted for negotiated solutions. Czechs and Slovaks parted by agreement, while Ukraine, Belarus and Moldova established their independence in relative peace.

As in the rest of Europe, the capitals of these nations display evidence of the glories and turmoils of the past. They bear the scars of the Second World War, and evidence of Soviet rule can be seen in the starkly functional architecture. Out of town, in the midst of remarkably well-preserved landscapes, there are pockets of appalling pollution caused by poorly managed industrial complexes – the legacy of years of communist rule.

Today, the states of Eastern Europe are seeking to redress the balance and re-establish their deeper historical roots as they build a future for themselves.

Bridging the continent   A satellite image shows Eastern Europe from the Baltic to the Black Sea. The area covers nine nations: Poland, the Czech Republic, Slovakia, Hungary, Romania, Bulgaria, Belarus, Moldova and Ukraine.

Marching sands The shifting dunes of Slowinski National Park on Poland's northern coast are one of the country's most remarkable natural features. The 46 000 acre (18 618 ha) reserve includes a stretch of shoreline between the Baltic and Lake Lebsko along which the main ridge of the dunes reaches a height of 132 ft (40 m) and extends for 3 miles (5 km). Every year, winds blow the dunes another 30 ft (10 m) inland, burying everything in its path, including the forest, and creating a desert-like landscape.

Smothered by the dunes Slowinski National Park is known for its forests of dwarf pines as well as its mountainous dunes. But the trees are progressively overwhelmed by the shifting sands. Decades later, as the sands move on, the skeletal remains of the woods re-emerge.

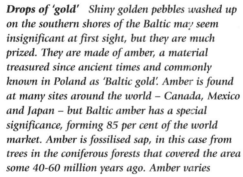

Drops of 'gold' Shiny golden pebbles washed up on the southern shores of the Baltic may seem insignificant at first sight, but they are much prized. They are made of amber, a material treasured since ancient times and commonly known in Poland as 'Baltic gold'. Amber is found at many sites around the world – Canada, Mexico and Japan – but Baltic amber has a special significance, forming 85 per cent of the world market. Amber is fossilised sap, in this case from trees in the coniferous forests that covered the area some 40-60 million years ago. Amber varies considerably in appearance, depending on the tree from which it originated. A drop may be more or less translucent, with or without little air bubbles, or grains of sand, or tiny scraps of vegetable matter. To the delight of palaeontologists, it may sometimes even contain a fossilised insect, frozen and eternally preserved. Such finds are rare; most Baltic amber – technically known as succinite – goes to jewellers, in particular to specialists in Gdansk who have long been experts at setting it in rings, pendants and brooches, or carving it into little golden-hued figurines, pipe stalks and cigarette holders.

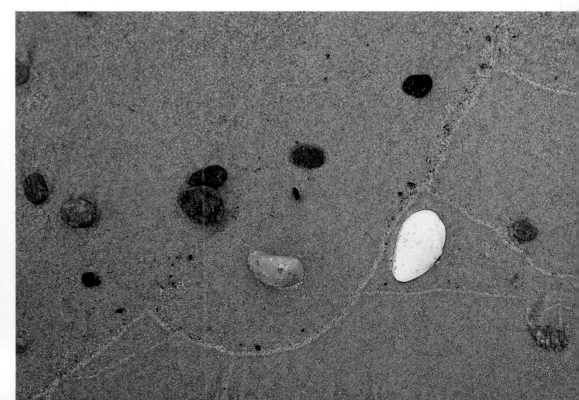

Mountain beauty A waterfall tumbles from the upper reaches of the River Vratna in the Mála Fatra range of north-western Slovakia. The peaks, rising to 5600 ft (1700 m), are part of the tangle of mountains that span the Czech, Polish and Slovak borders, gaining height as they run eastwards into the Carpathians. This region is celebrated for its charming villages, country roads, woods and streams. The village of Terchova is renowned locally as the reputed birthplace of the outlaw Juraj Janosik, a kind of Slovak 'Robin Hood'.

Hungarian idyll The headwaters of the River Szalajka carve steps in the Bükk Mountains of north-eastern Hungary. The surrounding forests of oak and ash make up the Bükk National Park, which is home to a wide variety of birds, such as the green woodpecker. The mountains are honeycombed with caves cut out by streams at the end of the last Ice Age.

Wild headland   Cape Kaliakra juts into the Black Sea a few miles north of the Bulgarian town of Varna. The rocky headland is one of the few remaining areas of wilderness along a coastline dominated by resorts from the border with Turkey northwards. In ancient times it was a base for Greek shipping, and a Greek fort remained in use on Kaliakra until the Turkish occupation in the late 14th century. This event was the source of a local legend, according to which 40 girls escaped from the Turks and, tied together by their hair, cast themselves into the sea from the cliffs.

Holiday playground   Olive, laurel and cypress trees dot Ukraine's rugged Crimean coast, renowned for its dramatic scenery and favourable climate. The winters are mild and in summer sea breezes relieve the heat. In the valleys, orchards and vineyards flourish. These Mediterranean-like conditions have attracted visitors to the Crimea since the 1860s when the Russian imperial family began to holiday here. Tsar Nicholas II built a palace at Livadia.

Black Sea spa Rocks protect the sandy beaches of Eforie, one of Romania's many Black Sea resorts. Tourists have been coming to the spa town since the early 20th century to sunbathe, swim, or take advantage of the saline hot springs and muds. These owe their existence to a nearby lake, Techirghiol, which is six times saltier than the Black Sea.

Poland's artery The Vistula, Poland's greatest river, has its headwaters in the Carpathian Mountains, near the country's southern border. It cuts right across the country as it flows northwards to the Baltic, linking the country's historic cities of Kraków, Warsaw, Torun and Gdansk. Its length alone (664 miles/1069 km) gives it the status of a national symbol.

Mighty waterway The Dnieper, Europe's third largest river after the Volga and the Danube, is the major waterway of Belarus and Ukraine. Rising 160 miles (250 km) south-west of Moscow, the Dnieper flows for 1375 miles (2200 km) southwards, through the Ukrainian capital of Kiev to the Black Sea. Its upper reaches cross swampy lowlands and then water the immense and fertile plains of Ukraine. Rapids at Zaporojie in southern Ukraine prevented navigation on this stretch of the river until 1932 when Soviet engineers completed the Dniproges Hydroelectric Dam, the largest power station in Europe at that time. The dam raised the river by 120 ft (36 m), eradicated the rapids and opened this section to navigation. The river's lower reaches, which once broke up into swamps and backwaters, were also transformed by a dam, which created the Kachovka Reservoir, a lake more than 100 miles (160 km) long. From the reservoir, the 250 mile (402 km) North Crimea Canal, built in 1971, provides irrigation for the Black Sea lowlands and links the Dnieper with the Sea of Azov.

Natural wonderland   Terns flutter across reedbeds in the Danube delta, which covers a huge area of swamps and side channels in Romania's eastern lowlands. The delta measures 1600 sq miles (4000 km²), one-tenth of which forms one of Europe's largest nature reserves. The area, on the main migration route between Siberia and Africa, offers sanctuary to vast numbers of birds. It is one of the few places in Europe where pelicans can be found. Other species include cormorants, flamingos, egrets, swans and storks. The waters of the delta contain more than 100 species of fish, and its woodlands of willow, poplar, oak and ash shelter ermines, otters, foxes, stoats and minks.

Rich harvest Poppies bloom in a field near Lake Balaton in Hungary. They were among the first crops cultivated by humans, a practice that is thought to have spread from south-west Asia to Western Europe, before reaching Eastern Europe. The shores of the 230 sq mile (596 km²) lake have rich volcanic soils which are especially suited to their growth. Though the best known of the 200 species is the one that produces opium, Hungary's poppies are grown for their seeds, which make oil and bread-seasoning. Nowadays, poppies are also much in demand for their decorative, papery blooms.

Reaching for the light With their slim white trunks and silvery leaves, birches like these in Belarus are one of the commonest sights in all northern forests. They have many uses: their even-grained wood makes them ideal for the manufacture of furniture. Traditionally, the bark was used by peasants to make rough shoes known as lapti. Birch sap is the main ingredient in a popular drink; it is also used in folk remedies.

Threatened sanctuary A meadow in the Czech Republic's Sumava National Park, which runs along the country's mountainous south-western border with Germany. Sumava forms the Czech part of the Bohemian Forest, which was preserved in pristine condition as a remote and inaccessible corner of the Soviet empire. In the early 1990s, with the Iron Curtain gone and the forest open for exploitation, UNESCO declared the area's spruce trees, peat bogs and glacial lakes to be of unique importance as part of what was termed the 'green roof of Europe'. But since then the forest has suffered from two kinds of assault: a natural one from bark beetles and a human one from loggers. In ten years its untouched core shrank from 22 per cent of the park to scattered enclaves amounting to only 13 per cent.

Natural arch Pravcicka Gate, a rock-bridge in the north-western mountains of the Czech Republic, is the symbol of an area known as 'Czech Switzerland'. The arch, 52 ft (16 m) high and 85 ft (26 m) across, is one of many outcrops created from the soft, golden sandstone that forms this part of the Erzgebirge (Ore Mountains). The Germans mined gold, tin, copper and iron here. And it was Germans from the neighbouring province of Saxony who gave the area its name, when the 18th-century Swiss painter Adrian Zinng was commissioned to record the landscape by Saxony's ruler. On his many visits with his engraver Anton Graff, Zinng fell in love with the mountains, and referred to them as 'Saxony's Switzerland', a nickname later adapted by the Czechs. Pravcicka Gate has always drawn visitors, who used to enjoy walking over it until it was declared unsafe in 1980. Today, the surrounding area is popular with hikers eager to explore the ravines and odd-looking outcrops. They also come in hope of seeing rare species such as black storks and peregrine falcons. The region was declared a national park in 2000.

Barrier and hideout The Rhodope Mountains (seen in the background) seldom rise above 6600 ft (2000 m), but they form a formidable barrier separating Bulgaria from Greece. One of the only ways through them is to follow valleys carved by the Struma and the Mesta rivers. Dominated by the massif of Musala (9596 ft/ 2925 m), the range protects Greece from cold northern winds. Its wild forests and remote valleys provided hiding places for rebellious Slavs during the 400-year rule of the Turks from the 15th to the 19th centuries.

A brief history

The peoples of Eastern Europe have always lived between two worlds: the open plains of the Asian nomads to the east, and the settled, urbanised cultures of the Atlantic and Mediterranean seaboards to the west.

Their land has been crossed continually over thousands of years by tribesmen seeking either to conquer or join their western neighbours – and sometimes both at once. In a sense, variations on this ancient theme are still being played today, as Eastern Europeans, left to fend for themselves

Pensive figures   Statuettes uncovered in graves in Romania date from c.5000 BC.

when the Soviet tide retreated in the 1990s, strive to find a balance between past and present, between East and West.

The mystery of the first arrivals

Ancestral humans – *Homo erectus*, Neanderthals, and our own *Homo sapiens* – crisscrossed Eastern Europe from 300 000 years ago. But the area's human history

Protected site   A model of a village near Biskupin, Poland, c.700-400 BC, shows a stockade, which indicates warfare in the region.

starts after the end of the last Ice Age, around 6000 BC, when hunter-gatherers first learned how to farm. Their 'tells' – mounds formed by disintegrating mud houses – have been found in the Balkans, Bulgaria, Romania and Ukraine. Later, 'Danubian' farmers, so named after their main archaeological sites along the River Danube, built large communal houses, used polished stone axes and buried their dead in cemeteries – techniques and traits that were used right across central Europe. Around 2500 BC, these peasant communities pioneered the use of bronze alloys to make tougher and more complex tools, which they traded across the continent.

Tribes on the move

Over the next 3000 years, Eastern Europe witnessed a succession of different cultures – Celts from the west, Romans from the south, Germans from the north and Asiatic nomads from the east.

The Celts emerged from Alpine Europe and spread out across the continent, forming an unruly eastern frontier with the Roman Empire in the 1st century BC. By then both the Romans and the Celts faced a new challenge: Germanic tribes who were

Thracians and Dacians

Both the Thracians and their neighbours the Dacians had lived in present-day Greece, Bulgaria and Romania long before the rise of Greek civilisation around 750 BC. They spoke an Indo-European language, but their origins are unknown. They were skilful goldsmiths. The Greeks adopted a god, Dionysus, from the Thracians, but regarded them as intractable barbarians, best left alone. The area remained a buffer zone between competing empires until Rome seized it in AD 106. The brutal conquest of Dacia imposed Roman culture, as reflected in Romania's name and language.

*Thracian treasure
A Greek-inspired gold drinking horn.*

expanding from the north. An overwhelming German victory in the Teutoberg Forest in AD 9 forced the Romans back to the Rhine and opened the way for German expansion to the lower Danube.

The final chapter in these epic tribal migrations belongs to the eastern nomads, shifting westwards from the Central Asian grasslands. The Scythians – accomplished

Artistic tribute   Thracian artistry is revealed in a fresco found in a 4th-century BC tomb in Bulgaria.

Holy Roman Empire

Being integrated into Holy Roman Empire

Kievan state

Byzantine Empire

Arab caliphates

VLACHS Tribal areas

Rival Christian capitals after Schism of 1054

Nomadic cook pots These 6th-century bronze cauldrons from Hungary reveal the presence of Huns at the time their empire was collapsing.

horsemen and archers – dominated the open plains of present-day Ukraine until the arrival of another nomadic people, the Sarmatians. From the 2nd to the 4th centuries AD, Sarmatians and Germans together assaulted Rome's eastern frontier, seizing present-day Romania. A third group of nomads, the Huns, ended Sarmatian rule. By the early 5th century, Northern Europe was a battleground between three competing groups: the nomads, Germans and Romans. With the collapse

Christian leanings The crown of Hungary c. 1000.

Russian conversion The baptism in 988 of the Varangian prince Vladimir, ruler of Kievan Rus, brought Orthodoxy to Russia.

of Rome, the two surviving cultures fought themselves to a standstill, a long, slow process that left Eastern Europe a patchwork of Germanic kingdoms interspersed with formerly Asian peoples, such as Slavs and Bulgars. As Latin Christendom developed in Western Europe, a final nomadic invasion around 900 brought the Magyars – who originated in the Urals – to their present homeland, Hungary, and the great age of migrations ended.

The rise of the Rus

The quest for trade, booty and new lands to colonise continued to occupy even the settled peoples. In Eastern Europe, the most ambitious were the Scandinavians, better known as the Varangians or Vikings. Brilliant sailors, restless adventurers, dynamic traders and notoriously ruthless, the Varangians ranged around the entire European coast and across the Atlantic. They also worked their way inland, exploring the 'river roads' across Eastern Europe, such as the Dvina and Dnieper. They were drawn by the wealth of Constantinople and the Byzantine Empire, and

the emergent world of Islam. Varangian and Slav settlements grew up along the rivers, including the principality of Polatsk, the future core of Belarus, and the medieval kingdom of Kievan Rus, the seedbed of modern Russia and its Orthodoxy. In Kiev, capital of modern-day Ukraine, the Varangians adopted Christianity from Constantinople with the conversion of Prince Vladimir in 988.

The coming of Cyrillic

In the 9th century, Moravia (now part of the Czech Republic) and Bulgaria were caught between rival empires, Rome and Constantinople. The Duke of Moravia commissioned two Slavonic-speaking brothers, Cyril and Methodius, as missionaries. He asked them to prepare a Slav translation of the scriptures. Cyril adapted the Greek alphabet to Slavonic, naming it Glagolitic (from the Slavonic *glagola*, 'word'). After his brother died, Methodius led the expedition to Bulgaria. There, under St Clement, a version of Cyril's alphabet took root, which was to form the basis of Russian Cyrillic.

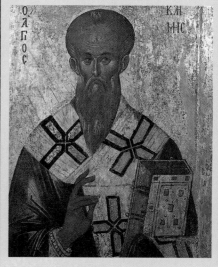

St Clement in a 14th-century icon.

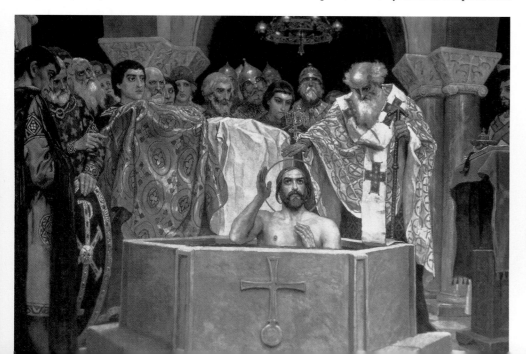

Northern barrier *Malbork, the fortress of the Teutonic Knights in northern Poland, blocked Polish access to the Baltic.*

The heretical Huss

In 1415 the people of Bohemia (now part of the Czech Republic) rebelled. They resented German domination and church corruption and had turned to the reforming cleric, Jan Huss. Huss was inspired by the translator of the English Bible, John Wycliffe. He, too, wanted to read the Bible and worship God in his own language. Huss was excommunicated for his outspoken criticism of ecclesiastical practices. In 1414, he was given a safe-conduct pass to appear before the Council of Constance. But, soon after arriving in Constance he was seized for preaching against papal orders. At his

Victim of treachery *Huss is burned at the stake in Constance in July 1415.*

trial he was prevented from defending himself and stoically refused to recant. In 1415 he was burned at the stake. His followers, the Hussites, rose up, drawing Pope and Empire into a 16-year war. In 1436, the Pope gave in to Czech demands, but the wounds remained. A century later, many Czechs became Protestant.

Genghis Khan's reign of tyranny

Eastern Europe's cultural and political borders were showing signs of permanence; but this was not the end of the ancient rivalry between nomads, Germans and Slavs. From the 10th century, Germans pushed eastwards, beyond the Elbe, colonising Slav lands, seizing Slavic locals as servants (thus

Prague's mentor *Charles IV, Holy Roman Emperor, turned Prague into a glorious capital.*

giving European languages the word 'slave'). In the 13th century, a new menace surged out of Central Asia – the Mongols of Ghengis Khan, bent not on migration, but destruction. Their mounted archers shattered armies in Poland and Hungary, bringing devastation to most of Eastern Europe. Stories of the horrors of that time remain alive in legend today. Some of Ghengis's heirs, known as Tatars, settled in Ukraine, where they ruled as the 'Golden Horde' (from Mongol *orda*, 'palace') for 200 years, a time referred to by Russians as the 'Tatar Yoke'.

A golden age

A turning point came in 1380 when the Muscovite Prince Dmitri defeated the Mongols on the Field of Kulikovo. The end of the Mongol menace allowed Eastern Europe to become an integral part of the continent socially, politically, intellectually and artistically. Charles IV (1346-78), king of Bohemia, Holy Roman Emperor and one of the most brilliant men of his time, turned Prague into the empire's leading city. In 1348, he established the university that still bears his name – the empire's first, rivalling Paris, Oxford and Bologna.

By exploiting its gold mines, Hungary completed its transformation from a base for nomad

raids into a wealthy kingdom stretching from the Adriatic to the Carpathians. In the north, Poles battling against the Teutonic Knights, a military order set on building a German colony, joined Lithuania in 1386. The result was a powerful new entity reaching from the Baltic to the Black Sea, to balance Russian influence.

The rulers of these young kingdoms – such as Hungary's Matthias Corvinus (1458-90) – matched their western rivals in power, wealth and ambition. To grace their burgeoning capitals, they attracted scholars and artists from France and Italy. Prague, Pest and Kraków acquired immense libraries and art collections. For two cen-

Eastern Europe, late 15th century

☐ Borders of Holy Roman Empire	Teutonic Order	Russian state
Habsburg possessions	Venice and dependencies	Poland-Lithuania (united monarchy)
Bohemia		
Other states of Holy Roman Empire	Ottoman Empire	Sweden-Denmark (united monarchy)

Medieval masterwork *A pentaptych depicting the life of Christ adorns the Church of St Mary, Kraków, Poland. The central doors open to reveal the five-panelled altarpiece, which was completed by Veit Stoss, a German sculptor, in 1489.*

turies, it seemed that Eastern Europe might one day dominate the West. But two unrelated events reversed the course of medieval history.

The coming of the Turks

The first event was a menace from the south: the Turks had been advancing from Central Asia for more than 300 years. The Byzantine Empire – the Orthodox heir to the Roman Empire's eastern wing – collapsed under their onslaughts. In 1353, the Turks made the symbolic step across the Dardanelles, from Asia to Europe. Though their progress was slowed by the sudden rise and catastrophic invasions of Tamerlane (Timur) in the east, Turkish advances continued, isolating Constantinople. In 1453, the great city fell, and with it the world of eastern Christian Orthodoxy. Turkish

Revered monarch *Matthias Corvinus (1443-90), one of the few kings to bring stability to Hungary.*

armies swept on northwards, seizing all the southern Balkans, inflicting a stunning defeat on Hungarian troops at Mohács in 1526. Hungary never recovered from this disaster. It lost two-thirds of the country to the Ottoman Empire.

The rise of the Habsburgs

At the beginning of the 16th century, the Habsburg family rose to 'sudden and immoderate greatness,' in the words of the

Astronomy's leading light

The scientific revolution that started in the mid 16th century has been called the 'most important event in European history since the rise of Christianity'. It was rooted in astronomy, and in the work of a Polish scholar, Nicholas Copernicus (1473-1543). The son of a merchant, he studied in Kraków and Bologna before becoming a canon in the Polish town of Frombork (Frauenburg). He was fascinated with astronomy, but unhappy with the theory that the Earth was the centre of the Solar System. By 1514, he had formulated his idea that the Sun lay at the centre. He hesitated for 30 years before publishing, and only saw his work, *On the Revolutions of the Celestial Spheres*, in print on the day he died. Acceptance of Copernicus's heliocentric system took almost a century. He is regarded as the founder of modern astronomy.

Nicholas Copernicus

Hungary's downfall *An Ottoman illustration depicts the Turks' victory at the Battle of Mohács, 1526, against the Hungarian king, Louis II, and his 20 000-strong army. The Turks moved north to capture Pest and Buda.*

Fall from grace Czechs toss German officials from Prague's palace window in 1618, an event that sparks the Thirty Years' War.

Bohemia shattered At the Battle of White Mountain in 1620, imperial troops won a decisive victory over the Czechs, and went on to root out Protestantism in Bohemia.

historian Norman Davies. Their success was due principally to the making of good marriages and the decline of rival dynasties. Charles V (1500-58) embodied the dream of a united Europe. Burgundy, Tirol, Bohemia, the Netherlands, Austria, Hungary, Spain, Italy, as well as Peru and the Philippines, were either ruled directly by Charles V or he exercised influence over them by marriage or relations. But the rise of Protestantism destroyed for ever his hopes for a united Christendom.

In 1522, Charles consigned his eastern dominions to his brother, Ferdinand, to whom the terrified Czechs and Hungarians turned when the Turks were victorious at Mohács. Ferdinand held the Turks at bay, restored an uneasy peace over warring Catholics and Protestants, and ensured Habsburg hereditary rule over Hungary and Bohemia.

Europe in turmoil

Protestant Bohemia remained resentful of its Catholic rulers. In 1618, the people reacted angrily when officials tried to prevent the construction of two Protestant churches. Prague's citizens tossed two imperial representatives out of the palace window – they fell 50 ft (15 m), but survived. The incident, the Defenestration of Prague, marked the start of the Thirty Years' War. This conflict, which drew in most of Europe north of the Alps, comprised several different wars: Catholics versus Protestants, Germany's princes versus the emperor, state versus state. In an early phase, Czechs were beaten by imperial troops at the Battle of Bilá hora (Weissenberg, or White Mountain) in 1620. It was followed by

Border guard Cossacks defended the Polish, later Russian, frontier against the Turks. In the 17th century they rose up in rebellion.

Turkish tolerance

Unlike Europe's Christian rulers, the Islamic Ottoman sultans made no attempt to convert their 'infidel' subjects in Bulgaria, Hungary, Romania, Greece and the Balkans. Christian or Jew, they were free to practise and teach in their own ways, as long as they paid their taxes (higher for non-Muslims) and remained peaceful within their *millet* (group). The Gregorian *millet* proved particularly useful to the Turks, ruling not only the Armenians, but also other minority groups, such as the Gypsies and Bogomils.

brutal repression. Czech nobles were executed and their lands were confiscated and given to German Catholics. The people suffered as hungry armies rampaged across Europe. By the final peace treaty, signed in Westphalia in 1648, France emerged as a dominant power, while in the Holy Roman Empire, Catholics and Protestants were acknowledged as equals.

With some peace and stability restored, Eastern Europe fought back against the Ottomans. The Austrians drove the Turks from Vienna and recaptured Buda in 1686 (it was not to be united with Pest for another 200 years). The Turkish frontier hardened farther south, across the Balkans.

Rivals for the borderlands

Russia finally freed itself from the 'Tatar Yoke' in 1480 and embarked on a long process of consolidation and expansion in the Baltic, Poland and southwards in Ukraine and Crimea.

Ukraine, long disputed between Russia and Poland, was a wild area in the hands of local Cossacks (from the Turkic word

Chosen to rule

Before the Habsburgs imposed a hereditary monarchy, the kings of Bohemia, Hungary and Poland were elected by a diet (assembly) of nobles. The system was at its most extreme in Poland, which was in effect a republic of nobles. A king might be chosen to rule more than one country, which was a cause of much dispute and instability. Matthias Corvinus, Vladislas II and his son, Louis, each ruled

both Bohemia and Hungary (Louis, notorious for loose living, lost a large part of Hungary to the Turks at the Battle of Mohács in 1526). Two kings, Louis I in the 14th century and Vladislas III in the 15th, both ruled Hungary and Poland.

*Switching allegiances
The Polish diet elects Henry of Valois king in 1573. In 1574 he returned to France as Henry III, leaving Poland in chaos.*

1772

1793

1795

Polish frontier
To Russia
To Austria
To Prussia

The Partition of Poland

The people's warrior *Tadeusz Kosciuszko, hero of Polish national resistance, is wounded in battle against the Russians in 1794.*

kozak, meaning 'outlaw'). Posing as the protector of the Orthodox against the Turks, Russia fought her way to the Black Sea, finally seizing Crimea from the Ottomans in the late 18th century.

Facing threats from Russia along its eastern and southern borders, Poland confronted another rival to the north-east, Prussia. When its old adversaries, the Teutonic Knights, were crushed in 1525, they left a German enclave on the Baltic that emerged in the 18th century as the new kingdom of Prussia. Prussia rose to power under its German rulers, the Hohenzollerns.

Hungarian victory *After a devastating siege, the Duke of Lorraine captures Buda from the Turks in 1686, securing it for Habsburg rule.*

Regal ruler   Under Maria Theresa, queen of Bohemia and Hungary (1745-80), the Habsburgs dominated Eastern Europe.

The end of Poland

Poland escaped the worst of the Thirty Years' War, but suffered attacks by Ukrainian Cossacks on her southern flanks in the second half of the 17th century. In 1655 Sweden invaded, took Warsaw, and seized Poland's Baltic territory. The country never recovered its strength from the five years of Swedish occupation, which became known as 'The Deluge'.

A century later, Austria, Russia and Prussia tore at Poland's frontiers, steadily reducing her size. The humiliation inspired Tadeusz Kosciuszko, a hero of the War of American Independence, to return home

Triumph of the Baroque

Wartime destruction in Eastern Europe in the 17th century gave architects the opportunity to rebuild on a grand scale. They did so in the Baroque style favoured by the victorious rulers, who were mainly Catholic supporters of the Counter Reformation. This was an age of absolutism, in which rulers aimed to achieve total control. Their palaces, churches and monasteries were richly decorated with ornate plasterwork, gilding and paintings, and exuded the wealth and power to which they aspired.

Painted gallery   Baroque decoration in the library of Prague's Strahof monastery.

25

Scholars and poets rally to the cause

In their struggle to found nations, people used their own languages and history as weapons to establish their rights. Slovak became a literary language only when the Protestant linguist and patriot Ľudovítstúr (1815-56) began to use it. Czech identity owed a debt to the nation's first historian, Frantisek Palacky (1798-1876). Poets, such as the Romanian Mihail Eminescu and the Hungarian Sándor Petöfi captured in verse the romantic spirit of national revival. They remain heroes in their countries to this day.

Voice of passion *Sándor Petöfi, revolutionary and author of the Hungarian national anthem.*

Romantic agony *The Russian eagle preys on a Poland flattened by the 1830 revolution.*

and lead a national uprising. It failed. In a final battle with the Russians, Kosciuszko was captured, and according to legend cried *'Finis Poloniae!'* (Poland is finished). In 1795 Poland vanished from the map of Europe and, except for a brief resurgence in 1812-15, it did not reappear until 1918.

Decades of revolution

At the end of the 18th century, four great entities – the Russian, Habsburg, Ottoman and Holy Roman empires – divided Eastern Europe between them. Elsewhere, in France and the USA, new ideas of government inspired revolution. For 25 years, the wars unleashed by Napoleon seemed likely to redraw the map of Europe, until the

Czechs humbled *Prague burns in June 1848 as Austrian troops bombard the rebellious city, prior to setting up a military dictatorship.*

Congress of Vienna in 1815 once again locked Europe into imperial borders.

But across Central and Eastern Europe the new ideas had taken root. Nationalist revivals were gathering force. In 1830, Polish nationalists rose against Russia, only to be brutally crushed the following year. In the Habsburg Empire, Hungarians, Croats, Czechs and other minorities all sought self-determination. In Germany, still comprising numerous mini-states, there were moves towards unification.

These forces led to an outburst of unrest across Europe in 1848, in what became known as the 'Year of Revolutions'. Violence spread from Italy and France to Austria, Hungary and Germany.

The Habsburg emperor, Ferdinand, vacillated. He granted a new constitution, then turned on revolutionaries in both Prague and Vienna. Under pressure from hardliners, he abdicated, leaving his successor,

Franz Joseph, to complete his policy of suppression the following year.

Meanwhile, Hungarians proclaimed their independence, only to have their hopes dashed four months later. In Germany, a national assembly in Frankfurt offered the throne of a united nation to the Prussian king; he refused, and unity was postponed for another 30 years.

Resurgent Habsburgs

Faced with the loss of possessions in Italy and with the rise of a rival in Prussia, the Habsburg dynasty reasserted its hold on its empire.

Still under pressure from Hungarians eager for autonomy, in 1867 Emperor Franz Joseph agreed to a federation between Austria and Hungary, by which Hungarians could administer their half of the empire – to the consternation of Czechs, Slovaks and Romanians.

Nevertheless, the creation of 'Austria-Hungary' stabilised the empire. For the next 50 years, the cities of Vienna, Prague and Budapest grew ever richer, both economically and culturally.

Imperial family *The autocratic but revered emperor of Austria and king of Hungary, Franz Joseph (1830-1916), with his wife, Elizabeth, and children, at the chateau of Gödöllo in 1869.*

Bulgarian vengeance *Two of the notorious Turkish irregulars, or* bashi-bazouks, *hanged by Bulgarians in the Balkan Wars, 1912-13.*

Balkan battle *Russians attack the Turks in 1877, aiding the cause of Bulgarian independence. Bulgaria became a Russian satellite state the following year.*

Imperial repression

To the north, Prussia continued its rise as the most powerful of the German states, a process that led in 1871 to the foundation of a German empire.

In Germany, the Polish population, though denied their own voice, at least benefited from Germany's rapid industrial growth. Poles living in the Austrian province of Galicia had a measure of autonomy. But in Russia, the fate of Poles was very different. An uprising in 1863-4 was brutally put down by Moscow, which decreed that Russian should replace Polish in Polish schools and Roman Catholicism should be outlawed. Moscow behaved in a similar way

Austria-Hungary in 1914

■ Germans	■ Poles	■ Serbs and Croats	■ Slovenes	■ Romanians
□ Czechs and Slovaks	■ Ukrainians		■ Italians	■ Hungarians

in Ukraine and Belarus. In Ukraine, nationalists had tried to emulate the freedoms achieved by their fellow Ukrainians (known as Ruthenians) in Galicia. But in 1876, Russia forbade the use of the Ukrainian language in schools and publications.

In Belarus, the local Uniate Church was abolished in 1839, and publishing in Belarussian banned.

Balkan uprising

The Romanians, too, wanted self-determination. In 1828, Russia advanced into the Romanian provinces of

Pumping oil *Peasant workers in Romania are employed to construct oil wells in the early 20th century.*

Wallachia and Moldavia, creating a buffer zone with the Ottoman Empire.

The major powers jostled for control of the region until 1878, when Romania's independence was eventually recognised by the Treaty of Berlin. But many Romanians remained either in Russian-held eastern Moldavia (Bessarabia) or in Hungarian-held Transylvania.

In the region's most bitter struggle, the Bulgarian uprising against the Ottomans in 1876 was put down with great brutality – 15 000 people were killed, 58 villages destroyed – events that became infamous in the English-speaking world as the 'Bulgarian Horrors.' The small Bulgarian

The rise and fall of an empire

At the beginning of the 20th century, the Austro-Hungarian Empire covered a vast area of Europe, including parts of Poland, Ukraine, Yugoslavia, Italy, Romania and what was to become Czechoslovakia. Its population totalled 51 million. The empire had come into being in 1867 under Franz Joseph, but it was beset by nationalistic unrest. In 1914, the heir to the throne, Archduke Franz Ferdinand, was assassinated by a Serbian nationalist. Austria-Hungary invaded Serbia in retaliation, a move that precipitated the First World War and led to the downfall of the empire in 1918.

Peace talks   *German, Austrian and Russian leaders gather in Brest-Litovsk late in 1917 to agree terms to end Russia's involvement in the First World War. The peace treaty was signed early in 1918.*

Brief coup   *Béla Kun (centre) announces a communist coup in Hungary in 1919. He faced strong opposition and fled five months later.*

state that emerged in 1878 was a core that Bulgarian nationalists sought to expand in complex disputes between Greece, Serbia, Bulgaria and four other Balkan mini-states. Two Balkan Wars (1912-13) achieved no final conclusion before spilling over into the First World War.

The end of empires

In June 1914, a Serbian nationalist assassinated an Austro-Hungarian archduke – and heir to the emperor – in Sarajevo. Austria-Hungary, with support from Germany,

attacked Serbia; Russia mobilised its forces in support of Serbia. Europe, and the world, descended into war. At the end of the bloodletting in 1918, the old empires of Germany and Austria-Hungary were gone, and a new one, Soviet Russia, had emerged. The peacemakers in Versailles backed the ideal of self-determination, and new nations rose from the imperial ruins. Hungary and Austria went their separate ways. Croats, Slovenes and Serbs united in Yugoslavia. Poland was reborn, Czechoslovakia was created, as were the Baltic nations of

Estonia, Latvia and Lithuania. Bulgaria lost territory to its neighbours, in punishment for siding with Germany and Austria. Romania seized Transylvania from Hungary.

No end to conflict

Self-determination proved an elusive ideal. Many ethnic groups remained embedded among others – Germans in Poland, Hungarians in Transylvania, Macedonians in Greece, Bulgaria and Yugoslavia – storing trouble for the future. Peace was confirmed in 1919-21 by the Treaty of Versailles and

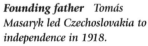

Eastern Europe in 1923

Map legend:
- States created after the war
- States that regained their independence
- Defeated states of the First World War
- States that increased their territory
- States that remained neutral
- Territories where referendums were held in 1920-21
- Territories under international administration

Founding father   *Tomás Masaryk led Czechoslovakia to independence in 1918.*

State visit   *Hitler honours Admiral Miklós Horthy, Hungary's conservative and pro-Nazi head of state, in 1938.*

After peace, more war

Western Europeans remember Armistice Day, November 11, 1918, as the end of the First World War. In the east, however, war dragged on into the 1920s. In 1918, Romania invaded Hungary, seizing Transylvania, and then in 1919, took control of Budapest itself for three months. Hungary was torn by a brief communist revolution, led by Béla Kun, before falling to right-wing nationalists under Miklós Horthy. In 1920, Poland seized Ukraine, only to be expelled by a revolutionary Russian army, but extended its frontier into both Belarus and Ukraine, before these two states joined the USSR in 1922.

the four adjuncts – the treaties of St Germain, Neuilly, Trianon and Sèvres – which confirmed gains and losses in Eastern Europe. But the treaties did little to address the root causes of unrest, and by imposing reparations on a defeated Germany, fuelled future conflict.

Peace might have had a chance, given economic progress. But in 1929, the Wall Street Crash in the USA ushered in a global economic downturn which came to be known as the Depression. The impact on the embittered and impoverished nations of Eastern Europe was dire. Everywhere – except in the region's one true democracy, Czechoslovakia – right-wing regimes came to power, asserting the causes of nationalism over international cooperation.

The greatest threat came from the most traumatised nation, Germany, where Adolf Hitler came to power in 1933, demanding

Cheers for Hitler *Sudeten Germans celebrate the Nazi takeover of their region of Czechoslovakia in September 1938.*

vengeance, and the fulfilment of Germany's historic 'eastward urge' (*Drang nach Osten*) by the creation of 'living space' in Slav lands. The first casualty in Eastern Europe was Czechoslovakia. Abandoned by her allies, the Munich Agreement of 1938 handed the rich western region, the Sudetenland, to Germany. Within a year, the Czechs were Nazi subjects, the Slovaks under German 'protection', and the nation dismembered. With German agreement, Hungary seized eastern Slovakia and Poland took its northern area of Teschen.

War, and a new order

Western nations hoped this was the end of Hitler's territorial ambitions. It was just a beginning. Next he turned to Poland, and the German enclave of East Prussia. Union between the two could only be achieved at the expense of Poland. A peace treaty with the Soviet Union removed Hitler's major source of opposition. The Soviet-German Non-Aggression Pact was, in effect, a cyni-

cal agreement to divide Poland between two dictators, Hitler and Stalin. Hitler was already dreaming of further war, Stalin hoping for peace. Briefly, both sides had their way. In September 1939, German forces invaded Poland. The Western allies honoured their pledge to protect Poland, and Europe was again at war. Germans met Russians in Poland, and Poland vanished again, partitioned between the powers.

After almost a year of ominous quiet, Germany turned westwards, into France, south-eastwards into the Balkans, and then, in June 1941, eastwards. The attack

Nazi Europe, 1942

■ German Reich	⧄ Front line, November, 1942	■ German satellites
■ Areas under direct Reich rule		■ Allies
■ German occupied areas	■ Italy (German ally) and dependencies	■ Neutral

The terror of the Holocaust

Between the wars, Eastern Europe was home to most of the continent's Jews. Despite the rise of anti-Semitism, Jews made vital economic and cultural contributions to their motherlands. In Czechoslovakia and Hungary they formed part of the urban bourgeoisie; in Poland and Ukraine they lived in Yiddish-speaking *shtetls* (Jewish towns). But Hitler considered them an inferior race. During the Second World War the Nazis launched a programme of extermination, transporting Jews to the concentration camps of Auschwitz, Treblinka, Belzec and others, in which 6 million people died.

Gateway to hell *Auschwitz's entrance led to death for 1 million people in 1942-5.*

300 000 'partisans' and other supposed anti-communists were deported to Siberia. Eastern Europe was now in the Soviet empire. This included the eastern sector of Germany.

When Stalin rejected an Allied offer to include Eastern Europe in the vast programme of reconstruction devised by US Secretary of State George Marshall, the Soviet empire closed in on itself. In Churchill's famous phrase, an 'Iron Curtain' had descended across Europe. Stalin set about establishing regimes in the Soviet image. Eastern European communist parties were purged of nationalists and repopulated with obedient Stalinist functionaries. More than 1

The big three   Churchill, Roosevelt and Stalin get ready to pose for photographs during the 1945 Yalta Conference, at which they decided the fate of postwar Europe.

February 1945, Poland's border would be shifted westwards so that the USSR could retain control of Belarus and annexe Galicia (once Czech, then Hungarian) and control Ukraine, which would in its own right take over other Romanian and Czech border areas. Thus Romania lost Moldavia to the Soviet Union and the plains of southern Dobruja to Bulgaria. The Hungarians had their prewar borders restored and handed back Transylvania to Romania.

These changes, confirmed at the end of the Second World War, involved massive population migrations as new governments moved their own people into recently acquired territories.

Behind the Iron Curtain

Brief experiments with democracy in Czechoslovakia and Hungary quickly gave way to communist rule, forcefully imposed by Soviet officials. In Ukraine,

Czech reformer Alexander Dubcek, first secretary of Czechoslovakia's Communist Party in the 1960s. His liberal policies inspired the Czech revolution of 1968.

Self sacrifice   Czechs mourn Jan Palach, a student who committed suicide by setting himself alight in protest against the Soviet invasion, 1968.

on the Soviet Union, planned long before the non-aggression pact, was a blow from which the Soviets took two years to recover, and forged an unlikely alliance between communist Russia and the capitalist West.

After defeat at Stalingrad in 1942, the German army was forced into retreat by the Soviet Union. Meanwhile, Western allies closed in on German forces in North Africa. In 1944, the Allies attacked Germany's mainland empire.

In Eastern Europe, a desperate rising by Poles in Warsaw, hoping for help from the advancing Red Army, led to the death of more than 200 000 citizens – a disaster that benefited Stalin's policy of seizing as much of Europe as possible. By April 1945 the Red Army controlled one-third of Germany and all of Eastern Europe.

Stabilising Europe

From 1943, the Allies debated the nature of the new order that would emerge from the ruins of war. As agreed at Yalta in

Workers' hero *Lech Walesa addresses the striking shipyard workers of his union, Solidarity, in August 1988. His success carried him to the presidency of post-communist Poland.*

Urging freedom *Václav Havel, the future Czech president, at the 40th anniversary of the Declaration of Human Rights, Prague, 1988.*

million party members were expelled, and show-trials – like those of the Hungarian party leader László Rajk, Czech foreign minister Vladimir Clementis and Czech party secretary-general Rudolf Slánsk – led to dozens of executions.

Stalin's death in 1953 brought hopes for liberalisation, and when Khrushchev denounced Stalinism in 1956, many Eastern Europeans thought the moment had come. But uprisings in East Germany (1953), Poland (1956) and Hungary (1956) were crushed in the old Stalinist fashion. Despite a cultural 'thaw' in the USSR, the Warsaw Treaty of 1955 confirmed that the political future of the East European states was to remain tightly bound to the Soviet Union.

Communist decay, Soviet collapse
Slowly, though, change came. In the 1960s, Poland de-collectivised its agriculture, and the Hungarian leader János Kadar allowed small private enterprises. These moves, however, did not usher in any political freedom. In Czechoslovakia, Alexander Dubcek introduced a freer, more open form of communist rule, dubbed 'socialism with a human face'. To the Soviets it looked like counter-revolution, and the

Way out *Hungarians dismantle the Iron Curtain on the Austrian frontier, September 1989. Many East Germans fled through the gap.*

The fall of Romania's dictator
In the late 1980s, as Eastern Bloc regimes tottered, Romania's dictator, Nicolae Ceausescu, received his comeuppance. His rule from 1965 was absolute. Informers infiltrated society, contraception and abortions were banned to increase the work force, his relations were appointed to senior posts and state funds were diverted into projects such as a 1000-room palace. Food became scarce, the economy declined and workers protested. In 1989 Ceausescu was overthrown and executed.

Burning the past *A protester consigns Ceausescu and his regime to the flames.*

tanks were sent in to end the experiment. But the people of Eastern Europe kept demanding freedom. In Poland in 1980, workers in the Gdansk shipyard went on strike. Their action was coordinated by a free trade union, something unheard of in Eastern Europe. Under the leadership of Lech Walesa, this union, Solidarity, gained the instant support of the Polish people.

In 1985, Mikhail Gorbachev's accession to power in Moscow introduced a thaw. Political parties were legalised and reformers such as Boris Yeltsin came to prominence. But the economy, now released from central control, nose-dived. In 1989, protesters tore down the Berlin Wall – a symbol of Soviet oppression – and the

empire began to crumble. Ukraine, Belarus and Moldavia, along with the Baltic States, declared their independence in 1991. Suddenly, the USSR was no more. It was replaced by a 'Commonwealth of Independent States'.

Towards European integration
The collapse of the Soviet Union came remarkably peacefully. Slovaks divorced themselves from Czechs. The transition to private economies was painful in Hungary, Poland, the Czech Republic, Slovakia, Romania and Bulgaria. But all could look forward to the possibility of affiliation with the European Union. Others were less fortunate. Ukraine, Belarus and Moldova were all left with shattered economies dependent on an impoverished Russia, which are taking longer to adapt.

Looking west *Hungary's new post-communist president Viktor Orbán receives his Czech counterpart Milos Zeman and Austria's chancellor, Wolfgang Schüssel, in 2000.*

The Place
and its
People

Eastern Europe is emerging from decades spent in a twilight zone. The old capitals of Prague, Budapest, Sofia and Kiev pulse with new life. Cafés enliven the streets. People share meals, revel in the flow of news and opinion, smile more easily. Outsiders are free at last to explore this newly open world, to discover ancient villages and forgotten churches, to hike over mountain ranges and cross the great plains, to wonder at the wildlife of the Danube delta and soak up the sun in colourful seaside resorts.

CHAPTER 1

NATURE'S GLORY

At first glance, there is little to distinguish the countryside of Eastern Europe from that of the West. Both have their summer cornfields, forests rich with autumn colours, snow-covered plains and peaks, and misty spring-time vistas. But Western Europe has no equivalent of the bare Carpathian uplands, the haunting mountains of Transylvania, the reedbeds of the Danube delta, Hungary's arid plains, the Pripet's dank marshes, or the dunes of the Baltic shore. Nature is wilder here, yet people are closer to it. Away from the sweeps of intensive agriculture and pockets of pollution, traditional farming methods have preserved a more ancient countryside, where bison, bears and wolves live on.

The Danube delta in Romania's eastern lowlands.

Along the Danube

The Danube is the lifeblood of Eastern Europe: a snaking highway through landlocked nations to the Black Sea, a source of water, power and food, and a major trade route. No longer is it as 'blue' as it once was. Wars and pollution have blocked its course and poisoned its fish, but the countries along its banks have agreed to make amends.

Rare resident *The common or white pelican is one of two species of pelican found in the Danube delta.*

Timeless scene *In Romania, a farm cart provides transport along the banks of the Danube.*

Ottoman Empire disputing its lower stretches, there was a mutual interest in ensuring the safety of shipping and the river became an important international waterway.

European trade route

After the Second World War the Danube linked the Soviet Union to several of its satellite states, and to Yugoslavia. For those decades, traffic was relatively light – only about half that on the Rhine. Since the end of the Soviet empire, crises in the Balkans have prevented any significant increase in trade.

From its source in the Black Forest of south-west Germany, the Danube crosses the continent to the Black Sea, passing through five Eastern European nations on its 2000 mile (3000 km) journey: Slovakia, Hungary, Serbia, Bulgaria and Romania. It is Europe's second largest river after the Volga. Fed by 300 tributaries, some from as far away as Ukraine and Moldova, its huge basin covers 315 000 sq miles (816 000 km²).

The Danube has influenced human life from prehistoric times. For centuries it has formed a natural frontier: its banks and high-points are dotted with the remains of Roman cities and medieval castles.

In the 18th and 19th centuries, as the Danube's strategic significance declined, it became a highway for the transport of coal and steel. With Austria-Hungary dominating the upper Danube, and Russia and the

As always, it seems that shipping on the Danube is to be limited by political complexities, as well as by its capricious currents. Yet the potential for trade along the Danube for the developing economies of Eastern Europe is enormous, especially as it is linked by canals to the other great rivers of Europe – the Main, Rhine and Oder – creating a vast transcontinental waterway network stretching west to the North Sea and south to the Mediterranean.

Bank to bank *In rural Hungary, far from any bridges, a ferry carries pedestrians, horses, tractors, trucks and cars across the Danube.*

Glorious past *The fortress near Visegrád, Hungary, was built by French princes in the 13th century. The Hungarian king, Mátyás Corvinus, transformed it into an opulent palace in the 15th century, but it was later destroyed by the Ottomans. Today it is just a shell.*

A barrage of bitterness

Work started in 1977 on a project proposed by Soviet engineers to dam the Danube between Hungary and Czechoslovakia to provide energy and improve navigation. Twelve years later, Hungary pulled out. Czechoslovakia split, and Slovakia completed the US$2.5 billion project by diverting 19 miles (30 km) of the Danube. The result was an ecological disaster, which left Hungary with a ruined flood plain and a water shortage. The ensuing row went to the International Court in the Hague, which in 1997 blamed both sides, but provided no solution.

Waterworld   The Danube delta's innumerable channels, lakes of still water, reedbeds and water lilies make life hard for the river-boatmen, but provide an ideal habitat for wildlife.

A source of energy and wealth

The Danube's immense flow – 254 000 cu ft (7000 m³) per second at its mouth – powers several electricity generating plants, two of them nuclear. A number of huge industrial complexes – such as those at Braila and Galati in Romania – have been built on its banks.

Fishing was once a rich source of income, but pollution from the industrial plants, which discharge effluents into the river, has caused a sharp decline in fish stocks (see box, right).

The Danube's many worlds

The Danube is as varied as the countries it crosses. Flowing along the Slovakian border and across the Hungarian plains, it passes countless islands. At Visegrád in Hungary and the Iron Gate on the Romanian-Serbian border,

Expert fisher   The raccoon dog, one of the rare species of the Danube delta, is a semi-aquatic fish-catcher.

it cuts through mountain gorges, foaming over reefs that once made navigation impossible until the construction of a side channel. Then its pace slows. Swollen by the run-off from the Carpathians, it snakes across the Romanian plains, before dividing into three channels. These – the Chilia, Sulina and St George – form its huge delta, covering up to 2180 sq miles (5600 km2). The delta is one of the great ecological wonders of Europe, with a multitude of lakes, channels, forests and islands, all home to a huge variety of fish and birds.

Pollution unlimited

In January 2000, fishermen on Hungary's River Tisza began to haul up dead fish. Within days, Eastern Europe was facing an unprecedented ecological catastrophe. In Baia Mare, northern Romania, a reservoir operated by the Aurul gold recovery company, a joint Romanian-Australian concern, had spilled 50-100 tons of cyanide-rich waste into the River Somes. A 25 mile (40 km) patch of poison flowed south into the Tisza, through Serbia and into the Danube, then onwards to the Black Sea. It not only killed fish by the ton, it also poisoned the food chain, from algae to wildlife. Millions of people were left without drinking water. Events such as this, as well as constant industrial and agricultural pollution, have destroyed 80 per cent of the Danube's wetlands and flood plains over the past 100 years. In 2001, at a summit organised by the Romanian government and the World Wide Fund for Nature, the countries of the Danube basin resolved to work together to clean up the river.

Unfolding disaster   Fishermen display a fraction of the 200 tons of fish killed in the poisoned rivers.

On top of the Carpathians

The wild beauty of the Carpathian Mountains is matched by the richness of their resources. This is the land of the Eurasian bear and sure-footed chamois. Recent exploitation of the minerals and forests, and an influx of tourists, is slowly changing the region's character.

The Carpathians form an amphitheatre of mountains that sweep for more than 900 miles (1500 km) through five countries. They are made up of a number of sub-ranges, divided geographically into western, eastern and southern.

The Carpathians arose in geologically recent times, pushed up by the same forces that created the Alps – the collision of the African tectonic plate with Europe between 185 million and 50 million years ago. But being farther from the impact zone, they never rose to Alpine heights. The highest peak is Gerlachovsky, which rises to 8711 ft (2655 m), only half the height of Mt Blanc.

Though the higher peaks have alpine features such as jagged crests, ice-formed valleys and deep gorges, they lack permanent snowfields and glaciers. These ranges are generally more like hills than mountains, with an average height of 3300 ft (1000 m). Uplands are typically grasslands, falling away through pine and larch forests to valleys of beech and oak.

Precious flower Primula halleri *is a rare long-stemmed primrose found in the mountains.*

The mineral-rich mountains

Although the Carpathians are poor in metals, they contain considerable mineral resources. Some areas are rich in oil and natural gas (both vital to the Romanian economy). Hungary and Slovakia mine brown coal (lignite), Romania has rock salt and Ukraine potassium. Bauxite, copper, lead and zinc all exist in abundance, mostly awaiting exploitation.

In the Middle Ages, the Bihor Massif of western Romania was well known for its iron ore,

Highland harvest *A farmer makes hay on the Polish side of the High Tatras, northern Carpathians.*

gold and silver mines, but a half-century of turmoil limited exploitation until after 1945.

Water power

Snow and rain turn the uplands into reservoirs from which flow countless streams and many rivers, forming a network of astonishing complexity, linking nations and ecologies spanning some 80 000 sq miles (200 000 km²). The Dnestr (Dniester) flows south-east to the Black Sea, while the Tisza,

Above the treeline *These open slopes are typical of the rolling, treeless uplands of the Carpathian Mountains. In the summer they are used as pastures for cattle to graze.*

Creatures of the forest

Until the mid 20th century, much of the Carpathian region was wilderness, with few people to threaten the wildlife. Then development and tourism began to take their toll on the environment. Two national parks – Tatra, in Poland, and High Tatra, in Slovakia – have preserved the highest and most dramatic areas from human incursions. Here, rigorous controls have allowed the recovery of the Eurasian brown bear, Europe's largest predator. Birdlife includes the black stork and the black grouse, potential prey for predators such as lynx and wolf. The middle slopes are home to chamois.

Rock climber *The chamois is a symbol of the Tatra parks.*

The Carpathian arc

Olt, Siret and Prut run from either side south to join the Danube. All are used to power hydroelectric plants and, on the lowlands, to water fields of cereals.

The Carpathians transformed

Since the end of the Second World War, development has brought enormous change to the rural economies of the Carpathians. Many people abandoned their traditional upland occupations as animal-breeders and pasturalists to work in the new industries in the lower-lying areas – mines, steelworks, chemical plants and machine and textile factories.

Valleys lost their forests to timber mills and wood-pulp plants. Industrial cities, such as Brasov and Cluj-Napoca in Romania, expanded. Natural gas plants and oil refineries supplemented hydroelectric schemes.

The region has become popular with tourists, attracted by its picturesque mountain villages and the opportunities for hiking in the remaining forests. New ski resorts, similar to those in Slovakia's Tatra region and Zakopane in Poland, draw wintersports enthusiasts to the slopes.

The real Dracula

Mention the Carpathians and images of castles, vampires and Dracula spring to mind. The anti-hero of Bram Stoker's novel, written in 1897, was inspired in part by Vlad Tepes, 'the Impaler'. Vlad was a 15th-century prince of Wallachia, on the lower Danube, who was famous locally for opposing the Turks, in particular for his habit of impaling captives on sharpened stakes. He was executed by the Turks in 1476. His reputation was made by German and Russian storytellers, who spun legends about Vlad 'Drakul' (Vlad the Dragon). But the historical Vlad had no connection with 'vampirism', or with Stoker's bloodsucking count.

Vanishing world In the High Tatras of Slovakia, a wooden village church spire stands out above the trees. Small communities such as this, backed by towering peaks, are typical of one of Europe's last unspoilt areas.

Remote wilderness The Prislop Pass in north-east Romania provides an extensive vista across spruce-covered slopes and snow-clad peaks.

The count's lair The castle of Bran, which guards the former frontier between Wallachia and Transylvania, is said to be the legendary 'Dracula's Castle'.

Jewels of the landscape

Eastern Europe's lakes sparkle like gems. They provide havens for wildlife, playgrounds for watersports enthusiasts and lovers of nature, and water for the cities. Masuria, in north-east Poland, is known as the Country of a Thousand Lakes, while Hungary has one lake, Balaton, which is more like an inland sea.

Lakes dot the landscape of Eastern Europe. There are more than 2000 in Poland's Masurian Lakeland alone, carved out by retreating glaciers at the end of the last Ice Age. The Rila Mountains of Bulgaria hold 200 lakes, while Balaton in Hungary, is big enough to be called an inland sea.

Balaton: timeless, yet changeable

Lake Balaton is considerably older than its smaller northern counterparts. About 1 million years ago, there were five small lakes divided by hills. Gradually the hills eroded and the lakes united. The remnants of one of the ridges still survives in the Tihany

Lakeland panorama   *Balaton's beauty inspires poets and artists.*

Fish eater   *The osprey, or fish hawk, is one of the 230 species of bird living on Balaton, which marks the southern and western limits of its range.*

Peninsula, which juts out from the northern shore. Today's lake is 50 miles (80 km) long, with an area of 230 sq miles (600 km^2) and a circumference of 125 miles (200 km).

At first glance, the lake seems utterly static, as its name suggests – Balaton derives from the Slav *blatno*, meaning 'stagnant'. In fact, the water is constantly changing. It reaches an average depth of only 9-13 ft (3-4 m), and would evaporate if it were not for the inflow of the several rivers, principally the Zara, and mineral-rich springs that infuse the water with

Rich catch   *A Hungarian fishing community heads for market along Lake Balaton's shoreline. At the time of this painting, in the 19th century, the lake's fish sustained a thriving economy, then pollution took its toll. A programme has now been implemented to restore the purity of the water.*

Balaton: Hungary's great lake

Somewhere beneath Balaton's surface, they say, is a drowned church where a young girl lives, weeping the tears that keep the lake's water pure and warm. This legend, one of many with which Hungarians have surrounded their lake, reveals how deeply Balaton has worked its way into the psyche of the nation. Stephen I, the first Christian king, founded a monastery at Zalavar in 1019. Fifty years later, Andrew I had himself buried on the Tihany Peninsula. In the 16th century, the caves in the lake's western cliffs became hiding places for those fleeing the Turks. Balaton inspired the romantic poet Sándor Kisfaludy (1772-1844), who founded the first national theatre in Balatonfüred, creating a base for Hungarian writing at a time when the official language was German. A monument to him stands on the promenade, surrounded by the villas of prominent Hungarians who, from the early 19th century, were drawn here to take the waters.

Guardian church   *The 18th century Benedictine abbey on Balaton's Tihany Peninsula.*

Hillside torrents   *The Seven Lakes of the Rila Mountains are fed by a mass of streams tumbling down from the snowy peaks.*

marshy reedbeds. The reeds are used as a roofing material. Each season brings its changes. In summer, when the temperature of the water reaches 25°C (75°F), holidaymakers crowd the spas. Sailing boats dot the surface, fleeing for safety at the hint of one of the lake's sudden storms. In winter, the surface freezes to a depth of more than 8 in (20 cm), to the delight of skaters.

Rila's 'Seven Lakes'

South of the Bulgarian capital Sofia, the land rises to form the Rila Mountains, topped by Mt Musala (9652 ft/2925 m). This is walking country. From hostels and chalets, hikers explore slopes covered with a rich variety of trees – oaks, beeches, elms, conifers and birches, with a scattering of rarer species, such as silver pines and hazels.

High up in the Rilas lie pastures where cattle and horses graze in summer, while above them cruise birds of prey – eagles, falcons, vultures and buzzards. Many paths lead through forests or down from the highland pastures to mountain lakes.

Of the 200 lakes in the Rila massif, some are hidden in high, ice-carved cirques. Others, like Sedemte Ezera (the Seven Lakes), are grouped together. The Seven Lakes were formed by ancient glaciers. They range downwards like a natural water garden from the highest, Ledenika (8907 ft/2715 m), to smaller ones at 7000 ft (2100 m). Lake Okoto ('Eye') is the deepest at 132 ft (40 m).

carbonates and sulphates considered to be health-giving. As a result, the lake's entire contents are replaced every three years or so.

Its slow evolution has given the lake a wide variety of land-forms. Along the flat southern shore stretch a succession of dunes, sandy beaches and spas.

The wilder northern shore is shingle broken by crumbly cliffs of loess. On the Tihany Peninsula, geysers – remnants of ancient volcanoes – have worked the landscape into columns and domes of basalt and chalk. Orchards and vineyards thrive on the rich volcanic soils, and Hungary's finest white wines are produced here.

In the south-east, in the region known as Little Balaton, the landscape changes to one of

In summer, the paths beside the lakes are popular with walkers. The waters are frozen from October until late spring, and then the forests are silent, except for the wind in the

Lone feline   *The lynx, a solitary night-time hunter, is one of the Rila Mountains' main predators, along with the wolf and bear.*

Pure waters   *Preserved within the borders of a national park, Sedemte Ezera (the Seven Lakes) supply water to the Bulgarian capital, Sofia.*

Watery heartland   Lake Mamry, with its reed-covered shores, reaches into the heart of the Masurian Lakeland.

trees and the occasional crunch of a passing animal. Chamois, wolf, bear, lynx and deer can be found on the slopes of the Rila Mountains.

Poland's Masurian Lakeland

Masuria is forest-covered and spangled with several thousand lakes and ponds left by Ice Age glaciers. This is known as the Country of a Thousand Lakes, but in fact there are about 2000, which between them cover a fifth of the lakeland's 20 000 sq miles (52 000 km²).

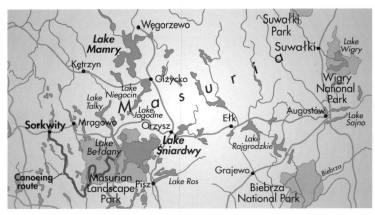

The lakes include Poland's two largest expanses of fresh water, lakes Sniardwy (44 sq miles/114 km²) and Mamry (40 square miles/104 km²). These two are at the heart of an area well protected by four parks – Suwalki, Wigry, Biebiza and the Masurian Landscape Park, which is subdivided into 11 nature reserves.

The area has a remarkable range of wildlife. The lakes provide habitats for some 50 species of fish, among which the most impressive is a species of catfish, the wels (*Silurus glanis*), which grows to 6 ft 6 in (2 m) in length. Thousands of water birds live here. The best-known resident is the white stork, a symbol of good luck in Poland and the emblem of the Masurian Landscape Park. Other species include swans, cormorants, greylag geese and a mass of

Woodland setting   The shores of Lake Warmie, like those of its neighbours, are covered with forest almost to the water's edge.

marsh-dwellers, which favour the Red Marshes of Podlasie, a complex system of depressions and peat bogs. The forests, too, have a wealth of bird and animal species, including rarities such as the white-tailed and lesser-spotted eagles. Roe deer, boar, beaver and otter attract hunters from all over the world.

The region's labyrinthine network of rivers, streams and canals also plays an important role in Poland's 'green' tourist industry. On the shores of lakes Sniardwy and Mamry, beaches provide good bathing in summer, and marinas have turned both lakes into playgrounds for amateur sailors. Kayakers can paddle a course from lake to lake.

Giant resident   The wels, a freshwater catfish, has been known to grow to 15 ft (4.5 m) long and weigh 660 lb (300 kg).

The Masurian Lakeland, Poland

The mazurka

The dance immortalised by Frédéric Chopin in some of his most famous piano works owes its name to the local tribe of the Masurian Lakelands, the Mazurs. Their stamping, three-in-a-bar folk dance was widely known in Poland in the 16th century. It became popular in society ballrooms around 1800, spreading to England and France, where it became all the rage. Chopin, Polish-born but French by choice, wrote 55 mazurkas as a way of capturing and disseminating Polish national folk music. The dance inspired other composers, among them Fauré, Debussy, and Tchaikovski (in *Swan Lake*). The composer Nichal Kleofas Oginsky also enshrined it in the Polish national anthem, Dabrowski's Mazurka.

Beneath the forest canopy

Poland and Belarus have combined forces to preserve the last remaining vestige of the primeval forests that once covered Europe. In the vast woods of the Bialowieski National Park, herds of European bison roam free once again, having been saved from extinction.

Venerable oaks *Each of the ancient trees in Bialowieza's Alley of Oaks is named after a Polish or Lithuanian king. Some of the oaks are 500 years old, with trunks that measure 6 ft 6 in (2 m) across.*

The Puzca Bialowieza is Europe's largest remaining original lowland forest. It spans the Polish-Belarus frontier, covering an area of 468 sq miles (1200 km²). The ancient forest blanketing the flat and often marshy soils owes its survival to the fact that from the earliest times it was owned by Polish kings, Lithuanian princes and Russian tsars who guarded it closely for their own use. A huge variety of plants and animals live beneath the oaks, spruces, hornbeams and pines: there are lynxes, elks, wolves, deer, beaver and around 120 species of

Second home *A herd of European bison live in Belarus's Berezina (Bjarezinski) Nature Reserve, a 300 sq mile (750 km²) forest created in 1925 between Minsk and Polatsk.*

The return of the bison

The European bison, or wisent, is a forest-dweller, rangier in stature than its North American counterpart. It was once common across mainland Europe, but was hunted almost to extinction by the 17th century. In an attempt to conserve the creature in the Bialowieza forest of Poland and Belarus, royal landowners forbade hunting, but the last wild wisent died in 1919. By then several animals had been sold to zoos where they were bred, and in the 1950s a herd of 54 was reintroduced to the forest.

The return of the bison has become a success story in the history of wildlife management. Today, more than 1000 wisent roam the forest. They consume 44 lb (20 kg) of grass a day and can run at speeds of up to 30 mph (50 km/h).

Winter foragers *Ducks in the Bialowieza forest on the Polish border patrol an ice-free stretch of river.*

bird. Only in the early 20th century did the area begin to suffer from timber exploitation. In 1920, the newly reformed Polish government decided to protect it and the Bialowieza National Park was set up. Now much enlarged, and called the Bialowieski National Park, it has a place on UNESCO's World Heritage list. The park is co-managed by both Poland and Belarus.

The national park's existence set the stage for the return of Bialowieski's star – the European bison, or wisent (see box), the continent's largest mammal. The wisent is similar to the American bison except that it has a slimmer build and stubbier horns.

At the seaside

Eastern Europe is often thought of as landlocked, but four of its countries border either the Baltic or Black seas. The coasts are very different: the Baltic is wild and windswept with towering sand dunes; the Black Sea, from Crimea to Bulgaria, is a summer playground for holidaymakers; while the area around the Danube delta is a haven for wildlife.

The Baltic and Black Sea coasts of Eastern Europe are like windows to the outside world for the countries of Poland, Ukraine, Romania and Bulgaria. They have long been popular with holidaymakers, and despite the industrial developments and creeping urban growth inland, the coastal regions have areas in which both nature and history are protected.

The northern dune-lands

Poland's northern province, Pomerania, is aptly named: *pomorye* in Slavic means 'by the sea'. Historically a region of wheat fields and forests, it belonged to Poland, Germany and Russia before settling into Polish hands in 1945. Its 200 miles (325 km) of coast is a string of pools and lakes enclosed by sand dunes. The most spectacular dunes rise to 130 ft (40 m) around Lake Lebsko, in the Slowinski National Park. Winds shift these great hills 30 ft (10 m) every year, gradually burying coastal forests.

Despite the chilly water, which barely reaches 20°C (70°F) even in high summer, holiday-makers flock to resorts such as Sopot, renowned for its annual song festival. Across the bay from Sopot, the Hel peninsula is a peaceful enclave of white sands and pines distorted by wind. In the estuaries of rivers such as the Leba and Slupia, ports still display the evidence of their ancient trading roots.

Feathered migrant *The red-necked goose winters in the Danube delta.*

A sea under threat

Away from well-protected habitats, the Baltic coast suffers from industrial and domestic pollution. The problem is at its worst in the Gulf of Gdansk, where the currents are too weak to disperse the water pouring from the mouth of the River Vistula with waste from the heavily industrialised port of Gdansk. Ecologists

Leader's outlook *In the Crimea, the dacha of the former Soviet leader, Mikhail Gorbachev, is set in a Mediterranean-like landscape.*

Shifting bulwarks *Dunes rippled with wind-blown sand form ever-changing barriers along the length of Poland's Baltic coastline.*

expect trouble from the Russian naval base of Baltiyisk in Kaliningrad, on the bay's eastern side. Here lies Russia's decaying Baltic fleet, whose nuclear-powered vessels increasingly threaten to leak radioactive waste.

In 1992, the growth of pollution and the possibility of ecological catastrophe led the Baltic nations to set up a council to protect

Tatar country

When the Mongols built their empire in the 13th century, they seized Crimea (in today's Ukraine) along with southern Russia. Their heirs, the Tatars of the Golden Horde, ruled Crimea for two centuries. A defeat by Tamerlane left Crimea as an independent Muslim khaganate under Turkish influence, until Russia seized control in the late 18th century. Germany held it in 1942-4, which was enough for Stalin to brand the Tatars as 'collaborators'. In 1944-5, as part of his clamp-down on suspect minorities, Stalin deported 200 000 Crimean Tatars to Uzbekistan. Their descendants have begun to return, and are seeking a restoration of their rights in a now independent Ukraine.

Black Sea grandeur *The elegant 19th-century promenade and casino in the Romanian port of Constanta.*

the environment and stimulate maritime trade links between Eastern and Northern Europe.

Summer in Crimea

The Crimean peninsula jutting into the Black Sea is a combination of Central Asia steppeland leading into a massif that rises to 5000 ft (1500 m). In the shelter of the highlands, the south coast basks in a climate that is almost Mediterranean. At the end of the 19th century, many seaside resorts sprang up here. The most famous, Yalta, owed its rise to the Russian royal family, who in 1860 began to spend their summers at Livadia, a village just to the west. In 1911, Tsar Nicholas II built Livadia Palace, which won Yalta worldwide fame in February 1945 when Stalin, Roosevelt and Churchill met there to decide the fate of postwar Europe.

After the war, the Crimea was the USSR's most popular holiday destination; it is the nearest thing in Russia to a Mediterranean beach. It suffered a decline in the 1990s when Eastern Europeans became free to venture farther afield, but its attractions – the

Sun worshippers *In summer, Bulgaria's Black Sea resorts are as crowded as any beach on France's Côte d'Azur.*

vineyards, fortified cities and palaces – survive as a foundation for future tourism.

The beach resorts of Romania and Bulgaria

South-west of Crimea, Romania's Dobruja coast is part of the protected area of the Danube delta. The exception is a stretch 31 miles (50 km) long between Constanta and the Bulgarian border, where the seafront and its sandy beaches are devoted to holidaymakers. Resorts such as Mamaia, Eforie and Mangalia have considerable charm. Others, with names like Olympus, Neptune and Venus, owe less to Greek mythology and more to the overdeveloped parts of Spain's Costa Brava. Farther south, mountains line the Bulgarian coast, with its mix of traditional fishing villages, holiday resorts and industrial ports, such as Varna and Burgas.

Fairy-tale castle *The Swallow's Nest, built in 1912, perches on Cape Ai-Todor, 6 miles (10 km) south of Yalta in Crimea. It is now a restaurant.*

The Kashubs of Poland

The region round Gdansk on Poland's Baltic coast has changed hands so frequently between Germany and Poland that its original occupants, the Kashubs, are often overlooked. About 210 000 Kashubian speakers live 60 miles (100 km) south-west of Gdansk in rolling countryside of forests and glacial lakes. Their language is the only surviving example of Pomeranian, a West Slavonic tongue like Polish and Czech. It has one close relative, Slovincian, spoken in just a few isolated communities. A related language, Polabian, died out in the 18th century.

Rural delight *Kashubia, a lakeland region in northern Poland.*

CHAPTER 2

PEOPLE AND RESOURCES

In the half-century of Soviet control Eastern Europe put
huge resources into industrial growth. New cities
grew up around immense factory complexes, and
rural populations drifted into these cities for work. As a
result, the nine nations are having to tackle a legacy of poor
farming methods, outmoded heavy industry, obsolete
nuclear power plants and widespread pollution. Together,
the countries possess valuable reserves of oil, coal and
minerals as a basis for the regeneration of their economies.
Information technology has grown with astonishing speed.
Tourism is thriving and traditional skills are making a
comeback. For nations such as Hungary, Poland and the
Czech Republic, who never lost their commercial drive, the
transition to a market economy has been easier.
For the others, progress is slow.

At work in the naval shipyard of Varna in Bulgaria.

Vista of wheat A rainbow arcs over a Belarussian wheatland. Despite the fertile soil and immense fields, yields have dropped recently and Belarus imports cereals from Western Europe.

The wheat belt

For centuries, the great plains of Eastern Europe helped to feed half a continent, from the Baltic to the Black Sea, from the Carpathians to the Urals. But in the postwar decades, when new means of production raised yields in the West, inadequate political and scientific policies combined to undermine the productivity of eastern farmlands.

Fields of wheat stretch as far as the eye can see across Poland, Hungary, Ukraine, Belarus and Moldava. This is the cereal-producing belt of Eastern Europe, where farming has shaped the rural landscape and way of life. Wheat predominates, alongside crops for industrial use and large swathes of orchards – together these underpin the economies of the plains.

Share cropper A Ukrainian state-farm worker helps to harvest potatoes. Part of her wages will be paid in kind.

The world of the plain-dwellers

Poland owes its name to the huge expanses of open countryside that roll between the river valleys across its central and northern regions – the word 'Poland' derives from one of the area's original tribes, the *Polanie* (the 'people of the field'). The conditions benefit

Vanishing scene Horses gather at a well on the Hungarian puszta – a sight, once commonplace, that is fast disappearing.

farming, and the yields are good. The plains of Wielkopolska ('Greater Poland') on the River Warta have become particularly productive, with large-scale farms that are unusual in a land of smallholders. On the good loess soils in the south, wheat, sugar beet and barley have taken over from other cereals and potatoes. Poznan, an expanding centre for stock-breeding, is renowned for its horses, which enjoy a prestige out of all proportion to their economic importance.

Much still remains to be done to increase the efficiency of Poland's farms, but the nation has recovered from the crises that beset it through the 1980s, and the empty shelves in the food shops are now hardly more than a bad memory.

The expansive Alföld

The Great Hungarian Plain known as the Alföld rolls east and south from the Carpathians and the Danube, covering half of Hungary, and reaching across borders into Yugoslavia and Romania. Far from any coastline, the climate is extreme. In summer, in the more fertile areas, mirages often shimmer

Colourful harvest A field of sunflowers in Bulgaria, one of several oil-producing crops.

Agriculture in Ukraine and Moldova

Stack of hay   Mechanisation is yet to make an impact on the farming community in parts of Slovakia.

rich in cereals but were also the former USSR's prime source of tobacco and grapes. Despite the occasionally violent resistance of the peasants, both regions had been forced to make the rapid switch from private estates to collective farms under communist rule, and these are still in operation today.

But their position is precarious. In the economic downturn following the collapse of the Soviet Union, Ukraine's wheat production plummeted. Despite its potential to be one of the greatest grain-producers, Ukraine now ranks only tenth in the world's wheat-growing nations. Bankrupt farms, lacking funds to buy fertiliser or equipment, have no means of reversing their decline.

Small is beautiful

Moldova shares the problems of Ukraine, but has an additional one of its own: 80 per cent of its agricultural products were until 1989 exported to the USSR. Now more than half the population live and work in a countryside dominated by oversized farms that are hard to run as private enterprises. Where, for example, would Moldova find investors for the wine cellars of Cricova, with their 75 miles (120 km) of underground galleries? Rather than devote themselves to such vast and declining enterprises, farmers prefer to cultivate their private plots, where they grow potatoes and other crops to eat at home and sell in the market.

Time off   Tractor drivers take a break on a cooperative farm in the Czech Republic.

over field upon field of grain. Others parts of the Alföld form semi-desert areas or *puszta*, a term introduced in the 15th century to describe the sheep-grazing lands abandoned under Mongol and Turkish rule. Idealised in the 19th century as the very crucible of Hungarian identity, the *puszta* has been on the retreat for decades in the face of irrigation schemes that make it possible to grow a range of crops, such as fruit, vines and maize.

Today, true *puszta* survives only in protected areas, most notably in the Hortobágy National Park, 44 square miles (115 km²) of marsh and grassland east of the River Tisza. Hortobágy became Hungary's first national park in 1973 and was proclaimed a biosphere reserve by the United Nations in 1979.

The farmlands of Ukraine and Moldova

The richest land in Ukraine and Moldova is part of the belt of 'black earth' that stretches from the Carpathians half way across Siberia. Traditionally, Ukraine was the granary supplying wheat, sunflowers and sugarbeet to a succession of empires: the Polish-Lithuanian kingdom, tsarist Russia, and finally the Soviet Union. In Soviet times, Moldova's plains were not only

Old ways   In Romania, smallholders continue to hang out corn on their fences to dry, as they always have done.

Black earth: a resource under threat

The dark soil of Ukraine's plains has evolved over millennia from the remains of plants mixing with wind-blown loess. But in many areas it has taken only a few decades of misuse for its fertility to be destroyed. Monoculture has impoverished the soil. Machinery has denuded it of its grassy covering leaving the ground vulnerable to rain, which gouges furrows in the earth, wind erosion and the summer sun, which dries out crops. Add to this the polluting effects of fertiliser and radioactive fallout from the Chernobyl nuclear reactor explosion (which made 12 per cent of Ukraine's arable land unusable) and a unique ecosystem faces destruction.

Farming today

The countryside has always played an important role in Eastern European society, despite the Soviet Union's drive to industrialise. On the farms, peasants only reluctantly adapted to collectivisation. Some countries, such as Hungary and Poland, were more enterprising than others and have successfully embraced the privatisation of agriculture.

Hay wain *The horse-drawn cart, such as this one in Romania, is still widely used in Eastern Europe.*

It is a common misbelief among Western Europeans that the agricultural sectors of their eastern neighbours are rooted in the collective farm. But this is not always the case. Each country has its own traditions, some of which survived the Soviet era, albeit with varying degrees of success.

Good results – and bad

In Hungary, the dairy industry was able to take advantage of considerable Western investment even during the decades of communism. Czech cooperative farms had also become enterprises that were well able to adapt to privatisation in the 1990s.

Belarus, however, retains its huge state farms, but these are no guarantee of self-sufficiency in food. The output of both Belarussian and Ukrainian collective farms is falling as a consequence of the debilitating influence of private allotments, although the economic significance of the private sector has never been great.

Between these extremes lie the small private enterprises run by Polish and Romanian farmers, often with outmoded techniques and almost no profit margins.

Family enterprise A Polish peasant family near Sandomierz, in the Vistula valley, prepares sugar beets for market. In Poland, family allotments survived communism, and traditional agricultural tasks still define the rhythms of everyday life in the countryside.

Collective lack of incentive

Nowhere do the returns from former collective farms match those expected from family-run concerns. Whether because there was no drive to make a profit on the collectives, or because of a lack of capital, or declining prices, entrepreneurial owners did not come forward at the onset of privatisation in the 1990s. The absence of long-term commitment combined with rural unemployment to accelerate an exodus from the countryside to the towns. In Poland, peasants whose incomes were in free-fall felt rejected by a society in transition. Only one country, Romania, has seen a reverse trend. There, unemployed labourers in the cities were confronted with such abject misery that they fled to the countryside.

Rural protest Farmers near Bialystock in Poland demonstrate for a better deal, 1999.

Nowy Dwór Gd.

Farmers-in-waiting

Eastern European farmers see their western counterparts as the well-off beneficiaries of quota systems and grants, and look forward to being a part of the system when their countries join the European Union. Westerners, however, look at these applicants with misgivings, wondering whether the Common Agricultural Policy could, or should, support them. To solve the problem, officials suggest creating new rural industries based on tourism and environmental protection. Farmers on both sides await developments.

New faces at the market

The move to the free market did not always go smoothly. In the former Soviet states, people had grown used to a 'command economy', where central government simply told each factory what to produce. These countries have found it hard to adjust to a market ruled by the complex and inscrutable laws of supply and demand.

Way ahead Skoda has made the switch to a free economy, and has even begun to shed the unstylish image it had in Western markets.

Most East Europeans saw the fall of the Berlin Wall as a political event. They believed that without its long shadow they would be able to bask in the sunlight of freedom. Many of them did not realise that the Wall also protected them from the bitter winds of the free market system. It was certainly brighter on the other side of the fence, but in purely economic terms it was distinctly chillier too.

False economies

The three westernmost countries – Hungary, Poland and the Czech Republic – had not lost the knack of entrepreneurship. There were enough people there with good business sense and sound ideas to make the market system work. But in Moldova and Belarus that tradition was extinct, and their communist-era economies were rusted solid. They were too outmoded and decrepit to be rebuilt.

Bag a bargain In a Minsk market, two women try to turn a quick profit on cheap carrier bags.

The Western banks which were managing the changeover to market economies did not grasp that these Soviet economies were beyond salvaging. So they insisted that price subsidies be abolished as a first step to reform. They hoped in one stroke to create a situation in which prices naturally floated to their true market value.

But price reform created such stratospheric inflation that money itself became an irrelevance. At every level of the economy, barter became the norm. Many factories simply swapped their product with suppliers and clients. They even paid their own employees in kind: streets were full of industrial workers trying to trade underwear or car parts for food and other essentials. State taxation became practically impossible – because how does central government tax the transfer of a lorryload of shoes from one factory town to another?

This moneyless economy also disguised an astonishing truth: that the output of most factories in the former USSR was worth less than the raw materials and labour invested in it. That is, the economy was *destroying value,* the exact opposite of what economic activity is supposed to achieve. Absurdly, it would have been better for the economies of Belarus and Moldova if their factories closed down and did nothing. But for their governments and the Western banks, the political consequences of that were too damaging to contemplate.

Eastern Europe online

Visitors to Eastern Europe over the past 50 years have been struck by the sight of peasants in headscarves. Now that cliché has been joined by another: young people with mobile phones clamped to their ears. Unreliable conventional phones made mobiles a necessity. Information technology is booming, too. Twelve per cent of city-dwellers have Internet connections.

Trading up Underpinned by the influx of capital into Hungary, the Budapest stock exchange is the most important in Eastern Europe.

Rare necessity In Belarus long food queues are still a fact of life – just as they were in the so-called 'hungry years' of the Brezhnev era.

Black treasure

Eastern Europe is the continent's 'black country', where coal deposits form the basis of heavy industry and the grimy face of the miner, the hero of the communist-era labour force, epitomises the working man. Only Romania has significant supplies of gas and oil.

The most extensive of Eastern Europe's coalfields are in Ukraine and Poland. For more than 100 years they supplied gigantic industrial regions that were, until the late 20th century, a pivotal part of the economy. Now, the mines are ageing, at best uneconomic, at worst a danger to their workers and the environment. With the coming of the post-communist era, the pits have been scheduled for restructuring, or closure.

Coal face *A Donbass miner enjoys a cigarette, one of the few pleasures left in a job of scant rewards and with many dangers.*

The rise and fall of the Donbass

The Donetsky Bassein, or Donbass as it is known, in southern Ukraine was the Soviet Union's largest coalfield. It played a crucial role in the development of the tsarist and Soviet economies. Reserves in the Donbass's 9000 sq miles (23 300 km²) total a remarkable 50 billion tons proven – with the

Coal ▼ Iron ■ Manganese ★ Mine ⚒

possibility that more than three times that amount exists in the region. In 1987, it had 60 per cent of the USSR's coal reserves and was producing a quarter of its output.

Today, the Donbass is in crisis. Even in the 1980s the most accessible deposits were beginning to run low, and miners had to start digging deeper, with a corresponding increase in technical problems and costs, and a reduction in output. The decline steepened, falling from a peak of 200 000 tons in the 1980s to 136 million tons in 1991, and to 68 million tons in 1998. To supply its heavy industries, Ukraine had to import coal.

Investment priority

Since the collapse of the Soviet Union, working conditions have worsened. The new republic had no cash to invest in the renovation of pits and equipment, some of which were 50 years old. The accident rate rose: in 1998, 350 men died in Donbass mines. The mines were kept open thanks to aid from the World Bank, which

Display of muscle *In 1990, 10 000 Romanian miners marched on Bucharest to protest at their working conditions. The new government listened, and promised wage increases. Here miners cross the River Jiu, 110 miles (175 km) east of the capital.*

Romania's oil bonanza

Oil was discovered near the little Romanian town of Ploiesti, south of the Carpathian Mountains, and in 1856 one of the world's first oil refineries opened here. From 1900, the oil town was the core of Romania's burgeoning industries. Germany seized the area in the Second World War, and it was the target of US bombing raids in 1943. After the war, the new communist government nationalised the oil industry. Ploiesti grew to a city of 300 000 inhabitants, and became

Eastern Europe's largest producer of oil and gas. Additional reserves were also found near Oltina in south-east Romania, along the rim of the Carpathians and on the Black Sea. Ten refineries now produce 12 million tons a year – a figure likely to rise with the discovery in 1999 of a new Black Sea oil field with an estimated value of $8 billion.

Mixed economy *A farmer in the oil-producing region of Oltina grazes his flock among the derricks.*

Heavy industry in the Donbass

The immense coal deposits in the Donbass fuelled the region's transformation into the industrial centre of Russia from the mid 19th century. In 1886, a railway linked the coal mines to the iron-ore deposits and steelworks of Kryvvy Rih. Nikopol, on the River Dnieper, grew as a result of its proximity to the world's largest deposit of manganese. The presence of sulphur, sulphuric acid and soda further attracted iron, steel and chemical industries.

Mining town   The city of Makiyivka, near Doneck in Ukraine, has 400 000 inhabitants and is one of the largest of the Donbass mining centres.

acknowledged Ukraine's argument that to close any pits would create more unemployment in an already impoverished area of the country.

The mines of Silesia

Poland, Eastern Europe's second largest coal producer, employs 540 000 people in the industry, of which 340 000 are miners. Silesia has the greatest coal deposits outside the former Soviet Union, with an estimated 45 billion tons. The 140 million tons produced annually are used to generate 70 per cent of Poland's electricity. Yet the high cost of extracting the coal has resulted in state support for the mines reaching $5 million a year.

Despite a 30 per cent decline in production over a ten-year period, losses approached $500 million in 1996. With World Bank help, the industry underwent complete restructuring to modernise equipment and return the mining sector to profitability. Today, Poland has fallen from fourth to seventh place in the world league table of coal producers. Major problems remain, such as tackling pollution in an area on the brink of ecological catastrophe.

Energy source   A mine in Katowice, Upper Silesia. The region's 50 mines contain 90 per cent of Poland's coal reserves.

Salt carvings

The salt mines of Wieliczka, 12 miles (20 km) south-east of Kraków, are one of the wonders of Eastern Europe. They are the oldest working salt mines in Europe and were a source of wealth for Polish kings from the 13th century. Over the years, miners created an immense 187 mile (320 km) network of galleries, some of which are open to tourists. The miners expressed their Catholic faith by sculpting altars, statues and bas-reliefs in three chapels and a 'cathedral' with chandeliers of salt crystal.

Underground worship   The 178 ft (54 m) long Blessed Klinga chapel, carved from a Wieliczka salt mine.

The Chernobyl syndrome

At 1.23am on April 26, 1986, a catastrophic explosion at Chernobyl in Ukraine blew the top off a reactor and caused the world's worst nuclear accident. Few places in Europe escaped the effects of the radioactive cloud that swept across the continent.

Survivor *A quarter of Belarus and 7 per cent of Ukraine was affected by the Chernobyl blast.*

The disaster started with a safety check of Chernobyl's Reactor No. 4. Scientists decided to test the plant's ability to provide enough electricity to cool the core if the main power supply was lost and before diesel engines delivered emergency supplies. But two teams – the one running the test and the one in charge of core operation – failed to coordinate their actions. This, combined with design faults and poor decision-making, resulted in catastrophe. A power surge caused overheating and triggered a violent explosion that blew off the reactor's 2000-ton cap and melted its core. It delivered severe, and in many cases fatal, doses of radiation to the 600 staff on duty; 31 people were killed and 140 suffered severe radiation sickness.

Radioactive vehicles *A fleet of contaminated cars and trucks await disposal.*

Nuclear power plants in Eastern Europe

A fatal cloud

For ten days a succession of fires and explosions released a plume of contaminating smoke. The cloud contained several radioactive elements – iodine-131, caesium-134 and caesium-137, the last representing 30-50 per cent of the core's total contents.

Blown by changing winds, the radioactive cloud first drifted across the Baltic and Scandinavia, then westwards over France and Italy, and finally dissipated over Greece and Turkey. Three-quarters of Europe was affected in some way.

The Soviet authorities at first played down the disaster, merely advising residents to close their windows. When it became obvious that suppression was impossible, 116 000 people were evacuated

Potential disaster *A Moravian woman tends her crop near the Bohunice nuclear power station in Slovakia. Two of the plant's reactors have been declared unsafe, but closure has been delayed to 2006-8.*

Fallen heroes A memorial commemorates the firemen who gave their lives fighting the catastrophic blaze at Chernobyl.

from within a 19 mile (30 km) radius of the site. 'Liquidators' were drafted in to make the plant safe. They worked in rotation for 90 seconds at a time, without protection and in so doing they were exposed to massive doses of radiation.

The final toll

Sixteen years after the event, it is possible to draw up a rough balance sheet of the human consequences of the Chernobyl disaster in which 9 million people could have been contaminated.

The main consequence has been a sharp rise in thyroid cancers among children: 1791 were diagnosed in 1990-8. It is estimated that 20 000-40 000 deaths from cancer are expected in the next 50 years as a result of the contamination. Other types of cancer have

not appeared, or at least not yet; nor is there evidence of congenital abnormality. But lesser complaints, such as nervous disorders, muscular dysfunction and eye problems, have jumped by 40-60 per cent in the affected regions of Ukraine, Belarus and Russia. A real, but hard to quantify effect is the emotional and psychological damage in a population frightened of the unknown and distrustful of authority.

An uncertain future

It will take many years to eradicate the effects of the disaster. The remains of Reactor No. 4 were blanketed beneath a concrete sarcophagus that was supposed to last 30 years; it already shows signs of leaking radiation from its still-active interior.

Clean-up operations included the use of earth-moving machines to bury irradiated bulldozers and trucks. Other radioactive waste was stored in 800 sites, with no long-term solution.

Moreover, to the astonishment of Europeans, the plant remained in operation. Only in December 2000 was the last reactor finally shut down, in exchange for aid of $715 million from the G7 group of advanced nations.

The surrounding area will remain contaminated for years. Yet many former residents have returned, especially the elderly, preferring to live as best they can in a ruined but familiar landscape than wait for death in some distant and alien place.

Air contamination Among Eastern European nations, Romania suffers the most from pollution pouring from its industrial complexes.

Chernobyl's end December 15, 2000: foreign guests watch as Ukrainian president Leonid Kouchma gives the order to press the button that will shut down Chernobyl's last operational reactor.

Bohemian specialities

The shift from central planning to a free enterprise economy posed problems throughout industry, but not in two areas of the Czech economy. In Bohemia, makers of both glass and beer relied on long-established traditions to enable them to rise to the challenge and compete internationally.

Ancient skill *A Czech glass-blower forms a semi-molten mass into a crystal goblet.*

Two of Eastern Europe's major success stories of the last decade are the glass and beer-making enterprises of Bohemia, in the Czech Republic. The production of Pilsner, centred in Plzen, increased during the 1990s and exports have risen.

Demand continues for the country's celebrated crystal glass, which is made in around Karlovy Vary (Karslbad). There are 200 glassworks in the Czech Republic.

Decorative effect *Finishing touches are added to a hand-crafted vase. Bohemian engravers are acknowledged masters of the art.*

crystal popular throughout Europe from then on. And not only Europe: in the 1930s, the King of Siam travelled to Bohemia to admire the techniques of manufacture, gilding, coloration and engraving – techniques that are still renowned today.

Glass: an enduring tradition

The many visitors who come to Bohemia to 'take the waters' in Czech spas almost always leave carrying three items: a stoneware flask of Valenbourg water, a bottle of Pilsner beer and a small object made of crystal. Those who are after something a little more discerning take the road westwards towards Cheb, to the famous Moser glassworks. Here, the huge exhibition hall and glass-making museum reveal much about the industry's history and techniques, but not all – parts of the process still remain a well-guarded secret inside the factory itself.

Glass-making skills have been passed down from generation to generation. Bohemian craftsmen began to make their mark in the 13th century. They came to the fore in the early 16th century, when a gem-cutter, Caspar Lehmann, began a tradition of glass engraving. Lehmann died in 1622, but around 1700, the tradition he established combined with the discovery of a new type of crystal-clear, potash-lime glass that made Bohemian

Portrait of Pils

Pilsner, the world's first transparent, golden beer, owes its subtle taste to the sweet must (unfermented liquid) of Moravian barley and the outstanding delicacy of Bohemian hops, which traditionally came from around Zatec, 43 miles (70 km) north of Plzen. The beer owes its clarity to the low temperatures at which it is made. Pilsner has been one of Czechoslovakia's main exports since the foundation of the state in 1918. It has been copied, but never equalled. Many towns have their own brewery and the Czech Republic prides itself on the many varieties of lager available in its thousands of bars.

A town that is a beer

Pilsner beer has transformed the little Czech town of Plzen where it was first made into a household name that became known across the world. Both town and beer came to the fore in 1295, when King Vaclav II gave 260 townsmen the exclusive right to act as makers of the brew known locally as *Prazdroj* (Original Source). Since Bohemia was ruled by Germans and Austrians, it became better known as Pilsner or Pilsner Urquell – Pils for short.

By coincidence, Pilsner was developed at the same time as mass-produced glasses began to replace tin and ceramic mugs. It is said that only in a glass can drinkers truly appreciate the beer's clarity and colour. By the time of the Thirty Years' War (1618-48), the town had 26 breweries, all underground to ensure the stability of their temperature, all with their own taverns. But for centuries, no one knew how to make beer last. It was only in 1842 that the brewers established their Mestansky Pivovar (Citizens' Brewery), and created a beer that could be stored and exported.

Original source *The Pilsner Urquell factory produces 3.4 million gallons (15 million litres) of beer a year. Its quality reflects that of its spring water, low-protein barley, hops and the chalk-hill cellars in which it is stored.*

Tokay and foie gras

There's more to Hungarian delicacies than goulash and paprika. The gentle volcanic slopes of Mount Tokay give their name to the country's most famous wine, which often accompanies another Hungarian speciality, foie gras.

Hungarian vineyards

Hungary has the perfect ingredients for viniculture: mild autumns, long sunny days, rich volcanic soils, protected slopes. The result: it produces Eastern Europe's finest wines.

The wine of kings

Ranking tenth among the world wine producers, Hungary makes 12.5 million gallons (55 million litres) of wine a year. Vineyards scattered across a score of different regions cover 585 sq miles (1500 km²). Abroad, one of the best-known marques is Egri Bikavér (Bull's Blood of Eger). Made in the Mátra Mountains, this wine owes its name to its dark red colour and its full-bodied taste. Farther east, close to the border with Ukraine, is the region that produces the syrupy white wine known as Tokay

Aszú, 'the wine of kings, the king of wines,' in the words of Louis XIV. Tokay, or *Tokaji*, derives from a Furmint grape first planted in the late 12th century. Furmints ripen late, and are affected by a mould (*Botrytis cinera*) that concentrates sugars and flavours to produce the characteristic honey-like sweetness.

Indulging a French passion

Hungary is also a top maker of foie gras, and is second only to France in its love of 'fat liver'. This rich pâté is made from the liver of a goose – geese in Hungary outnumber ducks and are bred mainly on the Alföld (Great Plain).

After force-feeding, 80 per cent of the birds, or their livers, are sent to the Landes region of south-west France, where they are processed with brandy, seasonings or truffles into pâtés and purées. It is this flow of goose products from Hungary, backed by a lesser trade from Bulgaria and Poland, that allows the French to indulge in their culinary passion.

Hand picked *Tokay's aszú grapes, covered by their taste-enhancing 'noble rot', are hand-picked in late autumn.*

Delicacy in the making *A flock of geese being raised in Hungary for the foie gras industry.*

Eastern Europe's undiscovered vineyards

As Eastern European wines permeate Western markets, wine drinkers may find some pleasant surprises in store. Slovakia makes excellent Tokays, and Moravian Rieslings, Sylvaners and Sauvignons are as drinkable as their Austrian equivalents. Among Romania's many wines there are some respectable but little-known whites such as the Cotnaris. Ukraine has some superb vintages, and a number of Moldovan varieties are remarkably similar to Bordeaux. Bulgarian wines have great possibilities, even if the quality is variable. The country has 44 500 newly planted acres (18 000 ha) that have yet to yield a vintage.

The valley of roses

May and early June is a magical time along the River Tundza in Bulgaria. Fields of roses in full bloom stretch as far as the eye can see. The valley of roses produces three-quarters of the world's attar, or essential oil of rose.

Celebrating harvest *Bulgarians in national costume pick the last roses during the annual harvest festival that takes place on the first Sunday in June.*

Damask rose.

According to legend, the first roses were brought to the land that now forms Bulgaria by Alexander the Great's soldiers on their return from Persia around 330 BC. Rose growing as a cottage industry was begun by a Turkish merchant in 1830.

An ideal environment

The conditions along the River Tundza are perfect for roses. The land lies below 2300 ft (700 m) and comprises a good mix of fertile soil, sand and fine gravel that allows water to penetrate fast. The heat of summer is tempered by cloudy skies and winds from the Black Sea. Rain falls gently and often. Humidity remains steady as the blooms turn the otherwise drab valley into one of Bulgaria's most popular tourist attractions in early summer. Harvesting starts in the second week of May and is completed by mid June.

Blooming fields

To ensure maximum exposure to the sun, the shrubs are planted in rows that in flat areas run in the direction of the prevailing wind, and in rolling terrain run horizontally up the slopes. Fields are carefully prepared, with 20 in (50 cm) deep holes dug four to six weeks before planting commences. Cuttings are taken from roses more than six years old and are placed in a bedding of topsoil. This uniquely Bulgarian technique, known as *kesme*, has been developed to produce the best growths and top quality oil. Of the two oil-rich species, the hardier white type, *Rosa alba*, is planted to protect the more fragile red one, *Rosa damascena*.

Each acre produces 3 million rosebuds, from which come 3000 lb (1400 kg) of blossom. The blooms are gathered in three hectic weeks, with work concentrated in the early morning hours between 3am and 8am, before the sun rises and starts to dry the oil. Donkeys transport the harvest to distilleries in Rozino, Karnare and Kazanlak where the greenish-yellow oil is made. Perfumiers around the world pay more than $45 million a year for this highly prized product.

Quintessence of rose

Rose oil is highly regarded by aromatherapists as an antidepressant and a stimulant for the circulation. It is also added to perfumes and soaps. A minimum of 2.4 acres (1 ha) of blooms are needed to make just 1.76 pt (1 litre) of the precious attar. It is an expensive product: about £37 for 1 oz (£13/g), or £7386 for 1 pt (£13 000/litre). Nothing is wasted in the production process: the residue of rosewater and pulp is used to make medicines, flavourings, jams and liqueurs.

Precious phial
A traditional flask of attar of roses from Bulgaria.

Constanta and Gdansk: awaiting a new dawn

Eastern Europe's ports are its windows on the West. The two greatest, Constanta and Gdansk, are the major links in the commercial trade routes between the advanced economies of Western Europe and the emergent ones to the east.

Constanta is not only Romania's largest port: it is the fourth largest in Europe, after Rotterdam, Antwerp and Marseilles. The port is well placed, lying on the west coast of the Black Sea. First mentioned in the 7th century BC as the city of Tomis, it owes its present name to Constantine the Great, who rebuilt it in the 4th century. It played an important role in maritime history from the 10th century, when it was used by Genoese and Byzantine traders.

A long period of stagnation ended in 1878 with the rebirth of Romania as a state. In 1895 Romania turned the little port – at the time hardly more than a village with 2000 inhabitants – into a base for its new navy and launched two steamboats, the *Medea* and the *Meteor*. The *Meteor* opened a new era by making a record 13-hour voyage from Constanta to Constantinople.

Today, the port is a crucial part of Romania's economy, receiving oil from the Russian port of Novorossiysk across the Black Sea, which is distributed to the rest of Europe. It performs many roles, supplying energy, and building, repairing and servicing shipping.

Along with its satellite ports of Mangalia and Midia, Constanta is south-east Europe's main gateway, and is well positioned to set the agenda for the economic development of the region.

Vanished wealth *These 18th-century waterfront trading buildings recall the days when Gdansk was the Baltic's most prosperous port.*

Gateway to Europe *When a canal linking Constanta to the Danube opened in 1984, it confirmed the port's pre-eminence on the Black Sea.*

Old guard *A Gdansk welder and Solidarity member witnessed the fall of both the shipyard and the union. Today the shipyard is showing signs of recovery.*

Future prospects

Gdansk grew from a small Baltic fishing port in the 9th century to become the Hanseatic League's most important trading centre in the 15th century. But it is probably best known to Westerners as the birthplace of Solidarity in 1980, the trade union led by Lech Walesa, who was to become president after the fall of the communist regime in Poland.

In 1992, at the height of the economic crisis brought about by the demise of communism, the total freight handled by Gdansk dropped by 50 per cent to 30 million tons. It took six years, and the closure and reopening of a shipyard, to regain lost ground. In 1998 tonnage topped 60 million tons. In 2000 the Polish government undertook to keep the shipbuilding yards full until 2002 to repay debts and complete the process of privatisation. Foreign investment is vital to the port's future prosperity.

The death and rebirth of Gdansk

On August 8, 1997, shipyard workers in Gdansk mourned the end of a world, and within a year were celebrating the dawn of a new one. Unable to obey the rules imposed by Poland's new market economy, the port had accumulated a debt of $160 million. In 1997, the shipyard – once one of the world's largest with 20 000 workers – closed. The very people who had started the anti-communist revolution in the 1980s had become victims of the system they advocated. Then in 1998, under a new chief executive, Janusz Szlanta, the rival shipyard in Gdynia took over Gdansk, and brought new hope. Now the Gdansk shipyard has a work force of 4000, sharing an order book for 65 ships worth $2 billion that will sustain both yards until 2004.

EVERYDAY LIFE IN EASTERN EUROPE

Few regions of the world could claim a more varied and passionate mix of peoples and cultures than those of Eastern Europe. New states have emerged from old, frontiers have shifted peacefully, and minorities are reasserting their individuality. Clichés about the tedium of life behind the Iron Curtain do not withstand a moment's scrutiny today. Here you can dance on the ice in Minsk, drink coffee in Art Nouveau splendour in Prague, bathe under a spangled dome in the thermal waters of Budapest, or gaze in wonder at the painted churches of Romania, while listening to a babble of different languages. Traditional celebrations, a love of sport, a deep religious faith, a passion for good food – these and many other comforts are all the more appreciated because they can, at last, be shared with the world.

A village scene in Bukovina, Romania.

Breaking free from the empire

In 1991, 15 new nations arose from the ruins of the former Soviet Union and 11 of them formed the Commonwealth of Independent States. It was a time of great rejoicing – the countries were free at last to elect their own governments, to run their own affairs. But for Moldova, Belarus and Ukraine the transition has not been trouble-free.

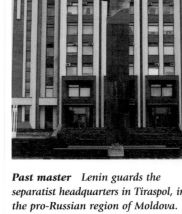

Past master *Lenin guards the separatist headquarters in Tiraspol, in the pro-Russian region of Moldova.*

Euphoria and despair: these were the two extremes of emotion experienced by Moldova, Belarus and Ukraine as they emerged as newly independent states from the western part of the former USSR. They faced a three-fold task – to assert their identities as nations, to make a difficult economic transition and to stop internal tensions breaking into conflict.

From Moldavia to Moldova

The republic of Moldova is the heir of the former Soviet Socialist Republic of Moldavia, but also of a succession of entities that were constantly swapped between Russia, Romania and Ukraine. Part of the region was known as Bessarabia (to the west of the River Dnieper), another part as Transdnistria (to the east, traditionally part of Ukraine). Medieval Moldavia sometimes incorporated Bessarabia, but today's border is different again. It was fixed in 1940 when Romania ceded its portion of Bessarabia to the Soviet Union.

During the time of Gorbachev's *perestroika* in the 1980s, Moldavia opted to make a show of independence by adopting Romanian as its official language. That decision, by leaders eager to rejoin Romania, prompted an instant reaction from the Ukrainian-Transdnistrian region, which seceded in 1990. Moldavia declared

Eyeball to eyeball *Russian president Vladimir Putin (right) and his Moldovan counterpart, Vladimir Voronin, meet to discuss their differences.*

independence in August 1991 amid rising tension that led to an armed confrontation between Romanian-speakers and Russian-speakers, the latter receiving support from Russian troops.

A ceasefire agreement, signed in July 1992, gave the 'Dniester Republic' the right to secede if Moldavia ever decided to unite with Romania. Since then, Russian troops have remained on stand-by, and Moldavia – Moldova as it now became – slipped into an economic crisis. It remains dependent on Russia for energy supplies.

Belarus: independent or not?

Belarus has no would-be secessionists, despite a troubled history and a potential split between Catholic and Orthodox religious traditions. This small state, wedged between Lithuania, Latvia, Poland, Ukraine and Russia, fell to Russia after the first division of Poland in 1772. Its borders changed many times until the end of the Second World War.

Belarus played a leading role in the establishment of the Commonwealth of Independent States in 1991 – formed in the wake of the Soviet Union – but then ossified into one of Eastern Europe's most conservative countries. In 1996, its populist president,

Military display *Ukrainian soldiers on parade in Sevastopol.*

Founder members *Moldovan, Ukrainian and Belarussian delegates take part in talks in Almaty, Kazakhstan, to set up the 11-member Commonwealth of Independent States (CIS), December 21, 1991.*

Hard-liner As leader of Russian peace-keeping troops in Moldova, General Lebed briefs the media. Lebed successfully negotiated peace in Chechnya in 1996.

Vyacheslav Lukashenko, won dictatorial powers in a referendum, after which he suppressed democracy and muzzled the press for criticising him.

Of all the former republics, Belarus is the most closely tied to Russia. Russian is the second language, the rouble the official currency. Reunification is more than a theoretical possibility. An act of union was signed in 1997, but awaits a revival of Russia's fortunes for realisation.

Ukraine: looking westward

At first glance, Ukraine and Belarus are similar – both are former Soviet breadbaskets, with histories marked by dislocation and division, their economies are in turmoil and they depend on Russia for energy supplies. But there the similarities end. Ukraine's leaders are doing their utmost to forge links with the West and assert their independence from Russia.

They have two major problems. First, negotiations with the International Monetary Fund (IMF) have not been straightforward – Ukraine stands accused of falsifying statistics and moving too slowly on economic reform. The IMF froze its loans several times before releasing them in 1999 and 2000 (loans that were in part earmarked to fund the closure of the Chernobyl nuclear power plant). Second, relations with Russia are enflamed

Honouring the leader Belarussian soldiers pin up a portrait of their president, Vyacheslav Lukashenko, in the lead-up to the legislative elections in 2000.

The mysterious Gagauz

Moldova is home to the little-known autonomous region of Gagauzia, situated in the south of the country. Its population of 173 000 people speak a Turkic language, but they are Orthodox Christians. Some say their ancestors were Turks who migrated to Bulgaria in the Middle Ages, some that they were Slavs who intermarried with Turks and Bulgarians, some that they were Anatolians who emigrated to Bulgaria under the Ottomans.

In any event, the Gagauz once lived around Varna on Bulgaria's Black Sea, and moved to Ukraine and Moldova in the late 18th century. They proclaimed a brief independence in 1990, a claim partially acknowledged in 1994 when Moldova granted Gaugazia its autonomy. With Comrat as its capital, this tiny, landlocked region makes good wine. It is acquiring its own oil terminal on the Danube to give it greater access to energy supplies.

by the question of Crimea. The peninsula was made part of Ukraine in 1954, but its mainly Russian-speaking population expressed a desire to break away in 1991. Crimea is an autonomous republic, but still part of Ukraine. Attempts at moving towards Russia, such as making Russian the official language and holding a referendum on reunification, have been overruled by Ukraine's Supreme Council.

The ex-Soviet Black Sea fleet, based in Sevastopol in Ukraine, poses another problem. Ukraine claimed a part of it. An agreement in 1991 gave Ukraine 162 of the 460 ships. In 1999, Ukraine agreed to lease the port itself to Russia for 20 years in exchange for relief from its oil debt.

New era On August 25, 1991, a cheerful crowd gathered in front of the Communist Party headquarters in Kiev to celebrate Ukraine's newly won independence from Russia. No longer was Lenin their hero.

Time for change Demonstrators cheer the fall of Ukrainian president Leonid Kuchma in 2001. The cartoon is captioned 'Kuchma kaput!' Despite implementing draconian measures, he failed to halt economic collapse and lost the support of the people.

A medley of ethnic groups

The redrawing of boundaries, particularly in the 20th century, divided regions and severed populations from their countries of origin. With the dawn of democracy in Eastern Europe, minority peoples felt free to demand rights that had for decades been subordinated to socialism.

Hungarians in Slovakia and Romania, Turks in Bulgaria, Germans in Romania, Poles in Lithuania – every country, it seems, has minorities enough to undermine the very idea of the nation-state. During the 1990s, a series of bilateral treaties ensured that the rights of almost all these groups are now protected.

Hungarians abroad

By the Treaty of Trianon, which formalised the end of the Habsburg Empire in 1920, a quarter of all Hungarians found themselves living in a country that was not Hungary. Today, these 3 million people form the most significant minority in Eastern Europe after Russians. About 1.7 million Hungarians live in the Romanian province of Transylvania, 570 000 in Slovakia, 380 000 in Serbia's Vojvodina province, 160 000 in Ukraine, 25 000 in Croatia, with the rest scattered in Slovenia and Austria.

Seen by Hungary as oppressed expatriates and by their host countries as potential threats to national unity, the 'Magyars' were a source of international tension from 1989 onwards.

Eager to find a way to protect Hungarians abroad without enraging neighbouring states, Hungary passed a law granting wide-ranging rights to its own minority groups (some 10 per cent of the population). This, combined with pressure from Western Europe, was enough to inspire other states to seek negotiated solutions to the problems posed by their own minorities and to acknowledge their rights.

A good read Papers in German for Germans in Hungary.

International handshake The mayors of neighbouring border towns of Slubice (Poland) and Frankfurt-on-Oder (Germany) exchange greetings in 1998 after the creation of a German-Polish university.

Rights for minorities

In 1996, after five years of discussion, Hungary and Romania settled a dispute over Transylvania, the loss of which in 1918 had never been accepted by Hungary. They signed a treaty by which Hungary agreed not to dispute the present frontier and Romania recognised the rights of its Hungarian minority. These rights were to find practical expression in a Hungarian-language university and in wider involvement in the administration of those areas in which Hungarians made up a majority – steps that so far remain unfulfilled.

These setbacks did not hinder the Democratic Union of Hungarians in Romania (UDMR) from taking part in a coalition government between 1996 and 2000, until elections upset the balance and returned the communists to power.

In 1995, Hungary signed a similar treaty with Slovakia, which came into force after the 1998 elections, when the local Hungarian party, the SMK, joined a new coalition.

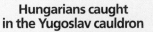

Anger on the streets Hungarians protest against oppression by the Romanian authorities in Tîrgu Mures, 1990. The banner asks: 'Where are those who disappeared?'

Hungarians caught in the Yugoslav cauldron

In Serbia in the 1980s and 1990s, the 380 000 Hungarians living in Vojvodina, in the north-east of the country, found themselves embroiled in a wider conflict that was to lead to the breakup of Yugoslavia. Their region, like Kosovo, was stripped of its autonomy by President Milosevic in 1990. The ensuing war in Kosovo drove one-tenth of the Hungarians in Vojvodina to flee to Hungary. The coming of peace, the fall of Milosevic and the reinstatement of autonomy for Vojvodina, has given the Hungarians renewed hope.

Turkish anger   In Kardzaly, Bulgaria, in the winter of 1989-90, Turkish-speakers protest against the vicious anti-Turkish, anti-Islamic nationalism unleashed by Todor Zhivkov's communist government. Both the campaign and the outraged reaction contributed to the fall of Zhivkov.

Bulgaria turns on its own Muslims

Bulgaria's population of 10 million is about one-tenth Muslim. Some 750 000 are Turkish-speaking descendants of those Turks who were resettled in Bulgaria as part of the Ottoman occupation which ended in the late 19th century; the remainder are mainly of Tatar and Slav origin, or descended from Christians who adopted Islam (known as Pomaks, meaning 'helpers'). Given their

Hungary's reach   In Cluj, Romania, a statue of the 15th-century Hungarian king Matthias Corvinus is an example of Hungarian influence in the city.

association of Islam with 500 years of Turkish oppression, Muslims have on occasion been victimised themselves.

In the 1970s, Todor Zhivkov's communist regime wooed popular support with a vicious attempt to integrate Muslims by ordering them to adopt Slavonic names and imprisoning those who refused. The campaign started with the Pomaks in the Rhodope Mountains with dire consequences. A riot in Pazardzhik left two officials dead, leading to a military clamp-down. In 1984, Zhivkov turned on the Turks in an even more brutal 'Regeneration Process.' The Turkish language was banned in public, Turkish newspapers and mosques were closed. When communism began to crumble and the frontiers opened in 1989, this outbreak of xenophobia inspired 350 000 Turks to flee the country for Turkey, intensifying economic and political decline in Bulgaria.

Zhivkov fell the same year, but only about half the exiles returned. Following elections in 1991, the Turkish language regained its status and a new party, the Movement for Rights and Freedoms, fought the Turkish cause in parliament. Minority rights were legally secured in 1999.

Of Macedonians, and others

Of all European minorities, the Macedonians are the most problematic. In the 4th century BC, Alexander the Great made his homeland part of the Greek world, and Macedonians played a crucial role fighting for

Instant suburb   This Transylvanian township was built as part of Ceausescu's plan to relocate Romanians and undermine the influence of local Hungarians.

Historic connections   The flag is Romanian, but this annual celebration by the Bolyai school in Tîrgu Mures recalls a centuries-old connection with Hungary. The town, on the short-lived 1940-7 Hungarian-Romanian border, is 40 per cent Hungarian.

Greek independence in the 19th century. But even then many Macedonians were also fighting for Macedonian independence, an aim that conflicted with the nationalist aims not only of Greece but also of Bulgaria.

A divided kingdom

To confuse matters further, when Yugoslavia emerged after the Second World War, Tito named his southern province Macedonia, to the chagrin of Greece. It is this small section of the ancient kingdom that now calls itself 'Macedonia'. Greece, fearful that this new

In Magyarpolány, in Hungary, German melodies provide the rhythm.

Macedonia wished to claim its share of the (Greek) old one, refused to acknowledge its existence except under the cumbersome title of the Former Yugoslavian Republic of Macedonia (FYROM). In their own drive for national identity, these Macedonians claimed their language as separate, though linguists label it a dialect of Bulgarian.

Meanwhile, a sizable minority of around 180 000 Macedonians still lives in Bulgaria. But these figures were obtained in 1956, since when the Macedonians have been systematically discounted, as if being wished out of existence. Only in 1999 did they find a voice again, along with other Bulgarian minorities, such as Gypsies, Gagauz, Vlachs, Armenians and the few Jews who remained after a major exodus in 1945.

The Germans of Eastern Europe

Before 1939, about 10 million Germans lived beyond the borders of Germany. After postwar migrations, less than a tenth remained. Today, there are 500 000 Germans in Poland,

200 000 in Hungary, 53 000 in the Czech Republic and a few thousand in Slovakia. Most of those remaining in Romania in 1945 opted to return to Germany, and others followed during the Ceausescu years. In the 1992 census in Romania, 119 000 people claimed German minority status.

Home country support

In the 1990s, Germany was keen to stem the flow of immigrants from Eastern Europe, and offered support for remaining communities of German-speakers beyond its borders.

German aid helped to create two German-speaking schools in Hungary. In Poland, a German minority has its own German-funded newspapers and educational network. But East Europeans have long memories. As a reunited Germany secures a central place in the region's economy, many fear a resurgence of the 'Drang nach Osten' (eastwards urge) – Germany's historic colonising impulse.

Local festival   At the pilgrimage of Simleu, in northern Transylvania, the local Hungarians, known as Csangos, perform ancient rites that reinforce their distinct identity.

Spirit of cooperation

German leaders have taken care to assuage such fears by signing treaties of cooperation with Poland (1991) and Hungary (1992), and confirming Poland's western frontier (1990). In 1996, it finally agreed terms to compensate Germans expelled from Czechoslovakia's Sudetenland after the Second World War – a direct consequence of the bitterness felt by Czechs at Germany's prewar seizure of this area. After half a century, it seems that old ghosts are finally being laid to rest.

Fighting for security   This Gypsy family is well off compared to many, who are outcasts in Eastern Europe.

The nomadic misfits

The Gypsies, one of Europe's largest minority groups, have been at best tolerated, at worst persecuted. The majority of Roma live in Eastern Europe, where they are confronting an upsurge of nationalist abuse and discrimination.

Musicmakers *A Gypsy band in Hungary.*

It is thought that 3.7 million Gypsies live in Eastern Europe – 450000 in Hungary, 750000 in the Czech Republic, Slovakia and Bulgaria, and 2.5 million in Romania.

The eternal victims

Having been targeted by Hitler in the Holocaust, when 400000 Gypsies (Romanies, or Roma as they call themselves) were killed by the Nazis, the surviving Roma were subjected to forced settlement by many of the socialist governments of Eastern Europe. The purpose was to control, count and tax the Roma who had traditionally led a nomadic life.

The fall of the communist regimes in the early 1990s brought no relief to the Roma, other than the freedom to speak their own language. They became victims of the free-market economy. Often illiterate, with no representation in political parties or unions, 70 per cent of Hungarian Roma and 80 per cent of those in the Czech Republic found themselves out of work.

The Roma are subject to frequent abuse. This may be in the form of discrimination and official harassment, such as in 1994 when the Czech Republic classified all Roma as Slovak, thereby depriving them of their rights. Often, racism leads to outright violence (as in Slovakia, Poland, Bulgaria and Romania). Authorities close their eyes to crimes committed against Roma by nationalist extremists. The perpetrators, if identified, even if arrested, are often acquitted. In Romania, oppression in the 1990s was so intense that many Roma fled west to Germany.

The bonds of family

Even when they settle, the Roma have a strong sense of family. Lacking both a geographical base and a written culture, they are held together by genealogy. Everyone is expected to be able to recite their family tree, reaching back many generations and across national bound-

On the road *About 10 per cent of Gypsies are nomadic, although they often camp in one place in winter. They arrived in Europe in the 14th century and are thought to have descended from metalworkers in northern India.*

aries. Therein lies their security, their identity and their moral code. It offers proof of continuity for an ever-shifting population, reaching back into the past and forward into the future. For this reason, children have particular significance and are the objects of special care.

Marriage, as the source of children and of new family links, is a ritual that involves large-scale celebration. This is very much a man's world, in which women have few rights. The girls are married young, often in their mid teens, and a 'bride-price' is paid by the groom's parents to the parents of the bride. Traditionally, the newly married couple live with the husband's parents.

Upwardly mobile – or not? *A family of Gypsies who opt for a settled life in the city may find themselves excluded from work through discrimination, and on a downward spiral into poverty.*

The buildings tell a story

From the medieval churches of ancient Kievan Rus to the glass and steel towers of modern Warsaw, the architecture of Eastern Europe provides an insight into the history and character of each region.

Shingled turrets *A wooden belfry in Szentendre's Village Museum is typical of those found in rural Hungary.*

The architecture of a place shapes its identity and reflects its history. Romania, for instance, was until the Second World War an agricultural country, in which the village was the main cultural unit and its houses a major form of artistic expression. The Maramures region in the north of the country is characterised from afar by its distinctive blue roofs. Close up, magnificently carved gates guard the fronts of the houses and enclosures where, for safety, families lived along with their livestock. The gates are decorated with symbols, such as the tree of life. Eaves and windows feature ornate woodwork. In Olt province, the dominant houses are big and solid with several storeys. They belonged to local boyars or landed gentry. On the low-lying southeastern coast of the Dobruja region, fishermen's houses are traditionally thatched with straw.

A museum of rural architecture

Szentendre (St Andrew) is a delightful town of alleys, hidden gardens, merchants' houses and hilltop churches, lying on the River Danube, 12 miles (19 km) north of Budapest. Here, an outdoor Village Museum forms a showcase for Hungarian ethnography and architecture. Its 113 acres (46 ha) include 300 houses from all over the country. A humble peasant dwelling from Kispalad stands beside a smallholder's cottage, a wooden belfry from Nemesborzova next to a German-style house from the Kisalföld in Transdanubia.

The German legacy

The area of Sibiu, founded by Transylvanian Saxons in the 12th century, still has a particularly German feel to it. Sibiu itself, known as Hermannstadt to German-speakers, is reminiscent of a south German town. It was strongly fortified in medieval times to protect its tight-knit community from raids by Tatars and Turks. Surrounding villages, such as Soars and Rodbav, are renowned for their Saxon architecture, fortified castles, and houses with solid

Stone guardian *Spissky Hrad, Eastern Europe's largest medieval castle, keeps watch over Slovakia's Spisské Podhradie region.*

walls flanking the streets. The fortified church of Cinsor and the monastery of Simbata, both near Soars, are fine surviving examples of this Saxon style.

Hungary, too, has a distinctive style of rural architecture as seen in the long, low farmhouses, painted in grey and white, found in villages of the Veszprém region, north of Lake Balaton. Wooden belfries are another feature of the landscape. At

Country living *The village of Krasnovo, 25 miles (40 km) north-east of Plovdiv, is an example of modern Bulgarian rural architecture.*

Devout sign *The wooden houses of Hungary's Transcarpathian region often display a crucifix.*

***Hungarian delight** Szentendre is a maze of painted houses. It owes its style to its founders, Serbian refugees from the Turks.*

***Carpathian grandeur** Peles Castle in Sinaia was built by Romania's Hohenzollern king Carol I in 1883. Seized by Ceausescu, it is now a museum.*

Nyirbator, in the north-east of the Great Plain, a 17th-century shingle-roofed belfry rises 66 ft (20 m) from a wide-skirted base, with a spire that resembles a wizard's hat.

In the Czech Republic, the countryside is dotted with chateaux, built with the wealth accrued by landowners despite numerous local wars.

***Hidden world** Interior courtyards are features of domestic architecture in the apartment blocks of Budapest.*

Urban styles

Cities tend to have an amalgam of styles reflecting various periods in their histories. Budapest has both the ruins of the Roman city of Obuda, which had an amphitheatre larger than the Colosseum in Rome, and Fishermen's Bastion, an observation platform looking across the Danube from Buda's Castle Hill, built in 1905. This undulating white rampart has seven turrets representing the seven Magyar tribes that first settled in Buda in the 9th century. Prague, the 'city with 100 belfries', is a mixture of Roman, Gothic, Baroque and Art Nouveau,

all cheek-by-jowl in the shadow of a 1000-year-old castle. In Kiev, the 11th-century golden-domed cathedral of St Sophia, the pride of Kievan Rus, is dwarfed by the monumental buildings of the Soviet era. The medieval architecture of Kraków in Poland remains largely intact and harks back to the city's golden age as the seat of kings and centre of learning. Meanwhile, Warsaw's architecture is largely mid to late 20th century, the city having been bombed extensively in the Second World War.

Changing places

When consulting a street map in Eastern Europe, it's always best to check the date of publication or prepare to be thoroughly confused. Squares and boulevards, streets and passageways are losing their Soviet-era names in favour of local heroes and national historical events. In Prague, Defenders of the Peace Street is now Milady Horakove, Pioneers Street has been renamed after the philosopher Jan Patocka, and the metro station that was once named after Lenin is now Dejvice.

***Czech glory** The arcaded 18th-century square in Ceské Budejovice, with a Baroque statue of Samson at its centre, reflects the wealth made by Bohemia's rulers from its silver mines and salt trade.*

A diversity of names, a diversity of cultures

The names of Eastern European cities have changed as frequently as the countries' borders, as each successive culture has imposed its own version. Towns have different names in Polish, Russian, German, Czech, Romanian and Hungarian. Slovakia's capital, Bratislava, for instance, is Pressburg to German-speakers, but Pozsony to Hungarians, whose ancestors claimed it as their capital between 1526 and 1784. Scores of Transylvanian places have Romanian, Hungarian and German names. Tîrgu Mures is Marosvasarhely in Hungarian; Brasov is Kronstadt to Germans. Ukraine's Chernivtsi is Czernowitz in German and Cernauit in Romanian.

Sporting zenith, sporting decline

Tennis, football, gymnastics, athletics: in these and other sports Eastern Europe has nurtured heroes and heroines by the score, won a multitude of medals and made new records. But the tradition of success demanded state support. When that slipped in the 1990s, so did the achievements.

Czech champion *Ivan Lendl, the world No 1, 1985-7 and 1989.*

Eastern Europe's prowess in international sport can be measured in terms of its record results. In many sports, from tennis to weightlifting, its athletes reigned supreme for the greater part of the 20th century. Among those who dominated the postwar history of the Olympics are the Polish sprinter Irena Szewinska (200 m gold in 1968, and six other medals), Hungarian light-middleweight boxer Laszlo Papp (three times gold medallist, 1948-56), the Romanian volleyball team, and the quintuple gold medallist in water-polo, the Hungarian Dezso Gyarmathi. For these and many others, it was a good life. Yet success had its down-side: it depended on official state support that was often obsessive, draconian, and even physically harmful.

Hungary rules

Hungary not only holds the record for the most medals in water-polo – six golds and 12 silvers and bronzes – but is also the only nation other than the UK to become Olympic football champions on three occasions (1952, 1964, 1968).

The Hungarians also excelled at fencing, particularly the individual sabre, in which its team won gold medals in seven successive Olympics between 1928 and 1960. Two Hungarian champions won double golds (J. Fuchs in 1908-12; and R. Karpati in 1956-60), while Aladar Gerevitch won seven Olympic titles in the individual and team events, 1932-60.

Gymnastics was a sport for which Eastern Europeans demonstrated a particular talent. The Czech gymnast, Vera

Magic boots *Ukrainian striker Andrei Shevchenko, star of Dynamo Kiev and of his national team.*

Golden foil *The fencing champion Timea Nagy of Hungary is tossed by delighted team-mates after winning the gold for the individual épée in the Sydney Olympics, 2000.*

Hungary's rebellious footballers

In 1956, when the Hungarian uprising was crushed by the USSR, it also brought to an end the golden age of Budapest's Honved football team. Honved (meaning 'Defenders of the Motherland') had emerged victorious under the politician and coach Gusztav Sebes. The squad won the Olympics in 1952 and twice beat England. To their countrymen, the players were gods. In the midst of the uprising, the team was touring Europe. Then they flew on to Brazil, to the fury of the Hungarian Football Association, which banned them from playing for a year. By the time the tour ended, Soviet tanks were in Budapest. Many players decided to seek exile, including their star, Ferenc Puskas, who went on to a glorious career with Real Madrid. Honved's glory days were over.

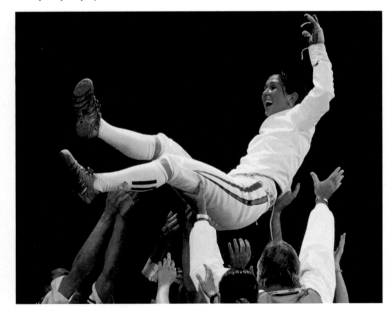

Victory in Europe *Steaua Bucharest, Romania's most popular team, celebrates winning the European Cup-Winners' Cup in 1986.*

Tennis superstar   Martina Navratilova, the Czech-born tennis star who defected to the USA, won 330 titles between 1973 and 1994, including 50 in the Grand Slam championships.

Pole-vaulting king   Ukraine's Sergei Bubka was world champion for six years between 1983 and 1997. He vaulted over 6 m (19 ft 8 in) on 40 occasions and raised the world record 35 times.

Caslavska, won five gold medals in two successive Olympics, 1964-8, Agnes Keleti (Hungary) won four golds (one in 1952; and three in 1956) and Romania's Nadia Comaneci took three golds and was the sensation of the 1976 Olympics.

Tennis supremos

Eastern Europe's sportsmen and women have excelled in all competitions, not just the Olympics. They have been particularly successful at tennis. Romania produced champions such as Ilie Nastase and Ion Tiriac, but Czechoslovakia takes the prize for the sheer number of winners.

Jaroslav Drobny, an exiled Czech, was the first to break the US-Australian monopoly over tennis in the 1950s, beating the Australian Ken Rosewall to win Wimbledon in a 58-game match in 1954. Jan Kodes won the French championship twice (1970, 1971) and Wimbledon (1973). Ivan Lendl took 70 titles in all in the 1980s (including the US and Australian championships). Czech-born Martina Navratilova, who became a US citizen, won the Ladies Singles champion at Wimbledon on nine occasions, including six successive tournaments, 1982-7.

In the 1990s, as state funding for athletes declined and banishments due to drug-taking took their toll, East Europeans began to disappear from the top of the rankings.

The young Czech hopeful, Petr Korda, was banned for drug-taking in 1998.

Few Eastern European tennis players will be remembered from the 1990s, other than Poland's Jedrejowska, Hungary's Takacs and its young star Andrea Temesvari, who played in ten world-ranking championships at the age of 15 and declared his brief and meteoric career at an end three years later. In 2000 the Belarussian tennis player Vladimir Voltchkov reached the semi-finals at Wimbledon.

Lifting for gold

Weightlifting was a tradition that preceded communism, starting with the gold won by the heavyweight Jaroslav Skobia of Czechoslovakia in the 1932 Olympics. After the Second World War, superb training facilities and state backing turned Eastern Europe into a seedbed for strong men, such as the lightweight Waldemar Baszanowski of Poland, who won gold in 1964 and 1968. Others followed – Mitkov and Zlatev from Poland, Becheru and Vlad from Romania, Rusev and Nikolov from Bulgaria. But as with other sports, disqualifications for taking performance-enhancing drugs have had a dire effect. In the communist years, coaches routinely dispensed steroids and the practice continued. At the 2000 Sydney Olympics, two Romanians were excluded before the opening ceremony and six Bulgarians were banned during the competition.

Disgraced winner   Bulgaria's bantamweight Mitko Grablev won the gold in Seoul in 1988, only to be disqualified for drug-taking.

Bar skills Nadia Comaneci, the gold medal-winning Romanian gymnast.

Nadia Comaneci, Romanian gymnast

At the 1976 Olympics in Montreal a new phenomenon was unveiled: teenage Romanian gymnasts who could accomplish astonishing feats on bars and beams. Under the dictatorial coach, Bela Karoly, the most breathtaking performance came from the 14-year-old Nadia Comaneci, who seven times took maximum points, amassing a total of 79.275 out of a possible 80. She left Montreal with three gold medals, one silver and one bronze. Her success and fame worldwide proved irresistible PR for Nicolae Ceausescu and his oppressive regime. It was not a role Comaneci was happy with. She retired to coach the Romanian team, then in 1989 she defected to Canada. After the fall of Ceausescu she was welcomed back to Romania as a national heroine, but continues to live abroad.

A winter wonderland

Dusted with snow, cities such as Prague can be magical places in winter. Dancing and skating, snowballing and eating hot strudels keep out the chill, and the tradition of the winter ball attracts partygoers from all walks of life.

Dancing the winter away *At a traditional celebration marking the end of winter in Minsk, a Belarussian soldier dances with his girlfriend.*

Imagine yourself in Prague, crossing the Charles Bridge. The silhouette of the castle and the old town loom through mist. This is one of Europe's most famous scenes, one that usually attracts a cast of thousands. But now you stand alone, without the usual horde of buskers and street artists, with only the bridge's 30 statues and the cold for company. There is silence. This need not be a dream: anyone can experience it if they happen to be on the bridge early on a winter's day.

The lure of the dance

After a day's walking in the cold, there's nothing like a dance to warm you up. Most visitors to Prague have heard of the glitzy Opera Ball. What they probably have not heard about is the mass of lesser-known balls that take place all across Eastern Europe.

A century ago in Budapest, winter balls were seen as subversive gatherings, encouraging political and cultural opposition to Habsburg absolutism. They still preserve their liberal character and welcome people of all professions, all ages, all communities – in theory at least. Some balls are more exclusive, and you need the right connections to be invited. You certainly will not have a chance of gaining admittance if you look too casual – dinner jackets and long dresses

Sweets for my sweet

Hot chocolate and cakes are an irresistible speciality of Eastern Europe. Fruit turnovers, doughnuts, apple strudels, white cheesecakes, chocolate gâteaux – if desserts like these remind you of Vienna, there is a good reason. In the days of the Habsburg Empire, young girls would flock to the capital to seek their fortunes. To charm their way into society and a good marriage, they learned to make a rich variety of *torten*, *kolacs* and *butchas*. If they returned to the provinces, they took their recipes with them and passed them on. Mothers in Habsburg lands, like mothers everywhere, impressed on their daughters that the way to a man's heart was through his stomach.

are *de rigueur* – or if you do not like the local beer. And you need to be fit: whirling, foot-stamping czardas soon take the chill off the air.

The joy of sport

After a ball, you will be expected to go tobogganing or skating the next day. Eastern Europe's parks are winter playgrounds for adults and children alike. Prague, in particular, has many open spaces, such as Letná Park overlooking the city. A huge statue of Stalin stood in the park before it was blown up in 1962 and replaced by a giant metronome. Stromovka ('place of trees') is another favourite spot for walking, jogging and skating. It was laid out by Rudolf II as a deer park in the 16th century.

Fun with snow *With Prague's cathedral dominating the skyline, young people play on Petřín Hill, the largest open space in the Czech Republic's capital.*

The light fantastic *Waltz, polka, tango and rumba: traditional-style dancing classes are a popular pastime in Prague.*

Of languages and alphabets

In addition to the nine official languages of Eastern Europe, there are scores of other major tongues, including Lithuanian, German and Turkish, and a mass of minor ones, too, such as the Gypsy language, Romany, which has several dialects. Two alphabets are in use: Roman for the predominantly Catholic countries and Cyrillic for the Orthodox nations.

Daily read *Absorbed in Magyar Nemzet (Hungarian Nation).*

Most Eastern Europeans speak a Slavonic language of some sort, with the exception of the Hungarians and Romanians.

The 13 Slavonic languages fall into three main groups. Western Slavonic comprises Czech, Slovak and Polish. Its southern relatives are Bulgarian and the languages of the former Yugoslavia. The eastern Slavonic groups comprise Ukrainian, Belarussian and Russian. Having separated from their parent-tongue in the 6th to 9th centuries, languages have overlapping vocabularies. Slight linguistic differences were intensified by the division in the Christian Church between Rome and Byzantium. Those languages that fell into the Roman Catholic

Romanised Slavonic *As shop signs in Kraków show, the Polish language uses Latin script, like all the western Slavonic languages.*

sphere (Polish, Czech, Slovak) are now written in Roman characters. Cyrillic, which developed from the alphabet devised by the missionary saints, Cyril and Methodius in the 9th century, is used for those languages traditionally under Greek or Russian Orthodox control (Bulgarian, Ukrainian, Belarussian). Orthodox influence gave this branch of Christianity its own lingua franca, Church Slavonic, which survives as a liturgical language.

Several other Slavonic tongues are also in minority use: Sorbian, spoken in eastern Germany, and two Baltic dialects, Slovincian and Kashubian.

The odd ones out

Of the the two non-Slavonic languages, Romanian derives from Latin, the language of its Roman rulers until the 5th century. It was written in the Cyrillic alphabet until the 19th century when the Roman alphabet was adopted. The Moldovan language is virtually identical to Romanian.

Hungarian was brought to Europe by Magyar nomads from Central Asia and the Urals in the 9th century. It is not part of the Indo-European family to which nearly all European languages, from English to Armenian, belong. It is distantly related to Finnish and Estonian. Though it uses Latin script, Hungarian is fantastically complex, and one of the hardest European languages to learn.

St Cyril's legacy *The Cyrillic script in Bulgarian newspapers is a reminder of Bulgaria's links with Greek Orthodoxy and Russian.*

Slav script *A Slavonic manuscript in Bucharest recalls the influence of Orthodox missionaries on Romania.*

A dream of unity

Esperanto was invented in 1887 by Ludwig Zamenhof in an attempt to create a universal form of communication. Zamenhof was an oculist from Bialystok, in eastern Poland, where Polish, Lithuanian, German, Yiddish and Russian all overlapped. He named his language after his pseudonym, Doktor Esperanto ('Doctor Hopeful'). It has 100 000 to 200 000 speakers, who preserve it in journals, translations and radio broadcasts.

Religion marches on

A thousand years ago the Churches of Rome and Byzantium broadly divided Eastern Europe with Catholicism to the west and Orthodoxy to the north and east. These boundaries still exist today, but conceal a more complex religious picture comprising Jews and Muslims and a multitude of Christian sects. Minorities, such as the Uniates of Ukraine, are re-establishing themselves after years of suppression.

The religious diversity of Eastern Europe is closely linked to the battles for supremacy between the region's dominant powers, whether Catholic or Orthodox, over the past 1000 years.

Catholic differences

Poles and Slovaks express a fervour in their Catholicism which is lacking both among the more reserved Hungarians and the Czechs. In Hungary, 15 per cent of the population is atheist; 66 per cent of Czechs say they have no religion at all.

There are historical reasons for these differences. In Poland and Slovakia the Church was the focus of nationalism, whereas among the Czechs it was discredited as a tool of Habsburg imperial rule.

In Hungary, the Church had its moment of glory during the uprising of 1956, when the anti-Soviet Cardinal Jozsef Mindszenty – newly released from prison by the liberal communist government – protested against the Soviet invasion and sought sanctuary in the American embassy.

Latter-day pilgrims *Pilgrimages such as this one near Bardejov, in north-eastern Slovakia, remain popular, especially among young people.*

Papal portrait *A poster honours the Polish-born Pope John Paul II, former archbishop of Kraków.*

The cardinal remained at the embasssy for 15 years. Meanwhile, the Church made its accommodation with communism, and lost credibility among ordinary people.

The appeal of Protestantism

Bohemia (part of today's Czech Republic) had a tradition of intransigence reaching back to the Jan Huss rebellion in the early 15th century. So when Martin Luther, the German religious reformer, broke with Rome in the 16th century, Bohemia provided fertile

Catholic festivals *Left: A procession in Lowicz, Poland, in celebration of Corpus Christi, the summer festival at which Catholics recall Christ's physical presence in the Eucharist. Right: Moravians in the Czech Republic mark the Assumption of the Virgin Mary, August 15.*

Polish pilgrimage In the Jasna Gora monastery, Czestochowa, celebrants honour the Black Madonna icon, thought to be of medieval Byzantine origin.

Hungarian reformers Bas-reliefs of the 16th-century Reformation preachers, John Calvin and Ulrich Zwingli, in the façade of the Great Reformed Church in Debrecen. Under their influence Debrecen became a centre for Protestantism in Hungary and the site of a Calvinist school.

Hungary's political and social life. The national anthem, written by a Calvinist poet, is used as a prayer to close every church service, whether Catholic or Protestant.

Polish fervour

In Poland, the dominance of Catholicism obscures the fact that for centuries this was a country of many confessions. From the Middle Ages, when the area's tribesmen were converted by Roman Catholic missionaries, it remained open to other sects and religions. Jews forced to flee Western Europe in the 13th and 14th centuries found refuge here under royal protection that lasted until the 17th century. The Reformation, which saw Lutheran churches established in Prussia and Lithuania, evoked no great reaction in Poland, and the effects of the Counter-Reformation were mainly evident in education. In the 17th century, when Ukraine and Poland were

soil. The Reformation split the country: though most of those who profess a religion in the Czech Republic remain Catholic, Protestants form a 300 000-strong minority, based mainly in the north.

Hungary is more evenly divided between Catholics and Protestants. Since the Habsburg rulers were Catholics and the Catholic Church was a focal point for national resistance to Ottoman rule, the majority of those Hungarians who profess a religion are Catholics. But in the late 16th century, local Lutherans and Calvinists put up a determined resistance to Rome's Counter-Reformation, securing the survival of a Protestant minority that amounts to about 21 per cent today. The two sects interweave in

Religious tensions A Carmelite nunnery stands abandoned next to the former Auschwitz concentration camp in Poland. The nunnery was built to commemorate Polish Catholic victims of the Second World War. It was vacated in 1993 after Jewish groups opposed a Catholic presence on a site of Jewish suffering.

Klausen Synagogue, Prague.

Ageing students Jews study in the first synagogue to be opened in Lviv in Ukraine in 40 years, but emigration has led to a decline in the population.

united, aristocratic land-owners tolerated the Orthodoxy professed by their Ukrainian and Belarussian peasants. On its southern fringes, where the Polish Empire touched the Ottoman Empire, Islam survived unscathed.

It was only with the collapse of Poland in the 18th century and the struggle for regeneration that Poles turned to Catholicism as a means to withstand German and Russian imperial aspirations, as expressed in Protestantism and Orthodoxy. With the destruction of the Jewish community in the Holocaust in the 1940s and the realignment of Poland's borders to the west, outside Orthodox areas, Poland became overwhelmingly Catholic – 93.5 per cent of the population claimed to be Catholic in the 1992 census.

Communist rule reinforced the position of the Church as the symbol of Polish history. In the later years of socialism, it took the lead in opposing state control, winning a position strengthened in 1978 when the Archbishop of Kraków, Karol Wojtyla, was elected Pope as John Paul II. In the summer of 1980, photographs of priests taking the confession of striking Gdansk dockworkers illustrated the central role of Catholicism in Poland's social and political life. Thereafter, with the Pope's encouragement, priests played a leading part in the reformist movement, spearheaded by the

Gdansk trade union, Solidarity. When in October 1984 one of the most active and popular priests, Jerzy Popieluszko, was assassinated by the secret police, the murder swung the entire population behind Solidarity, the Church and the reformers.

Since the fall of communism, the Poles' commitment to their religion remains undiminished – 6 million people took part in events to mark the Pope's visit in 1997. But 60 per cent of the population say the Church plays too large a role in political life. They disapprove of its condemnation of the new constitution, and its position regarding the restrictive abortion laws. The number of those applying to train for the priesthood has declined.

The Jews: destruction and survival

After 1945, it seemed that for the Jews of Polish origin the nightmare had ended when almost half of the 400 000 survivors in the USSR were deported or repatriated to Poland. Then in July 1946 there was an outburst of violence in the south-eastern city of Kielce, in which 43 Jews died and 50 were injured. Within months, 100 000 Jews had fled from Poland, leaving a hard core of 30 000, mainly those who were well-assimilated members of the intelligentsia. In March 1968, the communist government faced an internal crisis and – as Stalin had done 30 years before – accused the

Painted wonder The church in Voronets in northern Romania is one of several 15th-century monastic buildings that were painted with external frescoes depicting Biblical scenes.

Jews of conspiring in a Zionist plot and of being 'rootless cosmopolitans'. The campaign inspired another mass exodus that left just 1500 Jews in the country.

In Romania, the prewar population of Jews numbered 750 000. Anti-Semitism was particularly rife in the occupied territories of Bukovina and Bessarabia (present-day Moldova) and Transylvania. These areas bore the brunt of Romanian and German anti-Semitism: some 265 000 Jews perished during the Second World War. Of the 430 000 survivors, 40 000 left for Israel by 1948, another 100 000 by the early 1950s, and a steady stream followed in the face of low-level but relentless anti-Semitism during the Ceausescu years. About 20 000 Jews remain.

In Hungary, of the 470 000-strong prewar Jewish population, 140 000 survived, mainly in Budapest, which had held one of the most important Jewish communities in Eastern Europe. Many owed their survival to the Swedish diplomat, Raoul Wallenberg, who housed thousands of Jews under Swedish diplomatic protection. He vanished into a Russian prison camp in 1945, in circumstances that have never been explained. After the war, many Jews opted to stay, a decision reinforced from the 1960s by the relative liberalism of Jan Kadar's regime. The 80 000 remaining Jews were

Torchbearer In Minsk cathedral an elderly woman introduces her grandson to Orthodoxy.

able to re-establish a lively community, well assimilated but free to worship in their own way.

The world of Orthodoxy

Orthodoxy prevails throughout Ukraine, Belarus, Moldova, Romania and Bulgaria. In Romania and Bulgaria in particular, religious practice was the pillar of cultural continuity during the 500 years of Turkish occupation under the Ottoman Empire. When the empire fell in the 19th century, it was Orthodoxy that symbolised national regeneration for these countries. As the fount of Russian Orthodoxy, Moscow has maintained an involvement and, with its guidance today, Orthodox leaders across Eastern Europe now work closely with governments. The restoration of churches and a sense of religious community has in many areas provided stability in the post-communist years.

The Uniate hybrid

On the borders between Catholicism and Orthodoxy, the two mingled to form the Eastern rite Churches. They are composed of Catholics who acknowledge the Pope yet use Orthodox practices. The inspiration came from a desire to reunite Christianity in the 15th century, but the formal beginning was in 1596, when Poland's Catholic king ordered his Orthodox Ukrainian subjects to accept the primacy of the Pope. The hybrid, the Uniate Church, was looked down on by both the Russian Orthodox and Catholic Churches, but it thrived nevertheless. Ukraine's Uniates number 4.5 million. In Romania, where the 1.5 million Uniates were suppressed in the 1940s, only a few have re-established themselves. Hungary and Bulgaria also have small Uniate congregations.

New nations, new Churches

Orthodox Churches are organised as independent bodies on a national basis under an archbishop, bishop, metropolitan or patriarch. After a brief independence in the 1920s, Ukraine's Church was run from Moscow until Ukraine broke away in 1991. Belarus also acquired its own Church when it declared independence from the USSR. Moldova's Church is divided between the patriarchates of Moscow and Bucharest.

Monastic ways Restored in the 19th century, Bulgaria's Rila Monastery has sustained Orthodoxy for more than 1000 years.

Intimate worship Uniate worshippers of the Eastern rite Church often hold services in shrines set up in private houses.

Time to party

Whatever the date, there is sure to be a festival, whether to mark the arrival of a new season, express a desire for divine protection, or simply to attract good luck. Processing with a goat, throwing water at passers-by and making satirical nativity cribs are just some of the many customs.

Christmas and Easter hold pride of place among the many religious festivals of the nine countries.

Festive Poland

Christmas Eve in Poland has a special air of mystery and sanctity. Ancient superstitions are adhered to, such as no lying down or you will get ill, no borrowing money, and fasting until nightfall. Everyone takes part in decorating the house with apples, which symbolise health and beauty, nuts for a happy marriage, and straw and seeds for year-round prosperity. Activities are designed to involve both grown-ups and children.

The high point of the festivities is the Christmas Eve meal. In Polish homes, the appearance of the first star of the evening is the signal for everyone to gather round the table, at which one place is left vacant for any lost traveller who may need hospitality. To ensure prosperity in the coming year, each guest must taste every one of the 12 dishes – in honour of the 12 Apostles. The evening meal

Water fights and painted eggs

To celebrate the return of spring, on Easter Monday Poles are allowed to shower passers-by with water from their windows without fear of reprisal. They are obliged to show consideration towards children and the elderly, and keep their watery assault for those who can take total immersion from above (which, they may remind their victims, is a way of purifying them of their sins). They can make peace by offering eggs as symbols of rebirth. Sometimes these are *kraszanki* eggs, boiled in spinach, beetroot juice or onion peelings. Others, like the *pisanki* eggs pictured left, are painted to feature the pale green of spring grass and the yellow of the strengthening sun.

Macabre ritual A masked reveller at the Busojaras Carnival in Mohács, Hungary, a pagan spring festival that also reviles the Turks, who defeated the Hungarians nearby in 1526.

does not include meat – goose, duck and turkey are reserved for Christmas Day itself. Afterwards, groups of children dressed as the three kings, angels or shepherds go from door to door collecting small change and cakes. At midnight it is traditional to go to church for mass.

Carp and vodka

Throughout Eastern Europe, the main ingredients of the Christmas meal are flour, cereals, vegetables, fish and fruit. But each country has its own specialities. Czechs favour carp, and barrels of live fish appear on the streets in December. In Ukraine, the main course is roast pork. Romanians serve *cozonac*, a brioche-style plum dessert.

Orthodox Christmas starts on the eve of January 6, with the coming of Christmas Day marked by a midnight mass. Festivities

The Christmas cribs of Kraków

Polish Christmas cribs have been notorious since the Middle Ages for including certain elements that would not be approved of by the Church. They are nativity scenes in the traditional sense, but with a satirical bent that has won them increasing appeal. Since the First World War, local amateurs have modelled their cribs on the town's historical monuments – the Church of the Virgin Mary, Wawel Cathedral – and filled them with fantastical elements inspired by local characters and goings-on in the city. So popular have they become that the council has designated a spot on the statue in Rynek Glowny (central square, left) where they can be displayed on the first Thursday of December. The winning design – which could take up to 1000 hours to make – is announced the following Sunday.

Bulgarian revellers The feathered masks symbolise the triumph of life over death. Those who wear them are known as 'Survatsi,' and they wish people a happy new year with the cry 'Surva godena!'

Romanian merriment Locals dress in national costume and gather to make music during the winter festival in Sighetu Marmatiei, northern Romania.

end on January 19, with a baptism, when priests cut a cross-shaped hole in the ice of a river or lake and perform a mass nearby. Afterwards, those who feel brave and hardy enough take a dip.

In Ukraine, the coming of the new year is marked by an exchange of gifts, the singing of traditional songs and the consumption of liberal amounts of vodka. In Poland there are balls. Rural Romanians take a plough, decorated with leaves, from house to house to cut a furrow on each piece of land as a symbol of good health.

Charmed by a goat

The strength of rural tradition ensures that the changing seasons are observed across the nine countries, with every turning point seized upon as a chance to ward off evil spirits and attract good fortune in the coming year.

In Slovakia, the days between Christmas and Epiphany (January 6) are marked by processions of people wearing animal masks, with a goat in pride of place dispensing happiness, health and wealth. A mime play is performed in Romania with actors dressed as goats, bears and horses.

Czech villagers celebrate the arrival of spring on Palm Sunday by making a straw man or bear, which is ceremonially drowned or burned. In Poland, they mark the first day of spring by drowning

a scarecrow. In other places gifts are of particular importance: Bulgarians mark March 1 by spring-cleaning their houses and exchanging red and white confectionary figures known as *martenitsas* (the red is for Christ's blood, the white for winter's snow).

Looking for love

In western Romania, around 40 000 people gather every July on Mount Gaina in the Apuseni Mountains for the two-day 'Girl Fair'. Traditionally, this was an occasion at which young people from remote communities came together to find marriage partners, with everyone dressed to look their best. Nowadays, people come more for the processions, dances and songs. In Bulgaria, the arrival of summer is traditionally May 21, when villagers used to perform the 'fire dance' on hot coals.

Blessed meal Orthodox Romanians meet at a monastery to mark the end of Lent. They await the priest's blessing before a celebratory meal.

Goulash and paprika

The menus of Eastern Europe are rooted in peasant fare designed to carry farming folk through the harshest of winters when supplies are scarce. They have been enriched by the cuisines of the Habsburgs and Ottomans, whose courtly recipes and oriental taste added spice to the humble dumpling.

Eastern Europe has its staple dishes: well-done meats, often in the form of meatballs or ragouts, eaten with potatoes and cabbage in various manifestations, thick winter soups and thirst-quenching summer ones, followed by desserts designed especially for those with a very sweet tooth. But every area has its own range of specialities.

Southern taste

In Bulgaria, Romania and Moldova, the cuisine looks more to the east than the north – and for a good historical reason. Five hundred years of Ottoman rule left its mark, in the form of sticky desserts and strong 'Turkish' coffee. In the area's mild climate, fruits and vegetables grow in abundance.

Polish delicacy *Beef rolls – zraz zawijany – are made from thin slices of beef filled with salted gherkins and braised in wine and herbs. They are served with smoked veal breast.*

National fare   A table laid with a range of traditional Ukrainian dishes.

People enjoy grilled meat and cheese, mostly made of ewe's milk. No Bulgarian meal is complete without a *chopska* salad of cucumbers, tomatoes and grated cheese, the colours recalling the green, red and white of the Bulgarian flag. Bulgarians also consume immense quantities of yoghurt, often enriched with buffalo milk, which is traditionally thought to confer long life.

Pork is the basic ingredient of many Romanian and Moldovan dishes, where it is served as ragouts, grills (*muschi*), cold cuts and sausages such as the delicious little *mititei*. A legacy from Ottoman days is *ciorba*, a sharp soup made from fermented bran and sour cream. It is so popular that it has almost become the national dish.

Bread and cheese
This Romanian bread goes well with telemea, *a ewe's milk cheese.*

Fruit juices with attitude

Plum brandy – clear, fiery, famous for its kick – has many names: *slivovice* among Czech-speakers, *szilvapálinka* (Hungary), *sliwowica* (Poland), *slivova* (Bulgaria) and *tuica* (Romania, Moldova). Like its relatives made from apricots and cherries, plum brandy is reputed to have life-enhancing powers.

Spice of life Peppers (paprikas) dry on the wall of a house in Hungary before being made into spice. Shakers of paprika are often found on the table.

Ottoman flavours

The Ottomans also left their mark on Hungary's cuisine with paprika, the powder made from the seeds of red peppers. It is used to garnish dishes such as goulash (a beef and vegetable stew originally made by shepherds), *pörkölt* (a meaty ragout), the chicken-based *papkrikás csirke* and a fish soup known as *haláslé*.

Salamis are a Hungarian speciality. They were introduced at the end of the 19th century by Italians working for a pork butcher in Szeged, where the local climate encouraged the growth of the benign mould that produces their distinctive taste.

Hungarian chefs are also strongly influenced by the Habsburgs, whose tastes linked the culinary traditions of Hungary, the Czech Republic and Slovakia. Czechs have a particular fondness for whipped cream, which even finds its way into meat dishes, such as Prague ham and blueberry roast beef. Food is often breaded, not just meats but also vegetables and cheeses. The Czech national speciality are dumplings, known as *knedlíky*, that accompany a multitude of dishes. They are served plain, or stuffed with liver or bacon, and can even appear as a dessert, filled with plums or other fruit and garnished with icing sugar and poppy seeds. In Slovakia, the menu usually includes pork, *halusky* (a type of gnocchi made with potato and ewe's milk cheese), and a goulash similar to that of Hungary.

Recipes from the wheatlands

In the communist years, Ukraine was considered a leader in the culinary arts. A combination of extensive wheat fields and ingenuity gave rise to more than 70 varieties of bread, from wholemeal to refined, either plain or covered in poppy or sesame seeds, or mixed

Preparing for winter In Hungary, all the family turn out to make a hearty supply of pork sausages.

A taste for sugar

Drawing on both Turkish and Austrian traditions, Hungarian *pâtissiers* turned themselves into masters of the dessert. Compared to dessert menus elsewhere, Hungarian ones are treasure troves. Who could resist *dabostorta*, a creamy *mokka* cake glazed with caramelised orange; or *rétes*, apple or cherry strudels; or *gundel palacsinta*, flambé pancakes with almond cream and raisins topped with chocolate sauce; or *somlói galuska*, a dumpling made with vanilla nuts and chocolate with an orange and rum sauce?

Autumn fare In a Warsaw market, a stallholder spreads out ceps (Boletus mushrooms) collected in nearby forests. Poles are adept at finding recipes for mushrooms.

with nuts or honey. Cereals also come in the form of *kasha*, a porridge of wheat or barley, served with cabbage to accompany meat. But Ukraine, reaching as it does to the Black Sea, also looks south for inspiration. Seafoods are popular, as are vegetables that flourish in the Mediterranean-like conditions, such as peppers and aubergines. These form the main ingredient in the Ukrainian dish known as 'Poor Man's Caviar'.

Foraging for mushrooms

In Belarus and Poland, Russian-style soups are often on the menu, such as the beetroot-based *borshch* (known as *barszcz* in Polish) and *chlodnik*, a local equivalent of Russia's *okroshka* (cold cucumber soup) Mushrooms become a staple food in late summer, when mushroom gathering becomes a national obsession. They are either marinated or tossed into soups and ragouts, and make a nutritious addition to the winter menu. Since much of this area is far from the sea, fish finds little favour in Poland, Belarus and Ukraine, except that the Poles eat carp on special occasions such as Christmas, and also consider Baltic herrings a delicacy.

How to drink like a Pole

Every language has its similes for drunkenness. Unlike the English, a Frenchman does not 'drink like a fish' or 'get drunk as a lord', he 'drinks like a Pole'. The expression is attributed to Napoleon. Apparently, when he was in Spain in 1808, he was struck by the spirit of the Poles fighting for him. His aides said this was due to their consumption of alcohol. 'Well,' said Napoleon, 'drink like them, and match their bravery!' Today, Poles regard their drinking habits in a similar positive light, for every Pole claims to 'drink like a dragon'. It is considered a virtue to be able to knock back little glasses of *sliwowica* (plum brandy) and vodka without flinching, with a few gherkins to soak it up.

Powerful spirit Poland is renowned for its Zubrówka (bison grass vodka).

Bath time in the East

The Romans were the first to discover the therapeutic benefits of the mineral-rich hot springs flowing from the hills of the Czech Republic, Slovakia, Bulgaria and Hungary. The Turks and Habsburgs built splendid pools beneath spangled domes with colonnaded walkways, and by the 19th century Europe's elite were flocking to the fashionable spas.

In Hungary, a visit to hot-spring baths is as much a part of everyday life as going to a concert or passing an hour or two in a café. People go not just for treatment or to prevent illness, but also to relax, something they have been doing since Roman times. It is hardly surprising that the baths play such an important part in their lives, given the immense amount of mineral-rich water that pours from the 117 springs in the Buda Hills – 16 million gallons (70 million litres) per day. The practice declined after the departure of the Romans, but was revived in medieval times when the Knights of St John built a hospice on the site of the Rudás Baths. The Turks, who ruled Budapest from 1541 to 1686, ensured continuity, since Muslims are obliged to wash five times daily before prayer.

Four of the six major baths – among them the Rudás Baths – have colonnades and cupolas that reveal their Turkish origins. The 19th-century façade of the Kiraly Baths conceals their Turkish interior. The Gellért Baths, built in the early 20th century alongside the exclusive Gellért Hotel, have always had a reputation for being upmarket, which is reinforced today by a clientele of rich foreigners. Mineral baths are also a boon to the medical profession: the

Ottoman heritage *The 16th-century Turkish domed cupola over Budapest's Rudás Baths is pierced by little windows of coloured glass that allow a dim light to filter through to the octagonal pool.*

The spas of Eastern Europe

In ancient times, the Greeks ascribed magical qualities to hot springs and built cult sites nearby. The Romans took them over both for health and as places to meet and relax. They indulged in every type of treatment – steam baths, hot-water baths, cold-water baths, rub-downs and massages. They even laid down the rules that spa treatments should be varied and last for three weeks. The coming of Christianity, with its disapproval of pleasure, brought a reaction that lasted until the Renaissance revived the old practices. In the 18th and 19th centuries, taking the waters became fashionable. Scientists and doctors studied the effects of the mineral-rich hot springs, but whatever the medical advantages, thermal pools were acclaimed as places of wide-ranging, even miraculous, benefit. Towns sprang up around them, known as 'spas' after the Belgian town that became Europe's favourite hot-spring resort.

Prewar glory *Budapest's Gellért Hotel, built in 1913, is renowned both for its Art Nouveau architecture and for the hot springs that flow into its baths from the hill behind.*

Lukács Baths are the headquarters of Hungary's National Institute for Rheumatology and Physiotherapy.

High society

In the days of the Habsburg Empire, Karlovy Vary – in today's Czech Republic – was known by its German name, Karlsbad (meaning Charles Spa), a reference to the 14th-century emperor,

How to 'take the waters'

Swim in it, or drink it? That was the question about the mineral-rich water that concerned the early practitioners of balneology, as the science of water-curing is known. Some claimed that benefits came only to those who drank numerous pints a day or bathed for hours at a time, as if disease could be scourged from the body like evil spirits of old. Nowadays, the benefits are better understood. Neither bathing nor drinking works miracles, but both can improve some conditions and prevent the onset of others. Hot springs are classified by the chemical content of the water. Some, such as those containing radioactive elements, are suitable only for external use. Others, such as alkaline waters rich in hydrocarbons, can be swallowed. And some spas use both types.

Awesome architecture The Colonnade in Mariánské Lázne (Marienbad), built in 1889, is like a cathedral devoted to the mineral-rich waters that flow into its pools.

Greetings from Karlsbad A 1906 postcard from a German family in Karlovy Vary is a reminder of the turn-of-the-century days when the town was a haunt of the rich and famous from all over Europe.

Charles IV, who was said to have discovered the first of the 12 sulphurous springs that flow from the Bohemian hills. Nearby lies Mariánské Lázne (Marienbad, or the Baths of Mary), where 40 springs were owned by the local monastery until the monks built up the spa in the 19th century. Both towns became famous throughout European society, attracting the likes of Goethe, Chateaubriand, Beethoven, Chopin, Turgenev, Chekhov, Gorki, Peter the Great, King Edward VII and Wagner. Names may change, but not the ambiance. The mountain settings and the colonnaded, Baroque buildings still work their old magic on today's clientele.

Steam heat In Budapest's outdoor Széchenyi Baths, people like to play chess while enjoying water, which remains at a steamy 38°C (100°F) even in the depths of winter.

Mineral lake Holidaymakers swim in Europe's largest thermal lake at Héviz, in Hungary, a few miles from Lake Balaton's western shore. The waters, once used for tanning leather, offer relief from rheumatism and skin diseases.

Café society

From the moment coffee was introduced in the 18th century, cafés began appearing. In the 19th century they became favourite meeting places for writers and artists and were often lavishly decorated in the latest Baroque style. Today, they vie for popularity with beer halls and wine cellars.

Coffee and cakes *Gerbeaud's is a Budapest institution.*

In the golden age of café society at the end of the 19th century Budapest had 600 coffee-houses and salons where intellectuals and artists gathered to exchange ideas. They ate cakes and drank little glasses of sweet coffee strong enough to raise the heartbeat.

A Syrian, Theodat Damascenus, introduced coffee to Eastern Europe at the beginning of the 18th century, and the coffee-house soon became an important meeting place. Like their equivalents on Paris's Left Bank, the *kavarny* were hotbeds of gossip and new ideas, where people discussed literary periodicals such as *Nyugat* (The West) or the songs of Endre Ady, whose poems invigorated Hungarians with intense verses about love, war, politics and God.

Meeting places for the literati

Prague, too, had its café society. As a casual visitor to Café Archa in the early 20th century, you might have crossed paths with Max Brod, or seen Kafka playing the pinball machines, or spotted the rough draft of a soon-to-be-famous novel lying beside your cup. Here, or at Slavia's or the Union, you would have found members of the Devetsil group, founded by the avant-garde artist Karel Teige to celebrate modern life in 'picture poems' of images and words. Most of Prague's cafés would have had a dictionary and paper to hand.

Flavours of the past

Out of favour under communism, cafés once again spill out onto pavements from graceful interiors. In Budapest, a typical Baroque-style coffee-house with glass lampshades and painted ceilings, will serve *Hortybagy* pancakes (stuffed with braised meat) and grilled foie gras. These will be followed in Habsburg tradition by a pastry-based cream cake in Gerbeaud's or Angelika's, Budapest's most famous patisseries. In the Polish town of Kraków's inner city, there are 400 cafés, with chairs, tables and parasols spreading over the squares at the first sign of sun.

A pint and a pancake

Of all the eating and drinking establishments in Eastern Europe, pride of place must go to the wine cellars and beer halls. A visit to a tavern such as U Medvídku (The Little Bear) in Prague offers an insight into Czech life. Here you will fight your way

Music underground *A jazz band plays at Fat Mo's Music Club in Budapest. At other times, clientele in the vaulted cellar can hear rock or techno bands.*

The rebirth of Café Slavia

From the 1930s, Café Slavia in Prague became famous for its literary and political connections. It is renowned for remaining open right through the communist era. After the 'Velvet Revolution' in 1989, which preceded independence, it was sold to an American company and closed for 'renovation'. The Czech president Vaclav Havel, who had been a regular at the café in his days as a young dissident playwright in the 1960s, protested to the owners that they were spoiling relations between Czech intellectuals and American capitalism. After a long and bitter dispute, Café Slavia reopened on November 17, 1997.

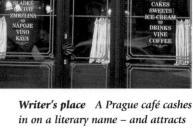

Writer's place *A Prague café cashes in on a literary name – and attracts a modern clientele with 'fast food'.*

Writers' retreat A Gypsy band plays czardas music in Budapest's ornate New York café, a popular meeting place for writers.

through the crowd to sample what Czech's call 'liquid bread'. Your half-litre of golden beer is likely to accompany a goulash or potato pancake, eaten while standing amid a confusion of loud talk and live music.

Out on the town

In terms of night life, Eastern European cities never sleep. Traditional entertainment takes the form of old-fashioned songs like the ones sung in Kraków's 'Yiddishe mama', or the wild strains of a Hungarian czardas.

Visitors to the Czech Republic have discovered the joys of Czech theatre, including avant-garde puppeteering and 'black theatre', in which black-clad actors holding props move almost invisibly across the stage to the accompaniment of music and sound effects. Some nightclubs specialise in revues. And these are just some of the ways that Czechs satisfy their hunger for artistic expression.

It is possible to dance until dawn, relax to the sound of jazz, absorb a classical recital in a church, or enjoy an opera or ballet

Beaded bubbles In a Romanian bistro, a waitress draws draught beer into half-litre tankards.

performance, all for a price considerably more reasonable than in Western Europe.

Theatrical and musical performances are often noted for their originality. Eastern European artists are not afraid to experiment with mixed genres. Prague's Jazz Club Reduta, for instance, hosts a unique form of literary cabaret which started in 1958, when an ideological thaw encouraged artists to combine sounds and words with traditional, Dixieland and rock jazz. The club is the city's most famous venue for jazz artists (and the place where the former American president, Bill Clinton, played saxophone when he visited in the early 1990s). Prague's International Jazz Festival in October is a major event in the jazz calendar.

Decorative charm An Art Nouveau-style café in the Municipal House, Prague's foremost concert venue, completed in 1911.

Supreme drinkers of supreme brews

The Czechs have the highest per capita consumption of beer in the world – 287 pints (163 litres) per person, followed by the Irish (264 pints/150 litres) and the Germans (223 pints/127 litres). It's hardly surprising considering that the Czechs have been drinking beer for 1000 years and invented Pilsner (see page 56). A half-litre of beer is often cheaper than a Coke or a cup of coffee. In most bars, you don't even have to order. The half-litre glasses just keep on coming, with the new total scribbled on your bill by the waiter. U Fleku in Prague brews what is reputedly the city's strongest dark beer (ordinary beers have an alcohol content of about 3.5%; strong ales have 11-12%; U Fleku's dark beer is 13%). The shaded courtyard and Gothic dining hall seethe with locals and German tour parties, drinking to the blast of a traditional Czech brass band. The back rooms contain brewing equipment from the bar's past.

Beer music An accordion adds to the ambiance at U Fleku.

CHAPTER 4

TOWNS AND CITIES

Golden domes and Gothic spires, Baroque façades and Art Nouveau motifs – from the smallest village to the grandest capital, Eastern European towns exude layer upon layer of architectural endeavour. Communist town planners have left their mark, too, with monumental buildings and sweeping boulevards, but nothing can mar the appeal of Bratislava's medieval backstreets, Kraków's Renaissance marketplace, Odesa's majestic wharves or Prague's glorious churches. Many smaller towns are urban jewels of colour-washed houses, clustered round a central bell-tower, secure within ancient walls. In such places, the strains of a violin sounding down an alleyway or the sight of an aged face seem suddenly to evoke the very soul of the region.

Bardejov in north-eastern Slovakia embodies small-town charm.

The golden ages of architecture in the provinces

Across Bohemia and the Great Hungarian plain lie many little-known architectural gems, including Cesky Krumlov, Telc, Kutná Hora and Pécs.

Tucked away in the hills of the Czech Republic are three Bohemian treasures, the towns of Cesky Krumlov, Telc and Kutná Hora. All are listed by UNESCO as World Heritage Sites. Farther south, in the softer climate of southern Hungary, lies Pécs, where European and Turkish cultures are evident in the buildings that survived war and revolution.

Medieval Cesky Krumlov

Cesky Krumlov has an artistic importance belied by its population of only 15 000 inhabitants, having survived more than 700 years of wars and revolutions virtually intact. The medieval town with its narrow cobbled streets and little squares is set around a hill in a bend of the meandering River Vltava as it winds northwards from the Bohemian Forest. Indeed, its name derives from the German 'Krumme Au' ('winding meadow'). The town grew up around

Postcard setting Cesky Krumlov occupies an idyllic position on the meandering River Vltava, on the edge of the Bohemian Forest.

a clifftop castle dating from 1240. Its population of Bohemians and German-speaking merchants and aristocrats started to build in the 14th century, under the auspices of their rulers, the Rozmberks.

As the town's wealth grew with the success of nearby silver mines, so the castle was transformed into a fine Renaissance palace. Cesky Krumlov emerged virtually unscathed from the Thirty Years' War (1618-48), and then enjoyed another golden age under new masters, the Schwarzenbergs, who sought to rival the glories of the Viennese court. Part of the castle was rebuilt to include splendid state rooms, a Masquerade Hall decorated with frescoes by Josef Lederer depicting scenes from a Venetian ball, and a Baroque theatre. The castle and many of the town houses acquired Baroque and Rococo frontages.

Noble families and well-off bourgeois both profited from their involvement in the brewing industry (Ceské Budejovice, the source

Shades of elegance Bordering the main square in Cesky Krumlov is a terrace of arcaded Renaissance and Baroque houses featuring ornate, brightly painted façades, some decorated with stucco.

Cesky Krumlov's majestic castle

The castle dominating Cesky Krumlov is the second largest of its kind in the Czech Republic after Prague's. It was built around 1240 by the Krumlov barons as an austere Gothic fortress. In the 16th century, it was transformed into a Renaissance palace and a round tower was added. The powerful Schwarzenberg family acquired it in 1717 and redesigned it in the Rococo style. The results of this make-over survive in the ballroom, dining room and Chinese 'cabinet' (in accordance with the French-inspired fad for chinoiserie).

Reaching skywards The castle is topped by a Renaissance tower.

Gilded glory *The Golden Hall in Telc's palace is just one of the sumptuously decorated Renaissance rooms. Each panel of its ornate coffered ceiling features a superb bas-relief.*

Theatrical backdrops *Telc is flanked by two lakes (right) that make a fine setting for the rows of decorated houses (below). Complete with sgraffiti ('scratched') wall designs, they seem to have been created for a stage set.*

of Budweiser beer, is 15 miles/25 km to the north), and competed with one another to build the most sumptuous homes. The two World Wars inflicted little damage and Cesky Krumlov remains an almost perfect medieval town, worthy of its UNESCO status.

Telc: Moravia's former ruler

Legend has it that Telc had its beginnings in a chapel built on the site in 1099 by a local ruler in gratitude for an unexpected victory. The town dates from the end of the 12th century when a group of Slavs settled near a ford on the River Telc. The village became a city in the 14th century, when the Hradec family built a castle, a parish church and a rampart.

Telc was destroyed by fire in 1530. It was rebuilt in stone, under the direction of the cultured and well-travelled Zacharias of Hradec (1527-89). Zacharias was so fascinated by what

Holy figure *The jewel in the crown of Telc's Renaissance and Baroque square is the 18th-century statue of the Virgin that stands at its centre.*

he had seen in Italy that he designed his castle as a Renaissance palace, with a vaulted ground floor leading up to state rooms and living quarters decorated with stucco.

Telc set the artistic tone for south-west Moravia, asserting its economic dominance by hosting four great annual fairs in the square, which is still lined today by a Renaissance arcade.

The last major addition to Telc's mixture of architectural styles came after the Thirty Years' War in the 17th century. The town escaped damage in the conflict thanks to the protection of the Habsburgs. With the Counter-Reformation in full swing, a devout countess brought the supposed remains of St Margaret to Telc. The relics attracted the Jesuits, who established a college and a church beside the palace. Their architect was an Italian, Domenico Orsi, who built in the Baroque style, with ornate gildings and curlicues.

With patronage from the rulers going hand in hand with donations and investments by wealthy locals, other Baroque additions were made to the square. Some of the houses acquired colourful, decorative

Gothic tracery *St Barbara's, Kutná Hora's Gothic cathedral, has an extraordinary array of flying buttresses and pinnacles. Building began in 1380 and took 150 years.*

façades. A statue of the Virgin provided the finishing touch in the 18th century. College, church, palace and square remain today as a glorious combination of Renaissance and Baroque.

Kutná Hora: the 'little Prague'

Around 1260, so the story goes, a monk named Anton had been working in the vineyard of his Cistercian monastery of Sedlec and had fallen asleep. When he awoke, he found that three rods of silver had sprouted up next to his head. He left his habit – '*kutná*' in Czech – to mark the spot and

Expression of wealth *The Stone House is one of Kutná Hora's most splendid Gothic buildings. It was built by a wealthy citizen in the 15th century, and has been added to on many occasions. It is now an art museum.*

reported the discovery. As is often the case, legend encapsulates truth. The monks had probably built on this spot in the valley of the River Vrhlice because silver had already been found in the area in the 12th century. Nevertheless, the discovery of silver in the Sedlec monastery prompted a silver rush, mainly from Germany, and the town of Kutná Hora, founded in the reign of Wenceslas II (1283-1305), began to grow.

The king made Kutná Hora his mint, striking a royal *groschen*, the coin used across his realm. In Sedlec itself, now a suburb of Kutná Hora, an abbey was established, in which local aristocrats were buried. Wenceslas IV (1378-1419) set up his court in a newly built palace, the Vlassky Dvur (Italian Court).

Benefiting from its royal status and its silver mines, Kutná Hora became fabulously wealthy. It soon emerged as the second most influential city after Prague. The German rulers constructed Gothic buildings with towering pinnacles and arches. A start was made on the great church of St Barbara in 1380.

In the early 15th century, the town and the abbey became the focus of the anti-German, anti-Catholic rebellion inspired by Jan Huss. It was here that Wenceslas IV issued his decree in 1409 that conferred

Timeless scene *Kutná Hora's patrician houses show a German influence.*

special status on Bohemians. In the war that followed, the Czechs expelled the Germans, seized the mines and set about rebuilding their devastated city. They completed St Barbara's, then added more buildings in the Renaissance style.

In the 16th century, German silver mines undercut the Czech industry, and Kutná Hora lost its position of prominence. After a final burst of creativity in the 17th century, when Jesuits added a few Baroque buildings, Kutná Hora entered a long decline. It survived intact as an enduring tribute to its former wealth and

Solid defences *After the Mongol invasion in 1241, Pécs was fortified with stone ramparts containing 87 bastions. The section backing the Bishop's Palace has survived intact for more than 750 years.*

architectural creativity. Wenceslas IV's palace, which became the town hall in the 18th century, has retained its splendid wooden roofs and its huge audience hall. St Barbara's remains a classic example of Gothic architecture, its flying buttresses and stone tracery unrivalled in the Czech Republic and much imitated elsewhere.

Pécs: a hidden past

Unlike Cesky Krumlov and Kutná Hora, Pécs in Hungary is no picture postcard small town. Its 180 000 inhabitants live in a place that is a cornucopia overflowing with the fragments of at least 2000 years of history, extending to 7000 years if archaeological finds are taken into account. Its surviving buildings are a mere fraction of what once existed as each successive culture superimposed its own styles on what had gone before.

People settled in the region because it lies on the edge of the Alföld (Great Plain), backed by

Focal point *From Széchenyi Square, in central Pécs, radiates a network of narrow streets reminiscent of a Mediterranean town.*

Cross and crescent

Széchenyi Square, the former marketplace in Pécs, is dominated by the mosque of Gazi Kasim Pashaa, a reminder of 143 years of Turkish rule. It was built in the 16th century from the stones of the medieval church of St Bartholomew. When the Turks were defeated in 1686, the victors, the Habsburgs, converted it back into a church, adding Christian statuary, but keeping the Turkish dome (below). Inside, ornate Turkish windows, a prayer niche and Koranic inscriptions combine with Catholic frescoes.

the Mecsek Mountains, with a soft Mediterranean climate ideal for almonds, vines and orchards.

The Romans exploited it as a trading town and as a border-post. Later, under Frankish rule, Pécs was a Christian centre, known as Quinque Basilicae (Five Churches). The Magyars followed in 899 and Hungary's first Christian king, Stephen, made it a bishopric and founded a cathedral in the 11th century. The cathedral was rebuilt in stone 100 years later. The town's bishops built superb libraries and created the first Hungarian university in 1367.

Little survived the Turkish assault of 1543. But Pécs's underlying advantages remained intact – its vineyards, its mills, its tanning industry, its trading traditions. The Turks transformed the city by adding wooden floors to stone houses, creating bazaars, using the cathedral as a mosque and building a further 17 mosques, two of which survive today.

After the defeat of the Turks in the late 17th century, Pécs discovered the sources of its present wealth: coal and uranium. The Habsburgs arrived and brought with them their style of Austrian Baroque. Meanwhile, the population grew tenfold, forming a thriving city whose history is among the richest and most varied in Eastern Europe.

Budapest, 'pearl of the Danube'

The Danube curves gracefully through Hungary's capital, linking the majestic, wooded hills of Buda to the broad avenues of Pest. The Romans built a garrison town here, the Magyars settled nearby, Turks added mosques and thermal baths, and the Habsburgs brought grandeur with Baroque palaces, Neo-Gothic state buildings and decorative Art Nouveau detailing.

***Danube crossing** Széchenyi Lánchíd (Chain Bridge), 1849, is Budapest's oldest bridge. Its reopening in 1949 symbolised postwar rebirth.*

Budapest was born in 1873, when the ancient Buda and Óbuda merged with the youthful Pest. There followed four decades of growth, which ended with the outbreak of the First World War. But these years of prosperity were enough to establish the city's look and its mix of Baroque, turn-of-the-century imperial grandeur and Art Nouveau (known as Secession Style in the Austro-Hungarian Empire).

Buda and Óbuda: the historic core

Ruins of baths and an amphitheatre uncovered near Óbuda (Old Buda) provide evidence of the time when this was the Roman garrison town of Aquincum. Around 900, when the Magyar Arpad dynasty arrived in the region, Arpad's brother, Buda, gave his name to a new settlement on a nearby hill.

Óbuda eventually became an attractive Baroque suburb of the dominant Buda, a huddle of low houses and narrow streets recalled in the nostalgic words of the early 20th-century novelist Gyula Krúdy: 'Here every street seems to shrink into itself, like a young journeyman beset by cold winds.'

That world all but vanished in the wars and upheavals of the 20th century. In Buda, virtually nothing original remains of Várhegy (Castle Hill) except its medieval street plan, for it was fought over and destroyed on no fewer than 86 occasions. It has

Ornate showpiece The 19th-century Neo-Gothic Mátyás Church, with its diamond tiling, spires and decorative balconies, adjoins a 13th-century church. The original building had been used as a mosque by the Turks and damaged in the siege that ended Turkish rule in 1686.

been almost entirely rebuilt from the rubble left after the Wehrmacht and the Red Army battled for the hill in 1945. A few porches and a chapel were incorporated into the palace, and some 13th-century remnants form part of the 19th-century Mátyás Church, named after the Hungarian king, Matthias Corvinus. The Neo-Gothic church, with its diamond-patterned roof and toothy spires, owes little to the more distant past, but centuries of Turkish rule are recalled by the existence of the city's thermal baths, with their Middle Eastern domes.

After the defeat of the Turks in 1686, Buda's wealthy inhabitants began to build across the surrounding hills. The most famous of these residential areas is Rózsadomb (Rose Hill) named after Gül Baba ('father of the Roses'), a Sufi who took part in the Turkish capture of Buda. His tomb lies between the hill and the river. There are fine examples of Art Nouveau houses from the late 19th century.

Pest: a playground for architects

While Buda was the domain of princes, Pest was settled by merchants and artisans.

Inspired by Vienna's radiating street plan, Pest comprises a fan-shaped series of tree-lined avenues intersected by semicircular boulevards, all defined by imposing buildings. Bold examples of 19th-century Neoclassicism, such as the National Museum, or neo-Renaissance, such as the Opera, vie with Art Nouveau buildings. In the early 20th century the city was a workshop for Secessionist architects. Their exotic, glazed-tile creations are much in evidence. The master of Secessionism was Ödön Lechner, whose creations included the Museum of Applied Arts, the Geological Museum and the Post Office Savings Bank building with its quilt-like façade swarming with bees (symbolic of savers).

From 1910 to 1930, architects turned to the more austere lines of Modernism, as can be seen in the apartment blocks of Napraforgó utca, and experimented with garden suburbs such as Wekerle.

After a brief interlude devoted to Stalinist Neoclassicism, designers reverted to building suburbs of monotonous apartment blocks.

A brief history of bridges

Nothing defines Budapest better than its bridges. They were late in coming: for centuries, the 1970 ft (600 m) wide expanse of water that divided the city could be crossed only by ferries and pontoons. The first permanent

Seat of power Buda's Castle Hill provides a grandstand view of the Parliament Building and Pest. Eighty-eight statues of Hungarian leaders flank the building, which is topped by a 316 ft (96 m) high dome. It was built at the high point of Habsburg rule and took 17 years to complete (1885-1902).

An empress's retreat

The Baroque palace at Gödöllö, 19 miles (30 km) north-east of Budapest, was the favourite summer residence of Emperor Franz Josef's wife, the beautiful and eccentric Elizabeth of Bavaria. Built in the 1740s by Count Antal Grassalkovitch, the palace was bought by the Hungarian state and offered to the Emperor in 1867. Elizabeth used it as a welcome retreat from the formality of court life in Vienna. She was assassinated by an Italian anarchist in 1898, after which it fell into disrepair. It was restored in the 1990s.

The palace at Gödöllö.

Street transport   Trams have been part of the cityscape since 1887. They mainly serve the ring road and the embankments.

Old-world character   Well-preserved houses in Fortuna utca on Várhegy (Castle Hill) date from Renaissance times. The majority are still privately owned, although today many are used as embassies or shops.

link across the Danube, the Lánchíd (Chain Bridge), was built in 1849. Legend has it that the sculptor who created the stone lions decorating the bridge's columns omitted their tongues by mistake, and committed suicide – a curious story, considering that their tongues are visible if you look closely. Perhaps not many people did, because until the end of the 19th century those who used the bridge were required to pay a toll, and in winter many people preferred to cross the frozen river on the ice.

Other bridges followed, only to be destroyed by the Germans in their efforts to stall the Red Army's advance in 1945. The Lánchíd's elegant ironwork, restored in the bridge's centennial year of 1949, now contrasts with the bold lines of the Erzsébet (Elizabeth) road bridge, rebuilt in the early 1960s.

Of undergrounds and trams

Budapest's underground railway has the distinction of being mainland Europe's oldest metro system. It sprang from the outburst of construction that accompanied the 1896 celebrations marking the 1000th anniversary of the Magyar conquest, when Heroes' Square was built. The single line linking Heroes' Square to the city centre had glazed tiling and wooden ticket offices, now restored to their old-fashioned charm. After the Second World War, the city acquired two new lines.

On the surface, Pest's avenues and boulevards are served by yellow trams, blue buses and red trolley buses, all interlinking with suburban railways.

Long-distance travellers use the three main stations, originally named after the areas they serve – Western, Southern and Eastern – which have nothing to do with their geographical position in the city. Changes to the services over the years have added to the confusion. Trains from the Western Station – designed by Gustave Eiffel's company in Paris – now serve both the east and the north.

Place of honour

Hősök tere (Heroes' Square) was built in 1896 to mark the 1000th anniversary of the Magyar conquest. At its centre, the 118 ft (36 m) column is flanked by Prince Arpad and his chieftains, who led the Magyars over the Carpathians. It is topped by the Archangel Gabriel, who, according to legend, appeared to Arpad's descendant, Stephen, in a dream a century after the conquest and offered him the Hungarian crown. King Stephen turned his people into a settled, Christian community. He was made a saint in 1083.

*Heroes' Square
Guards at the tomb of the Unknown Soldier.*

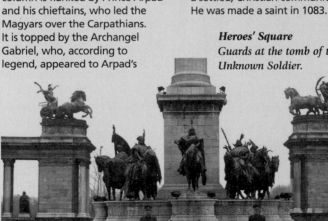

Green lungs

Budapest has a splendid location, and its citizens have taken care to make the best of it, as anyone who has walked along the Danube or in one of the many parks will testify. The countryside is an ever-present part of the city, the appeal of both changing with the season. Városliget (City Woods) is the city's largest park, situated on the eastern side of Pest. It was created – like its nearby castle – for the 1896 celebrations. The park's artificial lake, used for boating in summer, is transformed into a popular ice rink in winter.

A favourite way to reach the greenery of the Buda Hills is to take the cog railway through Svábhegy (Swabian Hill). Once there, it is possible to wander for hours with hardly a soul in sight. On the northern hills there are spectacular stalactite caves. Hang-gliders and mushroom hunters favour Háramashatár Hill, which offers the best view over the city.

In town, the open spaces are treated as stages by lovers of music and film. Summer concerts are held on Margit Sziget (Margaret Island), a popular recreation area with outdoor thermal pools, spa hotels and an open-air theatre. Locals flock to *kertmozi* ('cinema-gardens'), where screens are set up in the shady courtyards of apartment blocks. It is easy to escape the heat of summer in one of the city's swimming pools, many of which are fed by thermal springs and are open the year round. In winter, skating in the city and skiing on the Buda Hills are popular activities.

And any time of day in any season it is worth trying to pick up a bargain in the open-air secondhand bookstalls.

Winter playground Skaters glide across the frozen lake in Városliget (City Woods); the Rococo pavilion is used as a changing-room. In summer, boats bob on the water and the pavilion becomes a restaurant.

A merry-go-round of names

Not long after the end of communism in 1989, Budapest's streets and squares started acquiring additional signs. To the confusion of visitors, taxi drivers and locals, renaming was in progress, yet again. It had happened in 1918, after the Habsburgs departed. In 1989, the changes heralded the end of Hungary's Soviet mentors. The grandest, longest and most frequently renamed thoroughfare was originally named after the 19th-century statesman Gyula Andrássy. In 1949 it was dedicated to Stalin, and after he died it became the Avenue of the People's Republic, except that the elderly residents still knew it as Andrássy út, the name by which it is known once again.

The bus station named after Engels is now in Erzsébet tér (Elizabeth Square). Marx Square became Nyugati tér (Western Square) after the nearby station. Whether Moszkva tér (Moscow Square) will survive is anybody's guess.

Statues also have to fit in with new realities, or suffer the consequences. After Stalin was discredited in 1956, many statues were hastily despatched to Statue Park, a graveyard for discarded monuments dating back to 1919. In the 1990s several others joined them. Even the 100 ft (30 m) Liberation Monument on Gellért Hill has had its critics. The gigantic statue of a female figure holding a palm branch commemorates the Soviet soldiers who died freeing Budapest in 1945. It was given a white tarpaulin shroud in 1990 in an attempt to force its disappearance. In the event, only the statues of the soldiers and Liberation's real-life Soviet guard vanished. She herself survived to fulfil her original purpose as a symbol of the 'crusade against Bolshevism'.

A city in the throes of change

Once again, Budapest has been seized by a building mania. Work on the central market, the Széchenyi Baths, an exhibition centre and a new metro line is in progress as the process of Westernisation gathers pace. The dour years of the 20th century have given way to the glitter of neon lights. There is a new spirit of optimism among the 2 million citizens, who are now enjoying the old pleasures of strolling to a café along a tree-lined boulevard or listening to the sound of a violin beside the Danube.

Spirit of the age Budapest's central Market Hall, with its wrought-iron vaulted ceiling, is one of the best places to experience a colourful Hungarian food market.

Relic of the past A statue, completed in the 1980s, of Béla Kun leading his men in the Communist Revolution of 1919. It has been banished to Statue Park along with numerous other monuments from the Soviet era.

Sopron the faithful

The Hungarian town of Sopron in the Lövér Hills is a perfect example of medieval architecture, untouched by successive overlords. Lying on the border with Austria, Sopron earned its title as a 'faithful city' in 1921 when the inhabitants voted in a plebiscite to be part of Hungary rather than its German-speaking neighbour.

Gateway *The city's Baroque portal.*

Wandering through the border town of Sopron in north-west Hungary is like being in a time warp. Gothic and Baroque buildings mingle along narrow, winding streets to create one of Europe's most remarkable urban treasures. Spared destruction by Mongol and Turkish invaders, the town has survived almost unchanged since medieval times.

Sopron's most outstanding feature is the 201 ft (61 m) high Firewatch Tower. Constructed on Roman foundations, with a 10th-century base, the tower acquired an arcaded balcony and copper roof in the 17th century. From the balcony fire wardens kept watch over the town and blew a trumpet-call to mark each hour. The Fidelity Gate at the bottom of the tower was added in 1922 after the people of Sopron voted to be part of Hungary rather than Austria. It shows Hungarians being awarded the *civitas fidelissima* ('most loyal citizenry'). Nearby is the triple-aisled Goat Church, built in 1300, which is said to have been financed by a goatherd whose flock unearthed a crock of gold. A carving on one of the pillars shows an angel embracing a goat.

Historic huddle *Sopron's array of mellowing tiled roofs is punctuated only by a few church towers. The town is popular with day-trippers from Austria.*

A musical tradition

Every building has a story to tell. Rich patricians created mansions such as the Fabricius House with its blend of Roman, Gothic and Baroque styles, and the Renaissance Storno House, named after the 19th-century architect and painter who restored Pannonhalma Monastery, 32 miles (50 km) to the east.

Storno House's eminent occupants included Franz Liszt, who was born in 1811 in Raiding, 12 miles (20 km) to the south, and revealed himself as a musical prodigy when he gave his first recital in Sopron at the age of nine. Joseph Haydn (1732-1809) was Kapellmeister at the nearby castle of Prince Miklós Esterházy. In the late 19th century, Sopron's theatre hosted the first performances of operas by Karl Goldmark, who became one of Vienna's most popular composers. The musical tradition endures in Sopron's summer festival.

Treasures from the past *The Storno House flanks Sopron's Central Square, with the Firewatch Tower behind.*

Living in splendour

Prince Miklós Esterházy had a saying: 'Whatever the Emperor can do, I can do!' And he set out to prove it in his palace at Fertöd, 17 miles (27 km) east of Sopron. Completed in 1766, the palace had 126 rooms and a theatre, where Joseph Haydn produced his operas. After the prince's death, the palace fell into decay and is only now undergoing restoration.

1 The Philosophical Hall, one of the great libraries of the Strahov Monastery. Carved walnut bookcases 49 ft (15 m) high line the walls. The ceiling, by the Viennese painter Anton Maulpertsch in 1796, depicts the history of philosophy.

2 Charles Bridge (foreground), commissioned by Charles IV in 1357, was the only bridge over the Vltava until the 18th century.

3 The Old Town Bridge Tower (right) looms at the east end of Charles Bridge, with the Clementinum behind.

4 The Old Town Square, with Romanesque buildings as colourful as a stage set, is the focal point of Old Prague and a popular meeting place for tourists.

5 The Grand Hotel Europa on Wenceslas Square, built in 1903-6, is an exquisite example of Art Nouveau architecture. With its ornate façade of mosaics, balconies and gilded nymphs, it retains an old-world charm.

6 The former Jewish Town Hall lies at the centre of the Jewish Quarter in the Old Town. Built in the 1570s, it has a distinctive wooden clock tower and below it a dormer with a Hebraic clock whose hands turn anticlockwise. Before the Second World War, Prague had 50 000 Jews, of whom about 1500 remain. They are working to re-establish the synagogue adjoining the Town Hall.

Prague, the imperial city

Prague's roots, according to legend, lie in the 8th century, but it reached its height in the 14th century, under Charles IV, King of Bohemia (1346-78) and Holy Roman Emperor. Charles transformed his capital into the largest and most glorious city of its day in Europe. He commissioned a magnificent bridge over the Vltava, which still stands, to link Hradcany (the imposing 13th-century castle) and Malá Strana (the Little Quarter) with Josefov (the Jewish Quarter), Staré Mesto (the Old Town) and later Nové Mesto (the New Town). Each area exhibits a remarkable diversity of architectural and artistic styles – Roman, Gothic, Renaissance, Baroque, Art Nouveau, Cubist. Largely undamaged by wars and revolutions, they combine to give the 'city of 100 towers' and 1.2 million people an extraordinary power. The buildings of the Czech capital are an outward expression of cultural richness: artists, writers, musicians and academics have been drawn to Prague over the centuries. Every year thousands of tourists follow in their footsteps.

Melancholy graveyard The Old Jewish Cemetery contains 12 000 headstones and tombs all lying, leaning and standing in a higgledy-piggledy confusion across a dozen burial sites that may contain as many as 100 000 graves. Many of the monuments are decorated with animals or plants symbolising the name or trade of the deceased. Founded in 1478, the cemetery and the synagogues of Josefov (the Jewish Quarter) survive as evidence of 500 years of Jewish history.

Heart of Judaism The Old-New Synagogue, built in 1270, is Europe's oldest surviving synagogue. Within its clean-cut geometric exterior, octagonal pillars and rib vaulting support the steep roof. It remains at the centre of Jewish religious practice in Prague.

Timepiece The Astronomical Clock (Orloj) on the Old Town Hall has been working since it was built in 1490. Flanked by four figures representing Vanity, Greed, Death and Pagan Invasion, moving discs show the positions of the sun and moon, and the time. Below the clock is a calendar with 12 seasonal scenes – the 19th-century original is in Prague's City Museum.

Old Town Square The square began life as a marketplace in the 10th century and acquired its grand buildings in the 14th century. The dominant Gothic Church of Our Lady Before Tyn was a stronghold of the Hussites, 1402-1620.

National heart The Municipal House, built in 1906-12, is a stunning Art Nouveau creation by 30 artists who collaborated to design a cultural centre that would be the architectural high point of the Czech National Revival. It was here that Czechoslovakia's birth was proclaimed on October 28, 1918. Its rooms include Prague's biggest concert hall.

Arab inspiration *The Spanish Synagogue, built in 1868, was based on Moorish designs. It has a permanent exhibition on the history of the local Jewish community.*

1. Charles Bridge
2. Church of St Nicholas, Malá Strana
3. Wallenstein Palace
4. Strahov Monastery
5. The Loreto
6. Prague Castle: St Vitus's Cathedral and St George's Square
7. Royal Garden
8. The Belvedere
9. Old-New Synagogue
10. Old Jewish Cemetery
11. Church of St Nicholas
12. Old Town Square
13. Clementinum
14. Municipal House and Powder Tower
15. Wenceslas Square
16. State Opera
17. National Museum
18. National Theatre
19. 'Ginger and Fred' Building

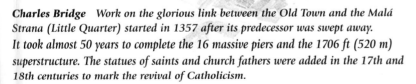

Charles Bridge *Work on the glorious link between the Old Town and the Malá Strana (Little Quarter) started in 1357 after its predecessor was swept away. It took almost 50 years to complete the 16 massive piers and the 1706 ft (520 m) superstructure. The statues of saints and church fathers were added in the 17th and 18th centuries to mark the revival of Catholicism.*

Baroque treasure *A statue in the Church of St Nicholas shows St Cyril, the 9th-century missionary who brought Christianity to the Slavs, pinning down the Devil. The church was built by the Jesuits, 1673-1755. It is a fine example of Baroque, designed by the father and son architects Christoph and Kilian Ignaz Dientzenhofer. The statue is one of four church fathers who form part of the four pillars that support the cupola. The roof painting in the nave, which portrays the life of St Nicholas, is Europe's largest fresco.*

Renaissance in Bratislava

Thrust into the limelight as the capital of the new state of Slovakia, Bratislava is looking forward to a prosperous future. For two centuries this city on the banks of the Danube reigned supreme as capital of Hungary while the Turks occupied Budapest. But after 1784 it was eclipsed first by Vienna and then Prague.

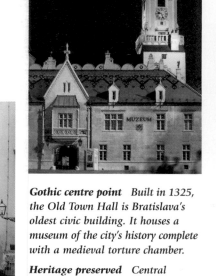

A glance at the map soon reveals why Bratislava has high hopes of securing a position among Europe's leading cities. As capital of Slovakia, it lies on a natural crossroads between Germans, Slavs and Hungarians. The country spans both the Danubian plain and the Carpathians and borders six other nations.

For much of its history Bratislava has been sidelined by the capitals of successive empires and nations – by Vienna as the capital of the Austro-Hungarian Empire, by Budapest (Austria-Hungary's second city) and, from 1920, by Prague when Slovakia became the junior and predominantly rural partner in the newly created Czechoslovakia. Even in its days of glory as the capital of a rump Hungarian state (1541-1784), when the Turks held Buda, it was known by its German name, Pressburg.

To express its Slovakian identity, Bratislava had to await the coming of independence in 1993. After the country's remarkably

Gothic centre point Built in 1325, the Old Town Hall is Bratislava's oldest civic building. It houses a museum of the city's history complete with a medieval torture chamber.

Heritage preserved Central Bratislava has many well-restored examples of Gothic, Renaissance and Baroque buildings.

peaceful parting from the Czech Republic, Bratislava has been able to capitalise on its historic heritage, attract foreign finance (60 per cent of Slovakia's foreign investment flows into the capital) and act as an anchor for the fledgling democracy.

The city that loves music

Bratislava's reputation for music is rooted in the time when, as Pressburg, it was the Hungarian capital. Mozart came here in 1762 as a six-year-old prodigy on the first of the European tours organised by his father. The young Mozart played to an amazed audience at one of the palaces owned by the Pálffy family, now known as the Mozart House. Ten years later, Joseph Haydn conducted a concert in the newly opened Grassalkovich Palace. But perhaps the city's most renowned musical son is Johann Nepomuk Hummel (1778-1837), a pupil of both Haydn and Mozart, and a composer and virtuoso pianist who influenced Chopin and Liszt. His house is now a museum in his honour. The city's hosts an annual music festival.

Dominating presence Bratislava's castle was founded in the 10th century. Its present outline dates from the 15th century and the towers were added 200 years later. Damaged by fire in 1811 and bombs in the Second World War, the castle was rebuilt as government offices and a museum in the 1950s.

Poland's three capitals

The tide of Polish history has washed the country back and forth across the map of Europe, leaving some cities stranded across the border. But three have survived as bastions of the nation's identity: Warsaw, Kraków and Poznan.

For three brief periods in 1795-1945, amounting to 62 years in total, Poland ceased to exist as a nation. Technically, in those years, there were no Polish cities. At other times, changing borders meant that some cities that were once Polish became Polish no more. Wilno and Lwow are now Vilnius, in Lithuania, and Lviv in Ukraine. But the three cities of Warsaw, Kraków and Poznan have reached the 21st century as enduring monuments to Poland's ability to survive, and as foundations for future growth.

Warsaw: Poland's soul

According to legend, a mermaid told two young lovers, Wars and Sawa, to found a city and give it their conjoined names. But neither legend nor town are very old. Warsaw was first mentioned in the 14th century. A century later it became the capital of a small state, Mazovia, which was soon incorporated into Poland. When Poland joined with Lithuania in 1569, it became the national capital. Thereafter, its story was one of constant destruction and rebirth.

It was burnt by the Swedes in 1656 and 1702, and ravaged by plague, then rebuilt in Baroque and Classical styles by the kings of Saxony. It

Capital founder *The bronze statue of Sigismund III, who made Warsaw his capital in 1596, towers over Castle Square. Warsaw's oldest monument, it was erected by Sigismund's son, Ladislas IV, in 1644.*

Monstrous present *The Palace of Culture towers 767 ft (234 m) over Warsaw's commercial sector. A postwar gift from Stalin, it is widely reviled: locals say the best view of the city is from the top, because it is the only place from which you cannot see the palace itself. It contains offices, cinemas, swimming pools, a conference centre and – as a symbol of changed times – a casino.*

reached a high point under Prince Stanislaw-August Poniatowski in the late 18th century, before Polish nationalism was crushed and the country partitioned between Russia, Prussia and Austria. None of these dramas approached the epic tragedy of the Second World War. Warsaw was the first city to be bombed by the Luftwaffe in 1939. Its Nazi occupiers subjected it to a brutally repressive regime and in 1940, the Jews in Warsaw were forced into a ghetto. When in

New lease of life *Warsaw's Old Town Square is a scrupulous reconstruction of the 17th and 18th-century original, which was flattened in the Second World War. Now it once again plays an important role as the centre of a historic town.*

Mixed styles Behind the Baroque façade of St George's Basilica lies Bohemia's oldest and, some say, most beautiful Romanesque building. Founded in the 10th century, St George's was rebuilt after a fire in 1142. Renovation in the early 20th century revealed original arcades and 13th-century frescoes. The adjacent convent is a museum of medieval, Renaissance and Baroque art.

Lighting darkness A window designed by the Czech Art Nouveau master Alfons Mucha in 1931 for St Vitus's Cathedral, showing the saints Cyril and Methodius. It is one of a group of 20th-century windows.

Wallenstein Palace The magnificent Baroque palace lying at the foot of the castle was the creation of General Albrecht von Wallenstein, the leading Catholic general in the Thirty Years' War (1618-48). It was designed by the Italian architect Andrea Spezza and completed in 1630. The gardens are in the Renaissance style, with geometric box hedges, statues and fountains.

Images in plaster A few buildings in Prague still display fine examples of sgraffito, in which plaster coating is scraped away to produce an image, as in these Renaissance-style portraits. The technique is also used to imitate masonry to create frameworks for historical, allegorical and Biblical scenes. External sgraffiti are rare, because they wear easily and require frequent renovation.

Sacred heart of Prague St Vitus's was founded by Wenceslas I (St Wenceslas) in 929. In the 14th century, Charles IV employed the architects Matthew of Arras, followed by Peter Parler, to construct a Gothic cathedral on the site. The building was finally completed, in meticulous imitation of Gothic, in 1929, after the period of National Revival.

Symbol of nationalism In the words of an inscription on its proscenium arch, the National Theatre was 'a gift from the nation to itself'. It was funded by public subscription. Just as it was due to open in 1881, the theatre was destroyed by fire. A second appeal raised enough to restore it for an opening in 1883 – for works in Czech, as opposed to German, the language of Prague's Austrian rulers.

The nation's stage Wenceslas Square, dominated by a statue of its namesake, is more like an avenue than a square. Designed by Charles IV in the 14th century, it was redeveloped at the end of the 19th century and lined with restaurants, hotels, shops and banks. Its size has made it the stage on which many great events – including the 1989 revolution – have taken place.

Doll's house barracks Crammed up against the inside wall of Hradcany (the Castle), the tiny houses of Golden Lane were built in the 16th century for the castle guards. A corridor runs through the roofs of all the houses. Legend claims that the lane was named after medieval alchemists who tried to manufacture gold here. In fact, the lane was named in the 17th century, when the city's goldsmiths lived in the street.

Proof of loyalty Troja Palace was the summer residence of Count Kaspar Sternberg. He built it in the Italianate style around 1700 to demonstrate his loyalty to the Habsburgs, whose hunting-grounds of Stromovka Park lay nearby. Formal French gardens surround the palace.

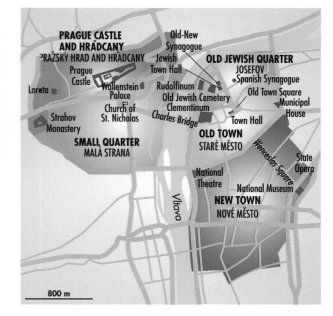

The historic centre of Prague

Cubism in stone This Cubist house in Vysehrad (High Castle) was designed by the architect Josef Chochol. He chose to build in Vysehrad because it was the nation's mythical birthplace. Other architects followed his lead. Their creations are noted for being the only architectural expression of Cubism.

Sound of music Everywhere in Prague, at any season and any time of day, music can be heard. In cafés and concert halls, streets and parks musicians perform (left). The musical high point is the Spring Festival in May and June, which draws crowds of tourists (below).

Prague

Blowing in the wind An eccentric shop sign in the Old Town Square. The square, like 85 per cent of Warsaw, was flattened in the Second World War.

Uprising in the Warsaw Ghetto

In 1939, Warsaw had the largest Jewish community outside New York with about 450 000 people, about one-third of the city's population. From 1940, as part of Hitler's policy to exterminate Jews, he ordered those living in Warsaw into a ghetto 0.6 miles (1 km) wide – which was like a huge prison – before being transported to concentration camps. By 1941, 1.5 million Jews were crammed into the ghetto. A quarter died of disease and starvation. Deportations began in summer 1942. In early 1943, only 60 000 people remained, of which a core – the Jewish Combat Organisation – rose in revolt. The Nazis took a month to crush the uprising. The leaders committed suicide, 7000 survivors were shot, and the remaining 50 000 were despatched to their deaths in Treblinka. The episode remains a symbol both of the plight of the Jews, and of their resistance.

Jewish tribute Warsaw's *Monument to the Heroes of the Ghetto, inaugurated in 1948.*

July 1942, they learnt that they were to be transported to almost certain extermination, they planned the revolt that broke out in April 1943, an act that led to their wholesale destruction.

In August 1944, the city as a whole rose up against its Nazi oppressors. In a fury, Hitler ordered Warsaw's elimination. The city was being systematically destroyed even as the Red Army advanced across the River Vistula. When the Soviets liberated Warsaw, only 120 000 Poles remained; 850 000 residents – two-thirds of the 1939 population – were dead or missing. There followed ten years of reconstruction, with the historic centre being rebuilt exactly as before, using old plans, photographs and paintings as a guide. Elsewhere, the new buildings were grim apartment blocks, which did not reflect Warsaw's cosmopolitan atmosphere and *joie de vivre*.

Kraków: the town that is a museum

Local legend claims that Kraków was founded by a mythical ruler named Krak. The truth is lost in time, for the settlement on Wawel Hill is ancient. Its fine position on the River Wisla was favoured by

Centre of learning The Aula, the main hall of Kraków's Jagiellonian University, features a Renaissance ceiling adorned with carved rosettes. University alumni include the astronomer Copernicus, and Pope John Paul II.

Medieval trading centre Kraków's Main Square (Rynek Główny) is the largest town square of medieval Europe. Once it was crowded with stalls. Now passers-by have an unimpeded view of the Cloth Hall (Sukiennice), rebuilt in Renaissance style after a fire in 1555.

The tale of Skuba and the dragon

Once upon a time, the people of Warsaw suffered from the depredations of a dragon which lived under Wawel Hill. One day the beast, which had until then been happy with a daily snack of cattle, seized seven local maidens and seven young men. A youth named Skuba, the son of a cobbler, came up with an idea: he placed a sheepskin full of salt at the entrance to the monster's lair. Having gobbled it down, the dragon was seized with such a terrible thirst that it threw itself into the river and drank until it exploded. In gratitude, the town's founder, Krak, gave the valiant young man his daughter in marriage.

Above the dragon's lair The 15th-century castle towers above Kraków on Wawel Hill. Below the castle is a cave which locals refer to as the Dragon's Cave.

Polish kings, who made it their capital from 1320 to 1596. It came through the two great destructive episodes, the Mongol invasions and the Second World War, virtually unscathed, and its historic buildings form a collection unrivalled in Poland. Kraków became a leading intellectual centre with the founding of the Jagiellonian University in 1364. Its architectural treasures include patrician houses by the score, 30 convents, 58 churches, a cathedral and one of the most glorious market squares in Europe.

After the third and final partition of Poland in 1795, Kraków was, in succession, part of Napoleon's Grand Duchy of Warsaw, then a free city (1815-46) and then it came under the auspices of the Austro-Hungarian province of Galicia. It was a famously liberal place, in which Lenin directed the international communist movement and printed *Pravda*. After reverting to the new Poland that

Design detail A Renaissance-style ceiling adorns a shop in Kraków's Cloth Hall. The Gallery of 19th-century Polish Painting occupies the upper floor.

The birthplace of Poland

Gniezno, 31 miles (50 km) east of Poznan, is the birthplace of the Polish nation. In legend, Poland's founder, Lech, chose it as his capital after he came across the nest (*gniazdo*) of a

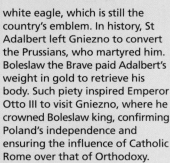

white eagle, which is still the country's emblem. In history, St Adalbert left Gniezno to convert the Prussians, who martyred him. Boleslaw the Brave paid Adalbert's weight in gold to retrieve his body. Such piety inspired Emperor Otto III to visit Gniezno, where he crowned Boleslaw king, confirming Poland's independence and ensuring the influence of Catholic Rome over that of Orthodoxy.

First Polish king *A statue of Boleslaw the Brave (966-1025).*

emerged in 1919, it was occupied by the Nazis in 1939-45. Post-war, it acquired a new suburb a few miles to the east, where a vast steelworks – Nova Huta (New Foundry) – arose as a symbol of the government's determination to overwhelm the city's traditional Catholicism with an atheistic proletariat. It did not work out as intended: in 1978 Kraków's archbishop became Pope John Paul II.

Poznan: city of trade, and war

Poland's most prominent western town is situated in a privileged position on the east-west route across the country, and on the mainline railway between Berlin and Warsaw. Poznan was at the heart of the 10th-century kingdom forged by Mieszko I, and remained a royal capital until the 12th century. When the court moved to Kraków, Poznan was granted duty-free trade privileges and grew to form a great medieval trading centre. Its heyday was in the late 16th century, when the Teutonic Order of German knights declined, the Hanseatic League of trading ports lost influence and Poland linked with Lithuania. The buildings of the Old Market Place are evidence of its success.

But the shadow of Germany loomed ominously. Berlin is a mere 125 miles (200 km) away, and Germans had been influential in the city since the 13th century. By the Second Partition in 1793, Poznan fell to Germany, officially becoming Posen. For this reason, it was a focus of Polish nationalism, even as it acquired more wealth as a growing industrial centre. Germans were forced out in 1918, only to return with a vengeance in 1939 when Poznan lost the majority of its population and 55 per cent of its buildings.

Rebuilding restored the ruined city after 1945, and with its annual trade fair it became once again an important commercial centre, as well as preserving its reputation for independence – in 1956, 50 000 people took to the streets to protest at Soviet domination and demand food.

Old Market Place *Poznan's 'Stary Rynek' is dominated by the Town Hall. Originally Gothic, it was rebuilt in the 16th century as a reflection of the city's commercial influence. It housed the provincial administration until 1939, and is now the city's history museum.*

Ancient and modern *Poznan's historic centre remains intact, but it no longer has its medieval walls, which were replaced by broad roads and tramways in the course of expansion in the 20th century.*

The cities of Belarus

Landlocked Belarus has been fought over and seized by the Tatars, French and Germans. Lithuanians and Poles have left their mark, but none more so than the former Soviet Union, which was responsible for the reconstruction of the country after the Second World War.

***Stalinist monument** The Pedagogic Institute typifies postwar Minsk.*

Belarus's two principal cities, the capital, Minsk, and Brest on the Polish border, both suffered wartime devastation. Both were rebuilt in the functional Soviet style of the 1950s, comprising solid, square buildings with little to distinguish them. Only Hrodna (Grodno in Russian) offers any historic charm, for it survived the Second World War intact.

Minsk: a shuttlecock between feuding nations

People seize on Minsk's name as a key to its character. It may derive from the root *myen*, meaning 'exchange,' which is a reference to its position astride the watershed that divides the rivers flowing north to the Baltic from those flowing south to the Black Sea. On the other hand, it could have been named after the giant magician Menesk or Mincz, who according to legend built a windmill that had the power to turn rocks into flour, and thus feed the populace. Or its name may be seen as a symbol of the

***Memorial column** Victory Square in Minsk centres on an obelisk erected in 1954 to honour those who died in the battle to free the city in 1944.*

many times Minsk has been seized: by the Crimean Tatars (1505), the French (1812) and the Germans (1918 and 1939). In the most recent occupation, half its 270 000 inhabitants died, including all its 50 000 Jews, and 80 per cent of the town was destroyed.

Minsk was rebuilt virtually from scratch. Only the 18th-century cathedral and a few backstreets in an old-town area east of the River Svislach retain an old-world feel. As a result, it is a perfect place to see Soviet urban planning taken to its logical extreme, with wide avenues, vast squares and parks, and forbidding official structures, such as the Government Building of 1934.

Minsk's attractions lie not in its buildings, but in the cosmopolitanism of its 1.7 million residents. With two airports, a modern underground system, concert halls and theatres, Minsk is both the driving force behind Belarus's economy and the country's shop window.

***High drama** Hrodna's theatre, built in the 1960s, reflects official Soviet approval of the dramatic arts.*

Historic highlights of Minsk

Recent restoration projects have revealed a hint of Minsk's ancient past. Of the 9th-century city that arose above the River Svislach there is no trace, for the densely packed wooden houses burned down in 1547. The site became Svabody Square. Poles founded a Catholic monastery here, with a Bernadine church in the shadows of the Baroque towers of the Orthodox Cathedral of St Dukhawski. Now the square has been restored to its former grandeur. The church houses the city archives and the monastery is a music academy. The renovated cathedral adds a graceful touch to the riverscape.

***Waterside** The Svislach river and cathedral.*

Model city Rebuilt after the Second World War, the greater part of Minsk is geometry in concrete, on a monumental scale. The style was intended to proclaim the dawn of a new proletarian age.

Brest and Hrodna: new for old

Brest and Hrodna have little in common except their proximity to the Polish border. Brest, the industrial frontier city, was completely rebuilt by the Soviets after the Second World War. Hrodna survived the episode almost unscathed. No two places could be more different.

Brest achieved international prominence when it gave its name – or rather its previous name, Brest-Litovsk ('of Lithuania') – to the peace treaty signed in the city by the new Soviet state and Germany in 1918. Like Minsk it was destroyed in the Second World War, but re-emerged as a busy border town. Its history can only be glimpsed in a couple of churches and in the excavated remains of medieval Brest, which now form the centre point of an archaeological museum.

Brest's main draw is its massive fortress. When it was built in the 19th century on the junction of the Buh and Mukhavyets rivers, the town was moved to its present site across the Mukhavyets. The German invasion in 1941 quickly overwhelmed the town, but the two regiments in the fortress held out for six weeks against forces that outnumbered them tenfold. Their heroism won Brest acclaim as one of the Soviet Union's 11 wartime 'Hero Cities', and the fortress remains as a grimly moving tribute to the fortitude of the defenders. Brest's monumental memorial of a man's head carved from rock commemorates the Soviet war effort.

Hrodna had the benefit of falling rapidly to the advancing Nazis, and was little damaged. Its past in Lithuanian, Polish

and Russian hands survives in two castles, two cathedrals and a fine collection of 18th-century houses. The 12th-century church of Saint Boris and Saint Gleb is one of the last surviving buildings from the days of Kievan Rus. Hrodna also has a botanical garden.

A city reborn Minsk gave Soviet planners the opportunity to build the city of their dreams. The result is an austerely practical place, stripped of excess and decoration, with many wide open spaces.

Symbol of heroism Brest fortress recalls the bravery of those who opposed the Nazi assault in 1941.

Kiev: jewel of Ukraine

Kiev exudes history from every golden dome and 1000-year-old stone. Situated on the river route to Byzantium, it was founded by Slavs and captured by Vikings. It rose to become capital of the first Russian state and the fount of Russian Orthodoxy.

Convert and converter *The statue of Vladimir, Kievan Rus's prince and saint, above the Dnieper in which he forced his people to undergo a mass baptism in 987.*

Big freeze *A snowfall offers the chance for some to earn extra cash.*

Archaeologists have traced Kiev's roots back to the 5th century, but the first documentary record places its foundation in the 8th century, when a Slav named Kyi settled here with his two brothers and sister and gave his name to the place. It was in a good position on the River Dnieper with high banks to support solid walls, and surrounding marshes for protection. A century later, Varangians (Vikings) from Scandinavia seized the settlement and made it the capital of their state, Rus. Kiev became the main link on the 'River Road' between the north and Byzantium, and a bulwark against eastern nomads. It was from Byzantium that Grand Prince Vladimir, sovereign of Kievan Rus, adopted Christianity in 987.

Past and present capital

For 300 years, Kievan Rus dominated Eastern Europe, until in the 13th century it was sacked by the Mongols and fell to Poland-Lithuania. With Poland's division in 1793, Russia took control again, with a spate of new building. It suffered brutal destruction in the post-Revolutionary Civil War and again in the Second World War, when 40 per cent of the buildings were flattened, half a million troops killed or captured and 80 per cent of its population made homeless. Babii Yar to the north of the city was a notorious killing field.

Postwar reconstruction made Kiev the Soviet Union's third largest city. Today, as capital of Ukraine, it has 2.6 million inhabitants.

The beauty of Kiev's site, the open country that surrounds it and its historic treasures, are all matched by the spirit of the city. Buildings of

Hermits' retreat *The Pecherska Lavra (Monastery of the Caves) is a complex of golden-domed churches, museums and underground labyrinths lined with cells, which contain the mummified remains of monks. Founded in 1051, it was Kievan Rus's intellectual heart. The Soviets made it into a museum. In 1988 it reverted to being a working monastery.*

Shevchenko: poet of the nation

There is one name that is closely associated with Kiev, or indeed with almost anywhere in Ukraine: it is that of the poet, novelist and painter Taras Shevchenko (1814-61). Born a serf, Shevchenko became the voice of Ukraine. He gave the language a literary form in his poetry and prose, and preached social justice with a passion. Although his work was banned by the tsars and he was exiled to Siberia, he remained a national hero to Ukrainians. Kiev gave his name to the city's opera house, a main avenue and a park, where his statue has a prominent place. There is a museum devoted to Shevchenko, which contains a library of his work.

A shining city *From the air, Kiev's history is revealed. Its buildings range from Orthodoxy's golden-domed churches to monumental Soviet-era blocks, interlaced with rich green spaces.*

bold design line the broad streets, which in spring are cloaked in the blossom of chestnut trees. The steep west bank is one long wooded park, which looks across to more woods and parkland on the low-lying east bank. White-sand beaches draw sunbathers and swimmers in summer.

A city of churches

The old town of Kiev, on the west bank, has superb monuments to the city's varied past (though the Golden Gate, named after a counterpart in Constantinople, is a 1982 reconstruction of the main medieval entrance to the city). Traditionally, Kiev for Christians was the 'city of 400 churches'. The Mongols called it the city 'of golden heads'.

The greatest example, St Sophia's Cathedral, survived the Mongol assault. Built in the 11th century it, like the Golden Gate, had a Byzantine model – Hagia Sofia Cathedral in Constantinople. The golden-topped Baroque domes were added in the 17th and 18th centuries, but much of the interior, with its

Mosaic masterpiece *An 11th-century mosaic of the Virgin dominates the central apse in St Sophia's Cathedral. Below, Christ presents communion bread and wine to his disciples.*

The killing fields of Babii Yar

On September 29-30, 1941, Nazi troops seized local Jews and forced them northwards to a gully known as Babii Yar, 'the ravine of women'. Here, 34 000 Jews were massacred in two days, before the place was turned into a concentration camp. In the following two years, 100 000 people died at Babii Yar. When the Nazis retreated in 1943, the bodies were exhumed and cremated. The site received worldwide attention in 1962 when the poet Yevgeny Yevtushenko wrote *Babii Yar* , an indictment of institutional anti-Semitism in the USSR. In 1976 and 1991, memorials were raised to commemorate those who were massacred.

choirs, five naves and exquisite mosaics, is original. St Michael's Monastery is far from original. A monastery was built on the site in the early 12th century, but in 1936 it was torn down to create space for a new Central Committee building. The war intervened and nothing was built. Now the complex has been reconstructed in its original form. On a nearby hilltop stands St Andrew's, a Baroque version of the traditional five-domed Ukrainian-style church by Bartolomeo Rastrelli, who designed many of St Petersburg's buildings in the 18th century.

Kiev's church-building tradition lasted into the 19th century, when St Vladimir's Cathedral was built with its seven domes, theatrical interior and Art Nouveau wall paintings.

Lazy afternoons *In summer, Kievans love to wander in the 3 miles (5 km) of parkland along the west bank of the Dnieper. Chestnut trees, which are symbols of the city, provide welcome shade.*

Centre point *Before Ukraine broke from the Soviet Union in 1991, Kiev's central open space was named the Square of the October Revolution. Now it is called Independence Square (Maidan Nezalezhnosti). It is flanked by Soviet blocks and crossed by the main thoroughfare, Kreshchatyk.*

Odesa's rapid rise

French governor *A statue of the Duke of Richelieu overlooks the harbour. He was Odesa's first governor in the early 19th century and a distant relative of the 17th-century French statesman.*

Ukraine's Black Sea port of Odesa is a vibrant commercial centre imbued with a mixture of Eastern and Western cultures and an air of the Mediterranean. Established as recently as the late 18th century, it soon became Russia's third city and a popular tourist resort.

Odesa was founded in 1794. As Russia's window on the south it rose rapidly to become the tsarist empire's third most important city after Moscow and St Petersburg. Europe, the Middle East and Asia come together at this Black Sea port, creating a tradition of enterprise. The city asserted itself most famously when its workers rebelled in 1905, backed by sailors on the battleship *Potemkin*. Today, its individuality comes through in the people – in their sense of humour and popular songs – in the buildings and in the cosmopolitan nature of the city.

Southern charm

In design, Odesa's sturdy buildings are central European; but their balconies and recessed windows and vine-swathed ironwork give a Mediterranean feel to a port where tradespeople of different nationalities and religions have always mixed easily. Wide pavements and tiled terraces are shaded by carob and plane trees, boulevards are interspersed with parks, esplanades are splashed with lilacs and acacias. In summer, cafés and bars spill out onto the main street of Deribasivska Vulitsya. Away from the town centre, beaches punctuate the rocky headlands, each with their attractions – Arkadia, the most popular, has an outdoor disco, Lanzheron has a cable car.

In search of a new role

Climate, beaches and buildings cannot hide the fact that Odesa is a shadow of its former self. Its glorious houses are decaying, the parks need attention.

Nevertheless, Odesa has the potential for a prosperous future, and is expected to reap the benefits of its participation in the Black Sea Economic Cooperation Pact, the 11-nation treaty signed by Ukraine and other countries bordering the Black Sea in 1992. The pact created a new regional zone to extend and counterbalance the European Union. Odesa is one of the principal cities in the group.

Stairway to fame *Odesa's flight of 192 steps, immortalised by Eisenstein in his film* Battleship Potemkin. *To trick the perspective, the bottom step is 30 ft (9 m) wider than the top.*

Sun-worshipping *Odesa's sandy beaches have made it a popular resort for Ukrainians and Russians.*

The return of *klezmer*

Odesa's Jewish quarter of Moldavanka was the birthplace of *klezmer*, the joyful music of the Jews which bears comparison to the free forms of jazz. After the 1905 Revolution, *klezmerim* fled, many to New York, where their playing influenced songwriters such as Irving Berlin. Now *klezmer* music is back, as an accompaniment to Jewish marriages and funerals.

Lviv: Ukraine's flag-bearer

Lviv, the capital of western Ukraine, looked west to Poland and Austria for most of its history. In 1939 it was absorbed by the Soviet Union. But under its many rulers it has remained the guardian of all things Ukrainian.

Lviv was founded in the 13th century as the capital of the new kingdom of Galicia, which until then had been a battleground for rival Hungarians, Polish and Russian rulers. A century later, Poland seized Galicia and held it for 300 years until it fell to Austria. Two world wars tossed control of Lviv to Poland, Ukraine, Germany, the USSR and finally back to Ukraine.

A living museum

Its buildings are correspondingly eclectic, with European Gothic giving way to the Renaissance, Baroque, Rococo and Neo-classical styles adopted by Eastern European rulers, all of which survived the Second World War. Its medieval ramparts enclose a maze of alleys, which open into parks and tree-filled squares where men while away summer days playing chess. The old town huddles round the Market Square (Ploshcha Rynok), with many churches that reflect the rivalry between Orthodoxy and Catholicism. Among them are examples of medieval design – the Gothic Roman Catholic Cathedral, the more restrained Armenian Cathedral, and the green-domed Byzantine St Nicholas Church. St George's Cathedral, the heart of Ukrainian Catholicism, was returned by the Orthodox to Catholic control in 1990.

On the east of the town lies Lychakiv Cemetery, a 110 acre

Potent symbol   On Lviv's Market Square, a stone Neptune brandishes his trident, the symbol of Ukrainian nationalism.

(40 ha) reserve of hilly woodland shading 3600 monuments. The cemetery, founded in 1786 when Austria banned further burials within the city limits, became a pantheon for eminent Poles and Ukrainians, including the Ukrainian poet Ivan Franko and the Polish novelist and playwright Gabriela Zapolska (1857-1921).

Lviv spells out its identity

Lviv is known as Lvov in Russian, Lwów in Polish and Lemberg in German. It was by its Russian name that it was known in the West from 1939. But this city nurtured Ukrainian nationalism more than any other, and it is the Ukrainian version of the city's name that has won the day. The well-formed Russian 'o' is replaced with the more intermediate sound of an 'i' in Ukrainian. Lvov is now well and truly Lviv.

Classic Rococo   With a façade uncluttered by decoration, the Dominican Church is a fine example of 18th-century architecture.

Chess lovers   Lviv's leafy squares are popular places for the town's chess players to meet for a game. Ukrainians are renowned for their chess prowess.

113

The paradox of Bucharest

Bucharest today is a patchwork of 19th-century Neoclassical and 20th-century brutalist architecture. It has been called the 'Paris of the Balkans' for its broad tree-lined avenues. But in the 1980s Nicolae Ceausescu tore the heart out of the Romanian capital to impose his own megalomaniac vision of modernity.

Bulldozing the past *In the 1980s, apartments pushed out family homes.*

For years after its foundation by the 15th-century prince, Vlad Tepes, Bucharest was little more than a huge garden planted here and there with mansions and churches. Even today, 20 per cent of the city is open space, justifying its epithet 'garden city'.

In the 19th century, rebuilding rolled back the effects of Ottoman rule, imposing a look inspired by Baron Haussmann, the architect of central Paris. Bucharest's buildings are Neoclassical; its Kisileff Avenue is a sort of Champs-Élysées. It even has its own Arc de Triomphe.

In the early 20th century, Bucharest was one of Europe's most charming and civilised capitals. The Second World War and an earthquake undermined its fabric and its image. Postwar construction introduced bland apartment blocks and suburban blight. In 1977, another earthquake killed 1400 people and flattened much of the city. Finally, Ceausescu's decision to remodel Bucharest destroyed what remained of its charm. Today, it takes patience and stamina to discover the few remaining corners of Parisian grandeur.

Romanian peasant life preserved

Although much of the traditional Romanian way of life has vanished, its essence has been captured in one of Europe's most remarkable displays, the Village Museum. Founded in 1936, along with the 494 acre (200 ha) Herastrau Park in which it stands, the museum was part of a project by a team of researchers to study Romanian village life. It began with 30 buildings and their contents drawn from all over the country. Today, it contains 300 structures, including wooden churches, carved timber and thatched peasant houses, farm buildings and windmills.

Street kids *Revolution in 1989 brought freedom and poverty – a combination that drove poor children like these to fend for themselves on the streets.*

Dictator's folly *The most notorious of Ceausescu's grand schemes was the People's Palace. He wanted it to be the world's largest building. In fact, it ranks second after the Pentagon. It took 20 000 workers five years to demolish one-sixth of Bucharest – 12 churches and 7000 houses – to build the 3000-room edifice. It is now the Palace of Parliament.*

Brasov and Chisinau

The cities of Brasov and Chisinau have a shared history of German, Hungarian, Romanian and Soviet rulers. Today they are striving to establish a new identity: Brasov in Romania and Chisinau as capital of Moldova.

In the early 13th century, Brasov was one of the seven fortified towns founded by Germans in what were then Magyar tribal lands. In succession, Transylvania (known in German as Siebenbürgen, the Seven Guarantors) became Turkish, Austrian and Hungarian, and finally in 1920 Romanian. Today's Brasov was previously named Brassó by the Hungarians and Kronstadt when it was in the forefront of the German-led Reformation.

Dominating the main pass from the Transylvanian highlands to the Romanian lowlands, Brasov became an important road and rail junction, and an equally important industrial and commercial centre for cars, food and textiles. Its heart is medieval, with the remnants of walls built in 1421 surrounding a ruined citadel, and several ancient churches, including the huge Protestant church and the Black Church (so-named from the blackening by a fire in 1689). New skiing facilities in the surrounding mountains have recently given Brasov a reputation as a winter-sports centre.

Historic centre Brasov's Sfatului Square, alive with shops and cafés, retains its medieval shape and fine Baroque façades.

From Kishinev to Chisinau

Moldova's capital, Chisinau, a place of parks and lakes surrounded by wine-rich plains, hardly seems to have the stature of a large city. Its quiet streets belie a dramatic past: conquered by the Turks, seized by Russia, ceded to Romania, retaken by the Russians, and occupied in the Second World War by Germans. The Nazis con-

ducted a notorious pogrom in which almost all Moldova's Jews were exterminated. It was recaptured by the Russians in 1944, with widescale destruction. When the Soviet Union collapsed in 1991, Kishinev became the capital of the new republic, under its Romanian name of Chisinau. But the broad streets and imposing monuments serve as a reminder of its half-century of Soviet rule.

Moldovan expansiveness Chisinau's wide avenues and vast apartment blocks are the legacy of its years as part of the Soviet Union.

The influence of the Hanseatic League

The hansa were unions of north German families, guilds or towns which sought to dominate trade across central Europe. By the mid 14th century, more than 100 Hanseatic League towns, many of them non-German, formed a sort of 'commercial state', with merchants working as far apart as Iceland, Spain and Ireland. The League's monopoly was finally undermined in the 16th century by the growth of English and Dutch rivals exploiting markets in the New World and the Far East. In the Baltic, its home ground, it was competing with Russia. The League's last diet was held in 1669.

Trading waterfront Gdansk in Poland was a wealthy member of the Hanseatic League.

Sofia: a choice capital

For 500 years, Sofia was little more than a link in the trade routes leading to the imperial heart of Bulgaria's Turkish overlords. Then, in 1879, Sofia emerged as the capital of independent Bulgaria, and never looked back.

Sofia is one of those cities that was neither born great nor achieved greatness; it had its greatness as a capital thrust upon it after several other candidates had fallen by the wayside.

Sofia's predecessors

Bulgaria's first capital was Pliska, headquarters of the tribal khan Asparuh, whose people migrated across the Danube in the late 7th century. Asparuh was officially recognised by the Byzantine emperor, Constantine IV. His city remained the Bulgarian capital for more than 200 years, and thus the place to which the followers of saints Cyril and Methodius came when they introduced Christianity and the Cyrillic alphabet into Bulgaria in the 9th century. In its day, it was a huge fortified town extending over 8 sq miles (20 km^2), but today the central ruins are of a palace with three lines of defence – a ditch, a wall with four gates and a brick rampart. The defences enclose two other palaces and a basilica, which once had piped water and central heating.

Bulgaria profited from the decision to opt for the Byzantine version of Christianity. Under Simeon I (893-927), the new nation grew into the so-called First Empire, and Simeon decided to build himself a new capital, one that would be a suitable match for Byzantium itself. He termed himself 'emperor and autocrat of all the Bulgars and Greeks,' and abandoned Pliska for Preslav. Here, palaces and churches arose that were the glories of their day. But

Preslav's heyday was brief. In 972, the Byzantines sacked and burned it. Little remains but ruins scattered over fields.

In the 12th century, Bulgaria regained its independence and acquired a new capital, Turnovo, which became known as Veliko (Great) in 1965. Turnovo has a stunning setting on three steep

Capital remnants *Graceful columns of the once magnificent capital of Preslav, created by Simeon in the 10th century.*

Clifftop views *Houses in Veliko Turnovo, Bulgaria's medieval capital, teeter above the chasm of the River Yantra.*

Plovdiv: the capital that might have been

Plovdiv, Bulgaria's second city, might have become the capital had it not been the scene of a nationalist revolt against Turkish rule in 1876. In the ensuing 'Bulgarian Atrocities' 15 000 people were massacred by the Ottomans. The Great Powers opted instead for Sofia as the new capital. Plovdiv owes its eminence to its position on the River Maritsa. Under Philip of Macedonia, it became a fortified Greek town, Philippopolis. Today it is a thriving industrial city with a historic core of Thracian, Roman, Macedonian, Byzantine and Ottoman architecture.

Roman past *Plovdiv's superb amphitheatre.*

Grand designs Central Sofia's broad streets and squares reflect a vision by 19th-century town planners to create a city on a scale to match that of Paris and Vienna.

hills, with near vertical slopes plunging 800 ft (240 m) into the tortuous, meandering gorge of the River Yantra. This, the capital of Bulgaria's Second Empire, held on to the nation's identity through 500 years of Turkish domination from the 14th to 19th centuries. The ruined citadel survives on Tsaravets hill, and on the neighbouring hill, Trapezitsa, rows of medieval houses huddle, 'like frightened sheep above the chasms, penned by stairways and steep, narrow lanes,' wrote the Bulgarian poet Ivan Vazov (1850-1921).

The newest capital

It was in Turnovo that the National Assembly gathered to draft Bulgaria's first constitution in 1879. Yet it was to Sofia that the Bulgarians turned as their capital. As a relative backwater, Sofia was a safer choice than the thriving, but politically sensitive Plovdiv. Sofia was also well placed. As Serdica, it had been an important commercial centre under the Romans. In an age of roads and railways, it could bind the nation and link it to the wider world better than any other. The town had the space to expand – its population of 30 000 grew fivefold by 1920. Today it has 1.2 million inhabitants.

Sofia has some fine Roman remains and ancient buildings, among them the 6th-century church of Sveta Sofia (Holy Wisdom) from which it takes its name and is considered to be one of the finest early Christian buildings in the Balkans. There is little trace of Turkish rule: only one working mosque, the Banya Bashi, remains. Sofia is essentially a late 19th-century city, laid out in a network of broad avenues and open spaces that owes much to Paris and ancient Rome. Boulevard Tsar Osvoboditel, with its rows of chestnut trees, follows an old Roman road. The new government buildings, churches and museums were built in a variety of styles: Neo-Byzantine for the Alexander Nevsky Cathedral, Neo-Baroque for the university, Neoclassical for the National Historical Museum, with Soviet-style postwar additions.

Liberation Avenue Boulevard Tsar-Osvoboditel (Liberator) honours Alexander II of Russia (1818-81), who supported Bulgaria's fight for freedom from Turkish rule.

Russian design Alexander Nevsky Cathedral (1884-1924) commemorates the Russian-backed war of liberation from the Turks. It holds 5000 people.

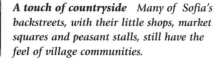

A touch of countryside Many of Sofia's backstreets, with their little shops, market squares and peasant stalls, still have the feel of village communities.

CHAPTER 5
CULTURE AND FOLKLORE

Every country, region and locality has its own way of expressing its identity, whether in music, art, verse or festival. Among them there are writers and composers, painters, photographers and film-makers who have achieved worldwide fame: Kafka, Chopin, Vásárely, Capa and Wajda to name but a few. Each generation has taken up the challenge to absorb and express, to champion a cause or contest a regime. At times of national revival, Eastern Europeans have looked to their literary and creative heroes for inspiration, even leadership. Festivals have always provided an excuse for donning national costume, striking up a tune and dancing. American television and Western pop music may intrude, but Eastern Europeans closely guard their cultures and their artists continue to move and astonish the world.

Spirit of the dance: Poles in festive mood.

A pen for all seasons

Fascinating and mysterious, the literature of Eastern Europe has a richness and diversity derived from constant political and social upheaval.

Eastern Europe's writers and poets have borne witness to the political events that have formed and reformed their nations. In their work they have preserved their cultures and languages and have often provided the inspiration for nationalist revival. Many have achieved international recognition, including the Czech writer Franz Kafka and the Polish poet Wislawa Szymborska.

Elias Canetti, cosmopolitan

Elias Canetti (1905-94), a Bulgarian of Spanish-Jewish extraction, wrote in German, but worked mainly in Britain. His formative experience was witnessing the riots sparked by Germany's hyper-inflation in Frankfurt in the 1920s. Canetti became obsessed with the madness of crowds, which formed the theme of his novel *Auto-da-Fé*, in which a scholar's life is torn apart in grotesque fashion. He emigrated to England in the 1930s, where he researched the same subject (*Crowds and Power*, 1962). His three-part autobiography, which contained scathing denunciations of totalitarianism, made him famous in Germany and infamous in Bulgaria, the more so when he was awarded the Nobel prize for literature in 1981.

Portrait of K *A painting captures Franz Kafka's haunted look.*

Romanian polymaths *Mircea Eliade (1907-86), religious historian and novelist (left), and the philosopher, Émile Michel Cioran.*

Svejk, the good soldier

Jaroslav Hasek (1883-1923) may not be well known outside his Czech homeland, but his 'good soldier Svejk' is renowned as a masterpiece of satire. Svejk originally made his appearance in a 1912 short story, but came into his own in four volumes written in 1920-3, after Hasek had served on the Eastern Front. Svejk is an anti-war anti-hero of such epic stupidity that, despite his apparent obedience to authority, he succeeds in paralysing the Austrian army. Triumphing over the forces of bureaucracy and elitism, he incarnates passive resistance to war, emerging as a character as original as Kafka's 'Joseph K' or Joseph Heller's 'Yossarian' in *Catch 22*. Translated into English in 1930, Svejk has been in print ever since.

Everyman, Czech style *A beer mat shows Svejk indulging in a favourite activity.*

Two Czech Ks

Franz Kafka (1883-1924) grew up in Prague at the centre of three cultures: Czech, German and Jewish. Together they gave him three defining qualities: dreamer, philosopher and purveyor of black humour. The Prague of Kafka's youth was a provincial Austro-Hungarian town, in which a foreign bureaucracy disguised incipient anarchy. Kafka had a tyrannical father and a tedious office job, and his only escape was through literature and fantasy.

In allegorical terms, he portrayed an individual – Joseph K, himself – in a seemingly normal world, yet isolated from his fellows and in a desperate struggle against arbitrary authority (of the type now known as Kafka-esque). Not that he lived an isolated

Tragic view *The Jewish-Romanian poet Paul Celan (1920-70) was consigned to a labour camp in the Second World War. Later, he wrote in German of the horrors of war. Celan committed suicide in the River Seine.*

JÓZSEF
ATTILA
«KÖLTÖNK
ÉS KORA»

Pre-war voice   Attila József on the jacket of a collection of his verses.

Hungary, land of poets

In common with other East Europeans, Hungarians care deeply about their poets, whether they are 19th-century romantics or the tormented souls who wrote of the horrors of the 20th century. They know by heart at least one poem by Attila József (1905-37), an idealistic communist whose sombre realism still retained a sense of optimism. János Pilinszky (1921-81) survived concentration camps to become a venerated poet, despite official disapproval of his Catholicism. There are few Hungarians who do not know the anguished work of Miklós Radnóti (1909-44), whose last poems were found in his pocket after he was shot on a forced march to a labour camp. In his words, Hungarian children grew 'pattering about in history ... not far from a prison, where the guards keep changing'.

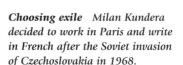

life – he had many friends, several love affairs and was widely admired by his intellectual peers.

Milan Kundera (born in 1929) is perhaps the best known of postwar Czech writers. Like Kafka, he expresses the alienation felt by the individual from society. His novel *The Joke* (1967) was an ironic portrait of the Czechs under Stalinism. His next novel was banned in his homeland, which he rejected in 1975 when he moved to France. His most famous work, *The Unbearable Lightness of Being* (1984), won him international fame, but was never published in Czech.

Poland's Nobel laureates

Henryk Sienkiewicz (1846-1916) is almost entirely unknown or forgotten by English-speakers today, but he wrote one of the most famous historical novels of the late 19th century, *Quo Vadis?* (1896). This story of the first days of Christianity in ancient Rome won him an international reputation, and the Nobel prize for literature in 1905. The book was translated into many languages. In 1951 it became a Hollywood film.

Czeslaw Miloscz (born in 1911), poet, translator and author of *The Captive Mind*, has had a life that seems to encapsulate the recent history of central Europe. Born in Lithuania, he was educated in Poland, where he was active in the Polish resistance, writing

Choosing exile   Milan Kundera decided to work in Paris and write in French after the Soviet invasion of Czechoslovakia in 1968.

Rising talent   Jáchym Topol, former underground writer, is a rising Czech poet and novelist.

and editing clandestine works. After the war he became disillusioned with communism. He emigrated, first to France and then to the USA, from where he condemned accommodation with communism. He was awarded the Nobel prize for literature in 1980.

Wislawa Szymborska (born in 1923) was well known for her poetry in Poland long before receiving the Nobel prize in 1996. Her verse, with its universal concerns expressed in spare and simple language, has been widely translated. In her poem *The Century's Decline*, Szymborska comments on the times: 'Our twentieth century was going to improve on the others/ It will never prove it now/ now that its years are numbered…. A couple of problems weren't going/ to come up anymore:/ hunger, for example,/ and war, and so forth.'

A booming book fair

Cluj-Napoca in Romania is as much Hungarian (in which it is known as Kolozsvar) as it is Romanian, and almost as German (Klausenburg) as both. So it is an appropriate place for the annual Gaudeamus educational book fair, which started in 1994. The fair attracts more than 150 exhibitors and 62 000 visitors. Educational publishing is a growing sector in Eastern Europe and is attracting considerable international attention. Book fairs have proved a success in Bucharest, Sofia and Prague, and it is hoped that Cluj-Napoca will be able to share in the boom.

Late acknowledgment   The work of Wislawa Szymborska had been studied by Polish schoolchildren for 20 years before she won international fame as a Nobel laureate for literature in 1996, at the age of 73.

Reading matter   The Globe in Prague is an American-run bookshop and café that is the hub of the foreign-language literary scene. Its floor-to-ceiling shelves hold the city's best collection of books in English.

On stage, everyone!

Romance and history, mythology and absurdity – all find a voice on the stages of Eastern Europe. Inspired by playwrights such as Stefan Wyspianski from Poland and Imre Madach from Hungary – whose historical dramas attracted large audiences in the 19th century – the people of Eastern Europe established a tradition of theatregoing that continues to this day.

Genius of the absurd *Ionesco accepts applause in Paris, 1989.*

Word play *The dream-like set for a 1994 French version of Slawomir Mrozek's* Love in the Crimea. *The Polish playwright is so popular that his name is used to describe an everyday absurdity.*

Theatre has had a long tradition in Eastern Europe, regardless of the ruling regime. It remained popular even when subject to censorship and actors always played to packed houses. Playwrights have often performed a role in a nation's cultural revival. The Czech National Theatre in Prague was so close to the hearts of the people that when it was destroyed by fire only days before its official opening in 1881, it took just six weeks to collect enough money to start rebuilding (see box).

The curtain rises

The 19th century gave the theatre the grounding it needed to flourish. People were eager for shows in their own languages. Light comedy was not enough, they wanted to see their mythologies and histories on stage. Actors became national heroes, performing repertoires that remain popular today. An example was *The Wedding* by the Polish playwright Stefan Wyspianski (1869-1907). He used the marriage of the poet Lucyan Rydel to a peasant girl as a context for a sweeping view of Poland's history. At its premier in Kraków in 1901, *The Wedding* became an instant classic. Hungarians look back to *The Tragedy of Man* by Imre Madach (1823-64), a 15-act drama portraying the past and future of mankind. Ferenc Molnar (1878-1952) won international acclaim with *Liliom* (1909), the story of a carnival owner who is killed and returns in spirit to check on his family. It was filmed by Fritz Lang in 1930, and inspired the musical *Carousel*.

Despair and absurdity

Exuberance and high hopes foundered on the reefs of war. Many playwrights expressed despair, or escaped it by turning to the absurd. Writing in France, Romania's Eugène Ionesco (1912-94) explored the theme of estrangement in plays that made surrealism popular on stage. Behind the Iron Curtain, the need to conform while criticising inspired irony and black humour, typified by the work of Vaclav Havel, the post-communist president of the Czech Republic.

Breaking the rules *The Polish playwright Tadeusz Kantor (1915-90) wrote himself into his productions, as seen here in* Let the Artists Die *(1985).*

Nazdar! A theatrical triumph

It took 20 years to raise the funds for Prague's National Theatre, and another 13 years to construct it. Then, just before the opening in 1881, it burned down. After an emotive public appeal the theatre was rebuilt. It opened in 1883 with the opera *Libuse*, written for the occasion by Smetana. The triumph was such that the subscription's slogan, 'Success (*Nazdar*) to the National Theatre' entered the language as a form of greeting.

Fiery end *Flames engulf the newly built Czech National Theatre in June 1881. Its successor stands as a symbol of Czech nationalism.*

The art of the poster

With their combination of poetry, bright colours and typographical tricks, posters have a particular place in contemporary Polish art. Designed as an essentially urban way of informing, enticing or condemning, they are the epitomes of their genre.

Modern poster design has its roots in French theatre advertisements of the late 19th century, when artists such as Manet and Toulouse-Lautrec were attracted to the medium's freedom, boldness and speed of production. Interest quickly spread to the rest of Europe, with new impetus from the growing demand for advertisements and political slogans (sometimes both together, as in recruiting posters).

In postwar Eastern Europe, the medium had particular appeal because posters are ephemeral – quick to design, quick to produce, quickly discarded. For the poster artist, any mundane cultural happening, whether a circus, play, film or sporting event, could inspire some new, and possibly subversive design.

An exceptional show

Warsaw is the mother-city of the poster, which makes it the natural home for the greatest of poster exhibitions. The International Poster Biennale started in 1966 as an expression of an art form that developed since the Second World War under the auspices of Tadeusz Trepkowsky and Henryk Tomaszewsky at Warsaw's Academy of Fine Arts.

Following their exuberant examples, which established Poland as the leader in the field of posters, other masters of poster art came to the fore, notably Jan Lenica, Roman Cieslewicz and Waldemar Swierzy. Jan Lenica (1928-2001) was born in Poznan, where he

Portrait of a goddess   Mucha's 1897 poster for La Divine Sarah.

Mucha's inimitable style

The Czech artist Alfonse Mucha (1860-1939) started as a scene-painter in Brno, moving on to Vienna, Munich and Paris. He found his métier as an Art Nouveau poster designer, winning fame when the actress Sarah Bernhardt asked him to design an advertisement in 1894. Later he produced posters for Bernhardt's triumphant *La Dame aux Camélias* and *Lorenzaccio*. Advertisements strengthened his reputation, while an American patron provided financial security. He also painted, worked in glass and – back home – designed banknotes for the Czech government.

trained as an architect before turning to satirical cartoons. His reputation spread when he started designing film posters in the 1950s, such as those for *The Wages of Fear*, *La Strada* and *Il Bidone*. He also designed opera posters and created surrealist-inspired animated films which he made from collages.

Roman Cieslewicz (1930-96) became the main exponent of new graphic techniques. After working as an artistic director in Paris, he taught graphic art and turned to the design of posters for films and humanitarian campaigns for hunger relief and human rights.

Waldemar Swierzy (born in 1931) is a set designer and illustrator. As a poster artist, he created a series of portraits of jazz musicians and the posters for Andrzej Wajda's films. As president of the Biennale from 1979 to 1997, he oversaw its rapid growth – it now shows more than 400 works from 36 different countries.

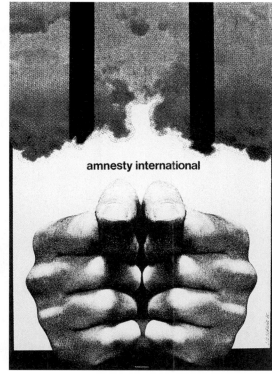

The Rite of Spring   *A Jan Lenica poster (left) for a Stravinsky concert at the Wielki Theatre, Warsaw.*

Cry freedom   *Cieslewicz's poster for Amnesty International, 1975.*

Lights, Camera, Action!

A small group of talented film-makers such as Andrzej Wajda worked through the censorious years of communism to develop Eastern Europe's embryonic industry. Today, films from Poland, the Czech Republic and Hungary are acclaimed in the West.

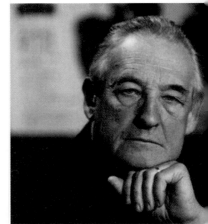

Before 1939, the film industry in Eastern Europe comprised a fledgling enterprise in Poland, with little of international note elsewhere. The Second World War hampered progress, which was further stifled by communist ideology. Irony, pessimism, despair, isolation, the uselessness of heroism, historical absurdity, carefully disguised criticism of the communist regime – these were some of the themes that exercised film-makers behind the Iron Curtain. They were not the most suitable subjects for an international audience. Many film-makers gave up in the face of low budgets and censorship, or went into exile. Only with Stalin's death in 1953 did life begin to return to the cinema.

Lasting genius Film director Andrzej Wajda provided the impetus for a revival in Polish film-making from the 1950s.

The 'Polish school' of film makes its mark
The film industry's revival was led by Poland's Andrzej Wajda, with a trilogy that won wide acclaim internationally (*A Generation*, 1954; *Canal*, 1957; and *Ashes and Diamonds*, 1958). They dealt in

On set *Polish director Andrzej Zulawski films* Chamanka *(1995), a story of a wild love affair between an anthropologist and a student.*

Homecoming *Roman Polanski, on a return visit to Warsaw after a long absence, films* The Pianist, *based on the autobiography of the Polish-Jewish composer Wladyslaw Szpilman.*

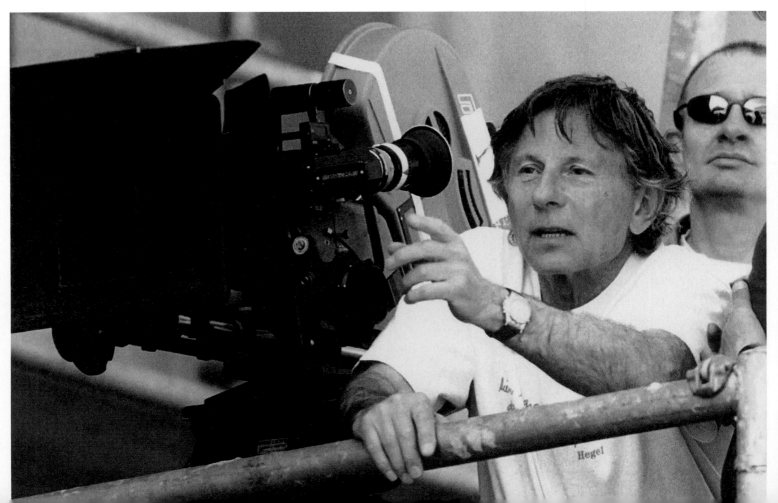

Death cry *In Skolimowski's* The Shout, *the character played by Alan Bates can kill with a cry. The film won the 1975 Prix Spécial in Cannes.*

symbolic form with Poland's wartime experiences: the German occupation, the Warsaw uprising, the postwar years.

Other film-makers in the so-called 'Polish school' followed his lead: Andrzej Munk (*Man on the Track*, 1956), who died in 1961 before completing *Passenger*, his film about the Holocaust; Jerzy Skolimowski (*Identification Marks: None*, 1964, among others); Wojciech Jerzy Has (*The Noose*, 1957) and Jerzy Kawalerowicz (*The Night Train*, 1959).

Every one of these Polish film-makers earned an international reputation, but one name became known to the public at large, Roman Polanski. He made his mark in 1962 with *Knife in the Water*, a short melodrama about a young couple who invited a hitchhiker to their yacht, and regretted it.

This upsurge of creativity faded under new official curbs during the 1960s, and production declined. Polanski fled into exile, followed by Skolimowski. Wajda remained, building a body of work that was both romantic and political, culminating in *Man of Marble* (1977), which denounced the absurdity of Stalinist rule.

With the rise to power of Solidarity and the democracy movement in the 1980s, other film-makers started to produce scathing social criticisms, among them Krzysztof Zanussi and Krzysztof Kieslowski. They, like their assistants Andrzej Zulawski

A renaissance in the East

In 1990, political freedom brought with it economic disaster. But a decade later, freedom has, after all, provided benefits. With borders open, companies and governments hungry for hard currency and prices low, co-productions with the West have been the salvation of the studios. In the Czech Republic, for instance, Prague's Barrandov studios have a wealth of experience and facilities to offer. Recently acclaimed productions from Eastern Europe include the Czech *Kolja* by Zdenek Sverak (best foreign film at Cannes and the US Academy Awards 1998); and from Hungary, Attila Janisch's *Long Twilight* (1998) and Ibolya Fekete's *Bolshe Vita* (1996), a cheery, cynical tale of travelling musicians.

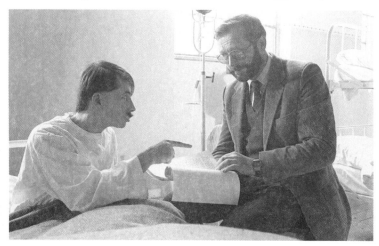

Polish-German link *Zanussi works on a television film,* Bygone Times, *with Markus Vogelbacher. Zanussi later turned to making feature films.*

Franco-Polish link *Irène Jacob and Jean-Louis Trintignant in* Red *(1995), the last of Kieslowski's French trilogy,* Three Colours.

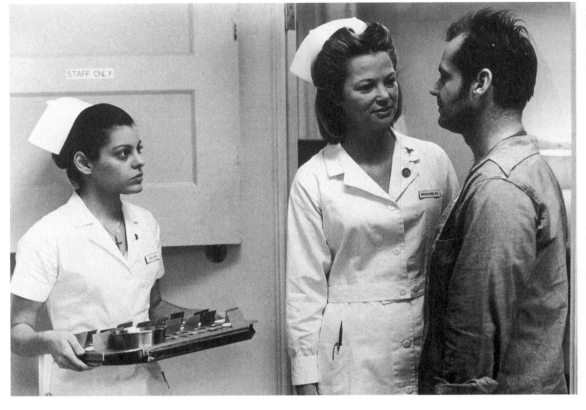

Oscar winner Milos Forman's One Flew Over the Cuckoo's Nest, *starring Louise Fletcher and Jack Nicholson, won five Oscars in 1975.*

and Agnieszka Holland, were silenced for a decade by General Jaruzelski, but flourished once again in the 1990s (though Kieslowski died in 1996).

Freeze and thaw

Prewar Hungary produced two great film-makers: Mihaly Kertész and Sándor Korda. But they had to go abroad to make their names. Kertész emigrated to the USA in 1926, and became the director Michael Curtiz. Korda made his first films in Budapest, but soon moved to Vienna, Hollywood, Paris and finally to England, where as Sir Alexander Korda he became one of the most successful film producers (*The Private Life of Henry VIII*, 1932, *The Third Man*, 1949).

Back in Hungary, repression lifted slightly between 1953 and 1956, with Felix Mariassy's *Springtime in Budapest* and Zoltan Fabri's *Professor Hannibal*. The 1960s nurtured a second renaissance, culminating in Istvan Szábo's *Mephisto*, which won an Oscar for the best foreign film in 1982.

Czech cinema followed a similar track. The National Revival inspired a few early successes, one being Gustaf Machaty's *Extase*, the first film to show

Czech master Istvan Szábo, director of Mephisto, *is acknowledged as one of the best directors of his generation. He has received more than 60 international awards.*

full-frontal nudity. It caused a sensation at the 1934 Venice Film Festival. Then came the Nazi occupation, war and Stalinism. Rebirth followed in the 1960s, with a 'new wave' best represented by Vera Chytilova (*Daisies*, 1966) and Jiri Menzel, whose comedy, *Closely Observed Trains*, was the Academy's best foreign film in 1967. This, too, proved a brief renaissance. It ended with the Soviet invasion in 1968, which drove Czechoslovakia's aspiring film-makers to the USA – among them, Milos Forman. Menzel himself made one more film, *Capricious Summer* (1968), before being forced to share the long silence, which is now being broken with startling success.

Poster and film A poster by Jan Lenica illustrates his animated film version of French writer Alfred Jarry's grotesque stage character, Ubu, king of Poland.

Imaginations running wild

Eastern European cartoon films form a genre with few equivalents in the West. Rooted in the traditions of puppet theatre, disrespectful of authority and highly imaginative, they have attracted creative geniuses such as Jiri Trnka (*The Hand*, 1965) and Jan Svankmajer (*Alice*, 1988) in Czechoslovakia; Jan Lenica (*Ubu Roi*, 1976), Jerzy Kucia and Walerian Borowczyk (*The Astronauts*, 1959) in Poland. This type of cartoon film is highly labour intensive and expensive to make. The films are rarely screened in the West and for the genre to continue and flourish they need financial backing.

Puppet master Jiri Trnka (1912-69) put puppets on film by changing their position frame by frame.

Strings attached

Every country in Eastern Europe has its tradition of puppeteering, and in Prague and Budapest, in particular, puppet shows are a popular form of entertainment. The techniques appeal to children, but the creations are often satirical and experimental, with story lines, scripts and images designed more for adults.

Puppet caricatures *Spejbl and Hurvínek on a book-owner's stamp.*

Puppet theatre has a long and eminent tradition dating back to the 16th century. Puppetry was common throughout Europe: the puppet hero (Pulcinella, Polichinelle, or Mr Punch) was the underdog with a well-developed disdain for authority. Haydn composed puppet operas for his Hungarian patrons, and Bohemian puppeteers acquired a status equal to their Hungarian peers.

The Czech equivalent of Mr Punch is Kasparek, who emerged in the 18th century. In the late 19th century, the Czech composer Smetana wrote puppet plays. Under communism in the 20th century, there was state support for puppet theatres.

Today, it is harder for puppeteers to make a living. They face stiff competition from computer games and television cartoons imported cheaply from the USA and Japan. Budapest's puppet theatre still functions in a fine Neo-Renaissance hall in Andrássy út, and Prague has a number of puppet theatres. Some puppeteers are adapting their work to make animated films.

Little and large *Gulliver discovers a giant in a puppet show performed by the Hungarian Véra Brody, who has often performed abroad.*

Spejbl and Hurvínek

The most eminent of modern puppet theatres is the Spejbl and Hurvínek Theatre in Prague. The theatre began life not in Prague, but in Plzen.

In 1917, Josef Skupa, a stage designer in Plzen, joined the local puppet theatre, and three years later devised a character, Spejbl, who was later joined on stage by his young sidekick Hurvínek. Together, they became as famous in Czechoslovakia as Punch and Judy are in Britain, though they are intellectually very different. The Czech characters comment on the world with grotesque humour and satire.

Skupa set up his own Spejbl and Hurvínek Theatre, in which he performed both the characters' voices, alternating between bass and treble. He was vocal in his opposition to the German invasion of 1938 and was soon arrested. After the war, Skupa opened the 50-seat Spejbl and Hurvínek Theatre in Prague, which he ran until his death in 1957. His roles were taken over by Milos Kirchner, who played the duo for 44 years, took them on world tours and performed in 18 languages. Martin Klasek continues the tradition in the same theatre, to the delight of children and adults alike.

Miniature Mozart *In Prague, the National Marionette Theatre stages regular performances of Mozart's* **Don Giovanni**.

Basketwork figures *These puppets show the inventiveness of their Polish creator, Adam Killian.*

Images in black and white

The first photojournalists came mainly from Hungary. They captured life at its most ordinary, its most poignant and its most significant. Their work has attracted worldwide acclaim and inspired successive generations of photographers.

The photographs are as familiar as Old Masters: a portrait of Picasso that seems to exude a life force, a Republican soldier being shot during the Spanish Civil War, Gypsy children embracing. These shots were produced by three Hungarians who became the founding fathers of photojournalism: Brassaï, Kertész, Capa.

'Avoid mere effects if you want to express reality,' Gyula Halasz (1899-1984) used to say. Born in Brasso (Brasov, then in Hun-

Working the land Collective Farm, by *Robert Capa; Ukraine, 1947.*

gary), Halasz moved to Paris in 1924 and adopted a new name derived from his native town: Brassaï. A friend of Picasso and other artists, Brassaï established his reputation with his book *Paris de Nuit* in 1933. André Kertész (1894-1985) had a talent for catching the spontaneous. He called these moments seized from everyday life 'little nothings'. But his 'nothings' influenced a generation of photojournalists. Robert Capa, born Andrei Friedmann in 1913, was the incarnation of the war photographer: adventurer, womaniser, gambler. 'If your pictures aren't good, you're not close enough,' he used to say. It was Capa who recorded the American assault on Omaha beach, France, on D-Day, 1944. It was an attitude that cost him his life. He died ten years later, when he stepped on a land mine in Indochina.

In the 1930s, Capa formed friendships with the radical French photographer Henri Cartier-Bresson, David Seymour (a Polish Jew originally named Szymin, known as Chim) and a quiet Englishman, George Rodger. In 1947, in New York, he suggested the four form an agency in order to retain the copyright to their pictures. They called it Magnum, and it became the soul of photojournalism. Over the next 50 years it grew to represent 80 of the world's best photographers.

Among them was the Czech, Josef Koudelka. He started as an 'absolute maniac' – in the words of a colleague – who climbed on

Russian tanks when photographing the 1968 invasion of Czechoslovakia. His pictures were later smuggled out to Magnum, which sold them to *The Sunday Times* and *Look* magazine for \$20 000, crediting him under the pseudonym 'Prague photographer'. Magnum's Elliott Erwitt then helped to engineer Koudelka's escape, and he was invited to join the agency. He became a French citizen in 1987.

Hungarian in Paris *Brassaï in his laboratory in the early 1930s.*

Inside story

Exhibitions often reveal talented new photojournalists, such as the Czech photographer, Hana Jakrlova-Kirkpatrick, born the year after Koudelka was climbing on tanks. In her black-and-white pictures of what remains of Old Europe, she maintains the prewar tradition of finding human depths in ordinary, everyday life.

Sweet melody Wandering Musician, *by André Kertész; Hungary, 1921.*

Dedicated to the Abstract

Many of the great names in 20th-century art – Kupka, Brancusi, Vásárely, Moholy-Nagy – came from Eastern Europe. They combined an enthusiasm for their work with the courage to experiment.

Contemporary art movements, such as Cubism, Surrealism and Abstract Expressionism, have been strong forces in Eastern Europe. Among the first of the modern artists to win international recognition was the Czech, Frantisek Kupka (1871-1957), who in 1895 settled in Paris. There he experimented with Fauvism and Pointillism, then developed into an early exponent of pure abstraction, a style of sweeping coloured curves sometimes referred to as Orphism, in line with Kupka's idea that colour could be used as a visual equivalent of music. At the same time, just before the First World War, Czech artists, writers and architects formed a group known as *Osma* (the Eight), which included the Cubist painters Bohumil Kubista (1884-1918) and Emil Filla, and the writer, Karel Capek.

Constantin Brancusi, The Cock, *1924.*

The search for simplicity and movement

In Romania, painters owe a debt to the Surrealist, Victor Brauner (1903-66), a close friend of André Breton and other French Surrealists. But the best-known Romanian artist was the sculptor Constantin Brancusi (1876-1957), whose spare creations are products of a yearning for geometric elegance. He owed his talent in part to the woodcarving skills he acquired as a shepherd boy in the Carpathians, a time to which he also owed his defining traits: simplicity, good sense, love of nature. Brancusi learned to read and write only in his late teens. Inspired by Rodin, he moved to Paris, and began his life-long work on natural forms expressed with ever greater simplicity of line. He became a French national in 1952, and was acknowledged as one of the century's greatest sculptors.

The Hungarian-born Victor Vásárely (1908-97) moved to Paris where he experimented with Post-Cubism, Expressionism, and a technology-based style of sculpture now known as

Moholy-Nagy Self-portrait.

Search for purity *Exhibits in the Vásárely Museum, Pécs, show the uncluttered forms that characterise much of the artist's work.*

kinetic. But it was only after the Second World War that he came into his own. In his sixties, he became one of the founders of Op Art, the 'op' being short for 'optical', a reference to its aim to create the optical illusion of movement by distorting simple repetitive geometric forms. Two museums – in Gordes, southern France, and Pécs in Hungary – are dedicated to his work.

Vásárely's compatriot, László Moholy-Nagy (1895-1946), was both a painter and a sculptor who used every possible technique – drawing, painting, photography, film – to achieve the dynamic effects he sought. In 1921, he worked in Berlin with the avant-garde Bauhaus school, designing an influential curriculum for arts education with a holistic approach summed up by his adage 'Everyone is talented'. Fleeing the Nazis in 1935, he settled in Chicago, where he founded the New Bauhaus, the first US school based on the Bauhaus programme.

Exploring three dimensions Lines, Surfaces, Depth, *Kupka, 1913-14.*

The music of freedom

In a part of Europe that lives and breathes music, Chopin from Poland, Bartók from Hungary, and Janácek, Dvorák and Smetana from the Czech Republic are just a few of the great names in the classical repertoire to emerge over the past two centuries.

Everywhere in Eastern Europe, composers seem to spring to the fore. Their music is often an expression of nationalism that in many cases won them international acclaim. The most remarkable of these musicians was Fryderyk Szopen from Poland, who became the Frenchman, Frédéric Chopin (1810-49). Drawing his inspiration from popular songs, Chopin composed polonaises and mazurkas that seemed to express the very essence of the national revival in his native Poland. They took his countrymen by storm, and then all Europe.

International impact

The nation whose music seems to restate its traditions most enduringly and have had the greatest impact on the outside world is the Czech Republic. Czech national music first found expression in Hussite hymns, some of which had roots

Local roots *Janácek found inspiration in folk music, as his Moravian songs show.*

Into the depths *Boris Christoff (1919-93), the Bulgarian bass, performs the role of Philip II in Verdi's* **Don Carlos.**

The New World – from concert hall to songbook

Dvorák's most famous work, his 9th Symphony, *From the New World*, was an instant success at its premiere in New York in December 1893. Its popularity sprang in part from its tunes, in particular its slow movement. Dvorák hinted that he had found his inspiration in 'negro melodies' and in 'local colour of Indian character'. Some listeners detect elements of *Swing Low, Sweet Chariot* in the tune. In fact, it is as much Czech as anything, for it is wholly original. It was a tribute to Dvorák's genius for rising above stereotypes that the touching melody was given words, *Going Home*, printed in songbooks and became a spiritual. Dvorák was director of the New York National Conservatory of Music at the time.

---

in pre-Christian dances and songs. But Czech independence was lost at the Battle of the White Mountain in 1620. For three centuries, Habsburg rule imposed Western Catholicism and Western models. The greatest 'Czech' musical event at this time was a very un-Czech occasion: in 1797 Mozart's *Don Giovanni* was given its

High society performer *Smetana plays to aristocratic admirers. He taught the family of Count Leopold Thun and ran a piano school before starting to compose.*

Player and composer *Dvorák's musical skill grew from playing the violin with local groups in his father's inn. He won international acclaim in his forties.*

Prague Spring Prague's major musical event, the Spring Festival, is held every May and June. It begins on May 12, the anniversary of Smetana's death, with concerts at historic sites such as the Wallenstein Palace (above).

premiere in Prague. The Czech composers of the 18th century – Zelenka, Myslivecek, Benda, Cernohorsky – were, and remain today, largely unknown outside their homeland.

Only in the late 19th century, with the Czech National Revival, did a truly indigenous music arise, when Bedrich Smetana (1824-84) reached back into the past and out into the countryside in search of the folk tunes that infuse his music and operas. His opera *The Bartered Bride* (1866) is a staple in the repertoire of companies the world over. Smetana's most famous piece is the six-part symphonic poem *Má Vlast* (*My Country*, 1874-9), the second part of which celebrates the River Vltava and could almost be described as a national anthem.

Classical additions

The same patriotic spirit drove Antonín Dvorák (1841-1904), the most widely loved of Czech composers. His 9th Symphony, known as *From the New World* (1893) because he wrote it while in the USA, has become one of the great popular classics, its slow movement accepted everywhere as a supreme expression of yearning. Leos Janácek (1854-

Genius honoured The Chopin Monument in Warsaw's Lazienki Park is a venue for concerts on summer Sundays.

March to independence

Czech music is not all classics and concert halls. Some of it is marches and bandstands. The nation's greatest composer for military bands was Frantisek Kmoch (1848-1912). His father was a tailor and a clarinettist in Kolin, 30 miles (50 km) east of Prague. Kmoch, a violinist, became a teacher, and then worked as a band leader for a movement known as Sokol, a nationalist physical education organisation that was officially discouraged, even banned on occasion, but survives to this day. Fired from his teaching post for his Sokol connections, Kmoch remained in Kolin as the leader of his band, for which he composed marches. They are still played in Kolin today, in a festival held every June in his honour.

1928) also looked locally for inspiration, as in his opera *Jenufa* (1904), based on a play by Gabriela Peissova about a stepmother who kills her stepdaughter's illegitimate baby to preserve the family's good name. His stupendous *Glagolitic Mass* looks back to medieval Orthodoxy that was later overridden by Catholicism. Both Janácek and his younger contemporary Bohuslav Martinu (1890-1959) are popular abroad, but were long considered a little 'difficult' in their homeland.

Rooted in folklore

The Hungarian composers Béla Bartók (1881-1946) and Zoltán Kodály (1882-1967) both recognised folk music as a root of national identity. In the early 20th century they travelled through Hungary and the Balkans, cataloguing the folk songs that were to prove so influential in works such as Bartók's opera *Duke Bluebeard's Castle* and Kodály's *Háry János*.

Musician of the people Béla Bartók, professor of piano at Budapest Academy (1907-34), gave Hungarian folk melodies a new lease of life with his arrangements.

Music of the Magyars Marta Sebestyén and her group Muzsikás are famous for their versions of Hungarian folk songs.

Bagpipes and panpipes

A special event, such as a marriage, a family reunion, or the arrival of an honoured guest, provides an excuse to strike up a tune. Panpipes, balalaikas and even bagpipes feature among the instruments.

National instruments can provide a valuable insight into a country's social history. Romanians favour panpipes, or *nai*, with their seven-note scale, continuing a tradition established under Greek and Roman influence. The cymbalum or dulcimer, a zither-like instrument played with hammers, originated in the Middle East, and arrived in Romania and Hungary in the 15th century, perhaps brought by migrating Roma (Gypsies). In Belarus and Ukraine, the triangular, three-stringed balalaika is the instrument of choice. Sometimes particular crafts or professions have their own preferences: Carpathian shepherds play the *kaval*, a sort of flute. Local Polish instruments include the *burczybas*, played by the Kashubians – a little cask that acts as a sounding box for a horsehair string – and the 'devil's violin', a sort of double bass with a top in the form of a devil and decorated with a tambourine, metal discs and bells.

The lure of the bagpipes

There is one instrument that is played everywhere, and everywhere has a local form: the bagpipes. The Romans and Greeks had early versions of the instrument, which was first recorded elsewhere in Europe in the 9th century. Sources are vague: since

Haunting sound The panpipe is Romania's archetypical instrument.

Shepherd's instrument With the Bulgarian version of the bagpipes (gaida), a master-musician can produce ornamented tunes of astonishing speed and rhythmic force.

bagpipes were simple combinations of animal-skin bags, cane and reeds, they were used by ordinary country people, whose ways were seldom considered worthy of recording.

Notes from a goatskin

Most types of bagpipe have either one or two 'chanter' pipes, a bass drone and a keynote an octave higher. The Bulgarian bagpipes (*gaida*) have a single chanter, the Czech (*dudy*) and Polish (*koza*, or *koziol*) versions have two. The scales preserve traditional intervals seldom used in classical music.

In Polish, bagpipes are called *koziol* (billy goat), because the instrument is made from goatskin, which is tough and remains airtight. They have been popular in Poland since the Middle Ages. A few 18th-century books refer to bagpipes being appreciated in manor houses and royal courts, where special bagpipe tunes and songs were composed. They seem to have lost nothing of their appeal, for they can be heard with increasing frequency in festivals and have at last won the attention of musical historians.

Wedding dance Accordion, clarinet and guitar are commonly played at country weddings in southern Bulgaria.

Maramuzical Festival

The pristine forests and mountains of Romania's Maramures region make a splendid backdrop for a festival of country music. This area has a pastoral tradition of violin playing: many farmers, loggers and miners are *ceteras* (violinists) who play at festivals and celebrations. At the instigation of the Maramures Country Association and with EU backing, the villages of Botiza and Leud, in the Valley of the Iza, hosted the first Maramuzical Festival in 1997. The four-day event drew hundreds of visitors. It is now an annual fixture in July, with violinists coming from Hungary, Ukraine and Romania.

Walls of wood, roofs of thatch

The houses of country people in Eastern Europe are more than simply examples of folk art. Whether the creativity is on show or hidden away, the homes reveal the interplay of traditional life with the natural world.

The house is the guardian of tradition, but in Eastern Europe it is a role that could only be played when stone began to replace the more ephemeral material of wood for building. Peasants started to use stone from the 10th century with the spread of Christianity. In the fortified proto-Slav village of Biskupin, 20 miles (30 km) north of Gniezno, Poland, archaeologists have reconstructed an Iron Age village that was founded in 550 BC. It was situated beside a lake that acted as a moat, and backed by a palisade of 35 000 stakes. The village was destroyed by war in 400 BC.

Even after the 10th century, stone was slow to catch on and the majority of country houses continued to be built of wood. The few examples that have survived the centuries reveal the varying traditions of the regions: the contrasting paints used to decorate homes around Kraków; the combination of wood and thatch that characterises north-eastern Poland and Belarus; the lime-whitened single-storey houses of Hungary, south of the Danube; the stone walls and nail-studded doorways of Zheravna, eastern Bulgaria. Even within the same country, different traditions reflect the availability of different materials. In Ukraine, the traditional wooden *isbas* of the north give way to houses of stone, brick or dried earth known as *khata*.

Painted village *Every June, the inhabitants of the village of Zalipie, near Tarnów in southern Poland, enter a traditional folk-art competition, painting bright floral motifs on houses, barns, and even dog kennels.*

The Country of Wood

In the Maramures region in northern Romania, the wooden carvings on the houses are works of art. This region is known as the 'Country of Wood'. Wondrous carved gates open to reveal walls made of massive oak beams hewn to fit, and intricately carved lintels. Inside the houses, painted wooden icons hang on the east wall, and furniture is incised with suns, crosses and other geometric patterns. Girls' dowries were packed in magnificent carved wooden chests.

World heritage

In eight villages in Maramures, the churches with their pointed wooden spires, are UNESCO World Heritage sites. An open-air Village Museum at Sighetu Marmatiei contains a collection of traditional peasant houses, mostly of oak.

The *chalupa*, where dreams come true

In the Czech Republic, clusters of little chalet-like houses dot the countryside. These are *chatas* or *chalupas* (mountain huts), the Czech equivalent of *dachas*. They can be anything from a one-room shack to a villa, but however modest in size, there is nothing modest about the pride invested in them. Owners spend every weekend in their second homes, making them the focus of their dreams. They sew curtains of patterned cotton, plant azaleas round the door, and turn each *chalupa* into a personal sanctuary. Vegetable plots are cultivated assiduously, berries picked, jams made. Some villages appear to be built in two halves: the village proper and alongside it another settlement of smaller, newer houses – the *chalupas*.

Home on the plains *Traditional Hungarian farmhouses were long, low and whitened with lime. But they are rarely to be found nowadays, except in outdoor museums such as this one in Hortobagy National Park.*

Made by hand

Commercial production and urbanisation may be sidelining traditional craftsmanship in towns, but not in the countryside. There you will still find carpet-weavers and lace-makers, woodcarvers shaping toys and potters at their wheels.

Table decorations *Hungarian doilies and clothes are delicately embroidered with floral motifs.*

Many visitors to Maramures in north-eastern Romania have shared the experience of arriving in a village in the valley of the Iza, perhaps on a Sunday. The women are dressed in their traditional flowery skirts. They make you welcome, you are invited into a house, offered a glass of *tuica*, the clear plum brandy, and within minutes you find yourself dressed as a Romanian, sporting a straw hat, felt waistcoat and leather sandals. Everything is handmade; the old handicrafts skills are alive and well in this region. Moreover, you cannot help noticing that the products also reflect a real economic need. It would be churlish not to buy something.

Pottery and porcelain fit for a queen

Such an experience could be repeated in many areas of Eastern Europe, where every region has its speciality and its own decorative traditions.

The Hungarian town of Hodmezovasarhely (meaning 'marketplace of the beaver's field'), a large market town on the Great Plain, had 400 potteries in the 19th century, and today pottery workshops are still thriving. Each district specialises in a distinctive style, the most famous being the black un-enamelled ceramics of Nádudvar, which are based on

Showcases for handicrafts

While the production of handicrafts is declining due to increasing urbanisation and pressure of time, the number of ethnographic museums is rising fast. There is a strong desire to preserve local arts and crafts for future generations. Budapest's Museum of Ethnography is one of the best in Eastern Europe, but every capital has its own, even Chisinau, capital of the smallest East European state, Moldova. Open-air village museums are increasingly popular as showplaces for rural skills. In many areas craftspeople are working together to sustain and market their goods.

Feast for the eyes *Overlooking Budapest's Parliament building, a Hungarian sets out her collection of embroidered tablecloths.*

Turkish designs. In the west of Hungary, 15 miles (25 km) from Lake Balaton, the village of Herend has a porcelain factory that was founded in 1826. It achieved international recognition when in 1851 it mounted a display at the Great Exhibition in London and Queen Victoria ordered one of its chinoiserie dinner services.

Pottery is one of the oldest of the traditional crafts in Romania. Evidence of the ovens in which the Roman goldminers of Rosia Montana (Red Mountain) baked ceramics has been found in Abrud in western Transylvania. In Sapanta, close to the border with Ukraine, there is a cemetery noted for its colourful wooden crosses and witty inscriptions. The cemetery was created by a sculptor, Stan Patras, who made decorative crosses from 1935 to 1977. The work is carried on by his apprentice, Dumitru Pop.

Hungarian stitchwork

Every region has its embroiderers. Women inherited their skills from mothers and grandmothers who grew up at a time when embroidery expressed both the spirit of the age and the status of the family. In the Hungarian town of Kalocsa, 75 miles (120 km) south of Budapest, women were respected as painters as well as embroiderers. Their embroidery, once limited to white, red and blue coloured

Pots in the old style *In Sarospatak in north-east Hungary, potters produce their wares in traditional colours and shapes unique to the area.*

Study in blue *Pottery and porcelain from central Europe is highly regarded for its craftsmanship.*

threads, evolved into startling multicoloured designs in the 1920s when the town's folk dancers achieved recognition and needed costumes that made an impact on stage. Women replicated the floral exuberance of the new designs in their paintings.

Art in the home

Often, even a humble three-room flat is like a miniature museum. Almost any Eastern European home will have some everyday object with decorations that identify it as a work of popular

Old skills, new markets   Carved wooden figures, such as these musicians, are one of many art forms using traditional skills that are aimed at the tourist market.

Cheerful graveyard   In Sapanta's Merry Cemetery, the 'gravestones' are wooden carvings showing the trade of the deceased, with portraits and humorous epitaphs.

art: a wooden bowl, a piece of pottery or glass, some embroidery or lace work. In Bohemia, the eye will be drawn to cloth embroidered with flowers. Slovaks give pride of place to a piece of majolica (pottery enamelled with tin), decorated with blue motifs on a white base. And many a wardrobe holds treasures of lace work. Since lace is not well suited to commercial production, women continue to produce their own.

Colourful carpets   Hand-coloured, hand-embroidered kilims (pileless carpets) are among the most sought-after products of Bulgarian craftsmen.

Maramures: independence and authenticity

The Maramures province of northern Romania was always famous for its independent spirit. Secure in their forests and mountains, the inhabitants fought off the Romans and even deterred the communists from imposing industry and collectivisation. As a result, this 'land of the free Dacians' retains many of its handicrafts,

notably carpet-making. In Botiza, women card the wool and colour it with vegetable dyes. In the next valley at Ieud – where the 14th-century wooden church housed the first document written in Romanian – they still make jackets and coats of felt.

*Country skills
A Romanian prepares wool for carpet-making.*

MAPS, FACTS AND FIGURES

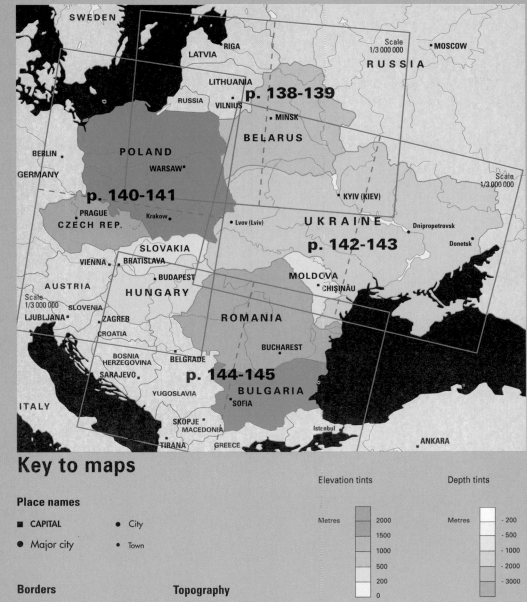

Key to maps

Place names

■ CAPITAL   ● City

● Major city   • Town

Borders

—————— International border

---------- Maritime national border

Topography

▲ G. Heverla
2081 m   Peak

CARPATHIANS   Mountain range

Elevation tints

Metres	
	2000
	1500
	1000
	500
	200
	0

Depth tints

Metres	
	- 200
	- 500
	- 1000
	- 2000
	- 3000

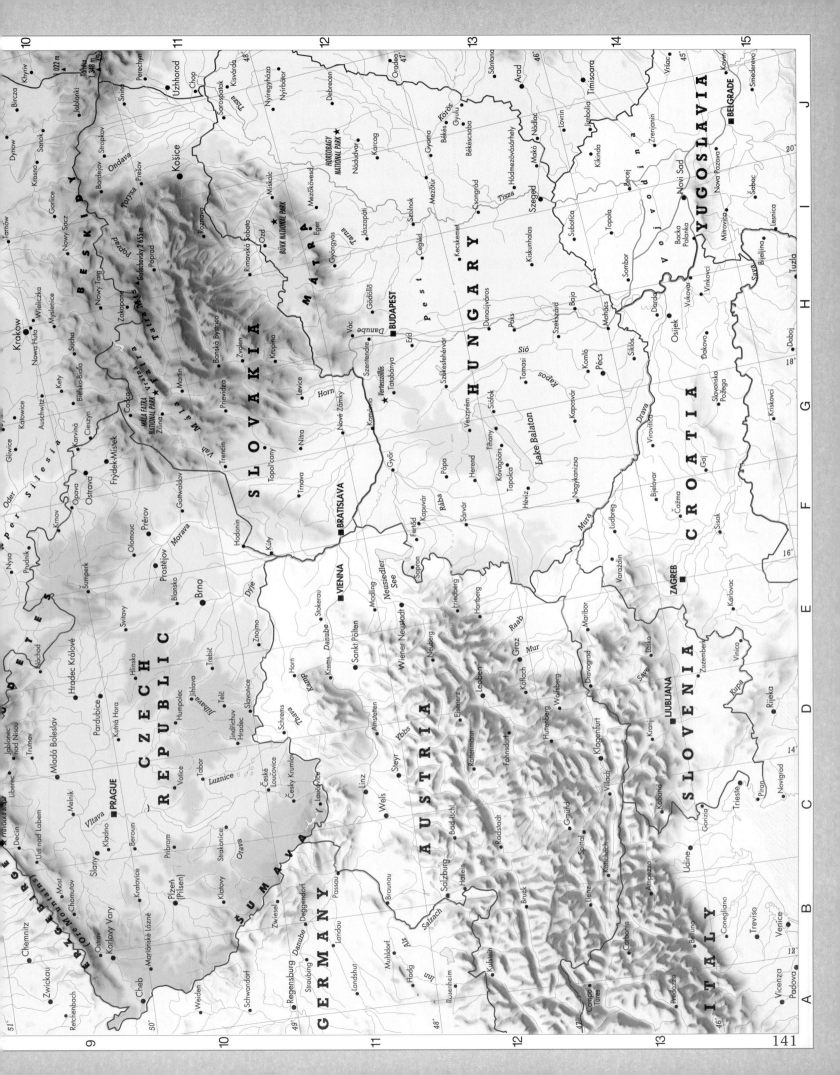

10

RUSSIAN FEDERATION

Krupets
Hlukhiv
-hostka
Korenevo
Aleksandroviskiy
Yakovlevo
Volokonovka
Valuyki
Mitrofanovka
Roven'ki
Sudza
Ps'ol
Belgorod
Urazovo
Aydar
Bilolutsk
Chertkovo
Kralevets
Vorozhba
Bilopillya
Myropillya
Shebekino
Borisovka
Bilokurakyne
Degtevo
Seym
Sumy
Vovchansk
Dvurechnaya
Kalitva
49°
Konotop
Tern
Terny
Grayvoron
Lopan
Kup'yansk
Starobil'sk
Bilovods'k
Millerovo
Romen
Romny
Lebedyn
Derhachi
Svatove
Borova
Aydar
Glinsk
Okhtyrka
Lyubotyn
KHARKIV
Chuhuyiv
Borova
Shchastya
Glubokiy
11
Zin'kiv
Kotel'va
Merefa
Balakliya
Izyum
Donbass
Proletarsk
Verchneye
Donetsk
Lokhvytsya
Komyshnya
Valky
Borki
Jama
Hirs'ke
Kirvosk
Luhansk
-dan
Dykanka
Krasnohrad
Krasnopaulivka
Slov'yansk
Stakhanov
Pyryatyn
Lubny
Myrhorod
Poltava
Lannaya
Donets
Kostyantynivka
Kramatorsk
Artemivsk
Krasnyy Luch
Gukovo
48°
Hrebinka
Pereshchepyne
Lozova
Samara
Dobropillya
Horlivka
Torez
Novoshakhtinsk
-biv
Khorol
Bilyky
Yur'yivka
12
U K R A I N E
Hlobyne
Hubynykha
Pavlohrad
Makiyivka
-hornobay
Kremenchuts'ku
Reservoir
Demuryne
Selydove
Donetsk
Matveyev
Kurgan
Cherkasy
Kremges
Kremenchuk
Dnipropetrovs'k
Vasylkivka
Pokrovka
Velyka Novosilka
Taganrog
Azov
-amyanka
Oleksandrivka
Dniprodzerzhyns'k
Volnovakha
47°
Znam'yanka
Pyatykhatky
Yelizarove
Dnieper
Rozivka
Talakovka
Syedove
Novomyrhorod
Nova Praha
Zaporizhzhya
Orikhiv
Polohy
Mariupol
Gulf of Taganrog
13
Mala Vyska
Kirovohrad
Petrove
Terny
Andriyivka
Yeysk
Kryvyy Rih
(Krivoy Rog)
Nikopol
Vasylivka
Tokmak
Dolzhanskaya
Rivne
Dolynska
Apostolove
Mykhaylivka
Berdyansk
Yasenskaya
Pomichna
Bobrynets
Inhulets
Kakhovske
Reservoir
Prymorsk
Primorsko-Akhtarsk
Bratske
Novyy Buh
Inhulets
Novovasylivka
Melitopol'
14
-anevka
Voznesensk
Bashtanka
Bila Krynytsya
Ivanivka
Achuyevo
Pivdennyy Buh
Nova Odesa
Kalininske
Frunze
Kyrylivka
Petrovskaya
Berezivka
Veselynove
Kakhovka
Partyzany
Herichesk
S E A   O F   A Z O V
Mykolayiv
Dnieper
Kherson
Brylivka
45°
Berezanka
Kalanchak
Valok
Kerch
Novorossiysk
Ochakiv
Chulakivka
Krasnoperekopsk
Dzhankoy
Lenine
Kerch Strait
Anapa
Vygoda
Skadovsk
Rozdolne
Kerch Peninsula
15
Odesa
Feodosiya
Illichivsk
C R I M E A
-horod
-vskyy
Chornomorske
Saky
Sudak
30 miles
-devka
Yevpatoriya
Simferopol' 1 253 m
0   25   50 km
B L A C K   S E A
Poshtove
G. Çatyrdag 1 527 m
Alushta
Bakhchysaray
G. Roman-Kosh 1 545 m
16
Sevastopol
G. Aj Petri
1 233 m
Yalta
Livadia
Mys
Khersones
Balaklava
Alupka
Foros

Bulgaria • Hungary • Romania

G H I J K L M N

11 Trnava • Nitra Levice MÁTRA Bicaz Bistrita
BRATISLAVA Horn Nové Zámky Vác Eger Mezokovesd Debrecen Marghita Olpret Dej Gherla Budesti Reghin
Komárno Szentendre Gödöllő HORTOBAGYI Zalau
48° Gyor Vertesszöllös Danube BUDAPEST NATIONAL PARK Nádudvar Oradea Huedin Cluj-Napoca Targu Mu
12 Fertöd Kapuvar Tatabánya Erd Pest Jászapáti Karcag Dobresti Turda Sighisoar
Rába Pápa Székesfenérvar Cegléd Szolnok Varful Mentele BIHOR Nucet Aiud Medias
Sárvár Herend Veszprem Mezötúr Gyoma 1 825 m Almas Slimnic
47° Tihany HUNGARY Dunaújváros Békés Körös PLATEAU Abrud Alba Iulia Sibiu Avri
Kóvágóörs Siófok Tamasi Paks Kecskemét Gyula Brad Sebes Varful M
Tapolca Héviz Lake Balaton Kaposvár Szekszárd Csongrád Hódmezővásárhely Békéscaba Sintana Deva Cugir 2 5
Nagykanizsa Kaposvár Kiskunhalas Arad Orastie 2 245 m
13 Mura Komló Baja Szeged Makó Nádlac Lovrin Bodo Hunedoara Petrila Brezol
Ludbreg Pécs Mohács Subotica Jimbolia Timisoara Lugoj Varful Peleaga Vulcan Petrosani
Drava Siklós Kikinda Caransebes 2 509 m Lupeni V. Parangul Mare
46° Bjelovar Virovitica Darda Topola Resita Anina 2 518 m
CROATIA Čazma Osijek Sombor Vojvodina Zrenjanin Bumbesti-Jiu Targu Jiu
Sisak Gaj Vukovar Backa Palanka Novi Sad Vršac ROMANIA Dragasc
14 Slavonska Pozega Đakovo Vinkovci Nova Pazova YUGOSLAVIA Kovin Varful Svinecea Mare 1 224 m Drobeta-Turnu-Severin Olténie Crai
45° Kriskovci Mitrovica BELGRADE Moldova Noua Iron Gates Vanju Mare
Banja Luka Doboj Sava Bijeljina Šabac Smederevo Danube Kucevo Negotin Bailesti
Krupa Teslic Tuzla Lesnica Krepoljin Vidin Lom
BOSNIA Kamenica Valjevo Rudnik Bor Dimovo
15 HERZEGOVINA Srebenica Rogacica Cacak Kragujevac Zajecar Montana
Zupa Dragnié Zenica Vares Olovo Uzice Kraljevo Krusevac Nis
Bugojno Rogatica Visegrád Ivanjica Raska Morava Prokuplje Pirot
CROATIA Prituka Duvno Neretva Kalinovik Lim Nova Varos Raska Leskovac Pernik
44° Sibenik Raska Gora Pljevlja Novi Pazar Kosovska Zemen
Trogir Split SARAJEVO Goranska Tutin Mitrovica Pristina Vranje Sto
16 Supetar Mostar Montenegro Berane Pec Kosovo Kjustendil Ri
Bol Starigrad Metkovic Kolasin Rozaje Prokuplje Pl
Ploče Niksic Dakovica Prizren Kacanik Kumanovo
43° Slano Podgorica Kotor Lake Scutari SKOPJE Stip
Dubrovnik Shkodër Tetovo Vardar Veles
17 ADRIATIC ALBANIA MACEDONIA Strumica
Virpazar Gostivar Kavadarci Valandov
Drini Debar Kruševo Prilep
42° Vieste SEA TIRANA Struga Ohrid Bitola Giannitso
18 Manfredonia Durrës Kavajë Elbasan Lake Ohrid Naousa
ITALY Lushnje Lake Prespa Veroia

144 F G H I J K

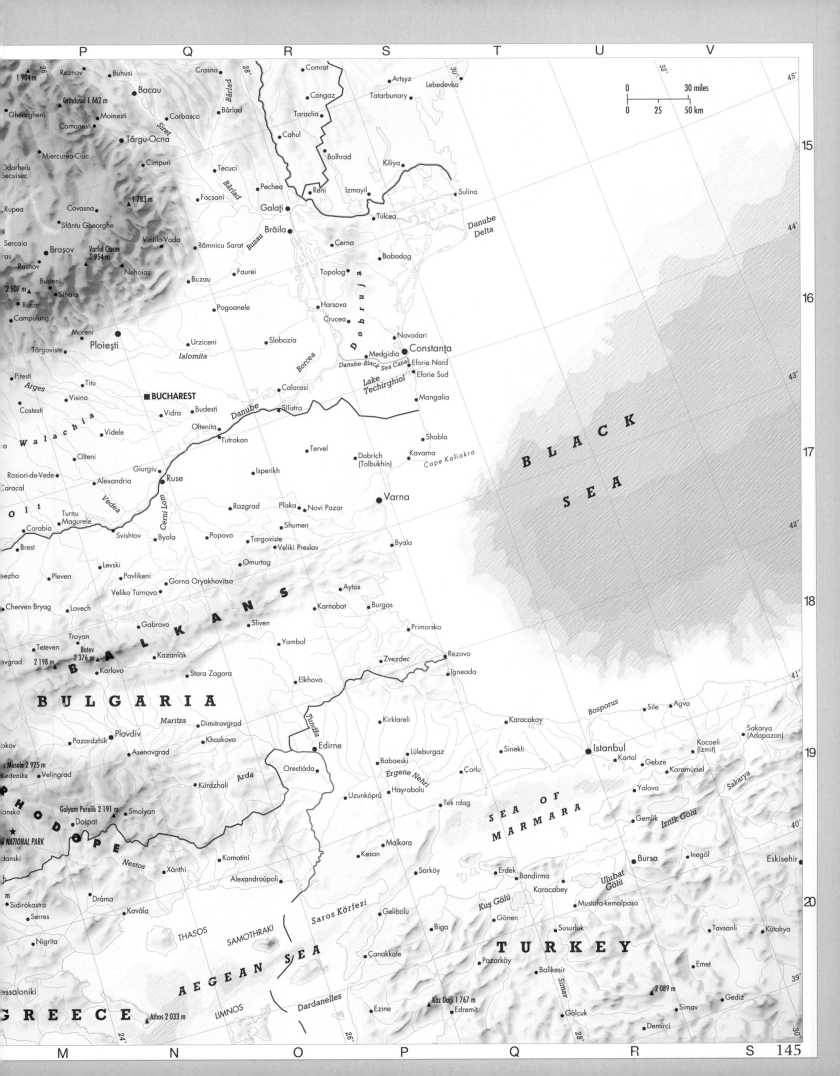

1 904 m
Roznov   Buhusi   Crasna   Comrat
Grindusul 1 662 m   Congaz   Artsyz   Lebedevka
Gheorgheni   Tatarbunary
Bacau   Corbasca   Bârlad   Taraclia
Comanesti   Moinesti   Cahul   Kiliya
Târgu-Ocna   Bolhrad
Miercurea-Ciuc   Cimpuri
Odorheiu   Tecuci   Reni   Izmayil   Sulina
Secuiesc   Bârlad   Pechea
                    Focsani   Tulcea
1 783 m   Galaţi
Rupea   Covasna   Sfântu Gheorghe   Brăila   Danube
Sercaia   Râmnicu Sarat   Cerna   Delta
Braşov Varful Ciucas   Vintila-Voda   Babadag
Rasnov 1 954 m   Faurei   Topolog
        Nehoias   Buzău   Harsova
2 507 m Busteni   Crucea
Rucar   Sinaia   Pogoanele
Campulung
        Moreni   Urziceni   Slobozia   Navodari
Târgoviste Ploieşti   Medgidia   Constanţa
Pitesti   Titu   Ialomita   Danube-Black Sea Canal   Eforie Nord
        Visina   Lake   Eforie Sud
Costesti   Arges   ■ BUCHAREST   Borcea Techirghiol
                    Vidra   Budesti   Calarasi   Mangalia
        Vidra   Danube   Silistra
Walachia   Videle Oltenita   Shabla
        Olteni   Tutrakan   Tervel   Kavarna
Rosiori-de-Vede   Giurgiu   Dobrich   Cape Kaliakra
Caracal Alexandria   Ruse   Isperikh   (Tolbukhin)
Olt   Turnu   Vedea   Cerni Lom   Razgrad Pliska   Novi Pazar Varna
        Magurele   Shumen
Corabia   Byala   Popovo Targoviste
Brest   Svishtov   Byala   Veliki Preslav   Byala
        Levski   Omurtag
nezha   Pleven Pavlikeni   Gorna Oryakhovitsa
        Veliko Turnovo   Aytos
Cherven Bryag   Lovech   Karnobat   Burgas
        Gabrovo   Sliven
Troyan Teteven Botev   Yambol   Primorsko
2 198 m 2 376 m Kazanlâk   Zvezdec
vgrad   Karlovo   Stara Zagora   Elkhovo Rezovo
                                            Igneada
BULGARIA   Maritza
        Maritza Dimitrovgrad   Kirklareli   Bosporus   Sile   Agva
Pazardzhik Plovdiv Khaskovo   Karacakoy
kov   Asenovgrad   Sakarya
c Musala 2 925 m   (Adapazan)
edenika Velingrad   Arda   Edirne Babaeski   Lüleburgaz Kocaeli
                    Orestiáda   Sinekli Istanbul (Izmit)
RHOD   Golyam Perelik 2 191 m   Uzunköprü Çorlu   Kartal Gebze
danski Dospat Smolyan   Karamürsel
NATIONAL PARK   Ergene Nehri   Tekrdag Yalova   Sakarya
                                Hayrabolu
OPE   Nestos   Komotini   SEA OF   Gemlik Iznik Gölü
Xánthi Kürdzhali   Malkara MARMARA   Bursa   Inegöl Eskisehir
m   Sidirókastro   Kesan   Erdek   Bandirma   Ulubat
Serres Dráma   Kavála   Sarköy   Karacabey   Gölü
Nigríta   Geliboru   Kuş Gölü Gönen Susurluk   Mustafa-kemalpasa
ssaloniki   THASOS   Saros Körfezi   Biga   Tavsanli   Kütahya
        SAMOTHRAKI   Gelibolu   Gölcük
AEGEAN SEA   LIMNOS Dardanelles Canakkale   TURKEY   Emet
GREECE Athos 2 033 m   Ezine   Kaz Daği 1 767 m Pazarköy   2 089 m Simav   Gediz
                        Edremit Balikesir   Simav   Gölcük
                                                Demirci

BLACK
SEA

SEA OF
MARMARA

Dobruja

Eastern Europe's states in profile

The nine nations of Eastern Europe form a cross-section of cultures, religions and languages. Since the collapse of the Soviet Union in 1991, these states have been in transition, turning away from their communist past towards a future based on democracy. Those closest to Western Europe – Poland, the Czech Republic, Slovakia, Hungary and, to a lesser extent, Romania and Bulgaria – can realistically hope to become European Union members one day. The other three – Ukraine, Belarus and Moldova – risk remaining forever on the fringes.

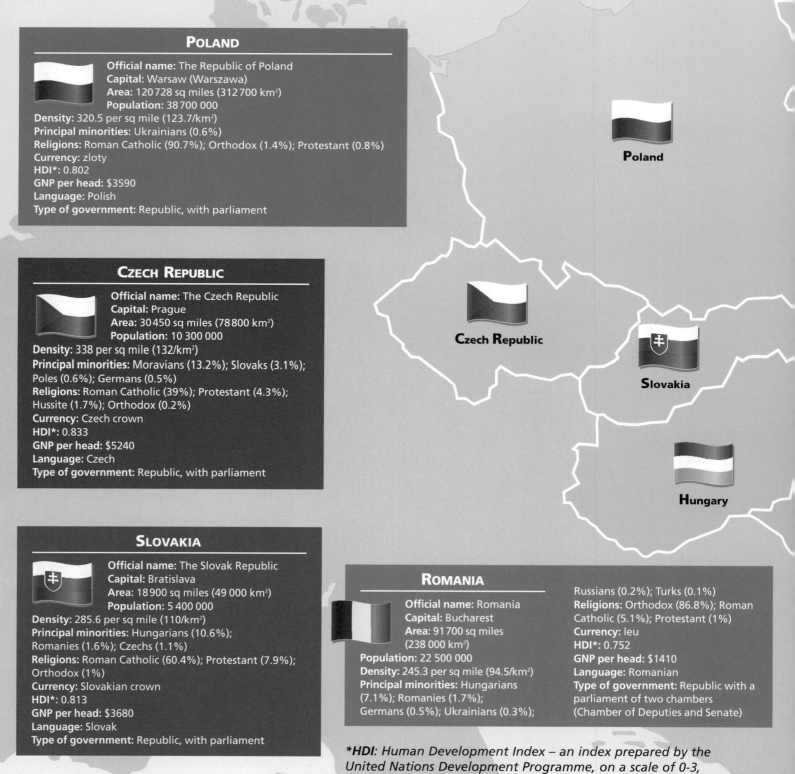

POLAND

Official name: The Republic of Poland
Capital: Warsaw (Warszawa)
Area: 120 728 sq miles (312 700 km²)
Population: 38 700 000
Density: 320.5 per sq mile (123.7/km²)
Principal minorities: Ukrainians (0.6%)
Religions: Roman Catholic (90.7%); Orthodox (1.4%); Protestant (0.8%)
Currency: zloty
HDI*: 0.802
GNP per head: $3590
Language: Polish
Type of government: Republic, with parliament

Poland

CZECH REPUBLIC

Official name: The Czech Republic
Capital: Prague
Area: 30 450 sq miles (78 800 km²)
Population: 10 300 000
Density: 338 per sq mile (132/km²)
Principal minorities: Moravians (13.2%); Slovaks (3.1%); Poles (0.6%); Germans (0.5%)
Religions: Roman Catholic (39%); Protestant (4.3%); Hussite (1.7%); Orthodox (0.2%)
Currency: Czech crown
HDI*: 0.833
GNP per head: $5240
Language: Czech
Type of government: Republic, with parliament

Czech Republic

Slovakia

Hungary

SLOVAKIA

Official name: The Slovak Republic
Capital: Bratislava
Area: 18 900 sq miles (49 000 km²)
Population: 5 400 000
Density: 285.6 per sq mile (110/km²)
Principal minorities: Hungarians (10.6%); Romanies (1.6%); Czechs (1.1%)
Religions: Roman Catholic (60.4%); Protestant (7.9%); Orthodox (1%)
Currency: Slovakian crown
HDI*: 0.813
GNP per head: $3680
Language: Slovak
Type of government: Republic, with parliament

ROMANIA

Official name: Romania
Capital: Bucharest
Area: 91 700 sq miles (238 000 km²)
Population: 22 500 000
Density: 245.3 per sq mile (94.5/km²)
Principal minorities: Hungarians (7.1%); Romanies (1.7%); Germans (0.5%); Ukrainians (0.3%); Russians (0.2%); Turks (0.1%)
Religions: Orthodox (86.8%); Roman Catholic (5.1%); Protestant (1%)
Currency: leu
HDI*: 0.752
GNP per head: $1410
Language: Romanian
Type of government: Republic with a parliament of two chambers (Chamber of Deputies and Senate)

*HDI: Human Development Index – an index prepared by the United Nations Development Programme, on a scale of 0-3, based on longevity, education and income

BELARUS

Official name: The Republic of Belarus
Capital: Minsk
Area: 80 155 sq miles (208 000 km²)
Population: 10 200 000
Density: 128.5 per sq mile (49/km²)
Principal minorities: Russians (13.2%); Poles (4.1%); Ukrainians (2.9%)
Religions: Orthodox (32%); Roman Catholic (18%)
Currency: Belarussian rouble
HDI*: 0.763
GNP per head: $2150
Languages: Belarussian, Russian
Type of government: Republic with parliament of two chambers (Chamber of Deputies and Council of the Republic)

Belarus

HUNGARY

Official name: The Republic of Hungary
Capital: Budapest
Area : 35 900 sq miles (90 000 km²)
Population: 10 100 000
Density: 281.3 per sq mile (108.6/km²)
Principal minorities: Czechs (1.6%); Slovaks (1.1%)
Religions: Roman Catholic (63%), Calvinist (18%); Lutheran (8%); Jewish (1%)
Currency: forint
HDI*: 0.795
GNP per head: $4510
Language: Hungarian
Type of government: Republic with parliament

UKRAINE

Official name: The Republic of Ukraine
Capital: Kiev (Kyiv)
Area: 233 090 sq miles (603 700 km²)
Population: 51 000 000
Density: 218.7 per sq mile (84.5/km²)
Principal minorities: Russians (22.1%); White Russians (0.9%); Moldovans (0.6%); Bulgarians (0.5%)
Religions: Orthodox (60%); Uniate (7%); Protestant (3.6 %); Roman Catholic (1.2 %); Jewish (1 %)
Currency: hryvnia
HDI*: 0.7221
GNP per person: $1040
Language: Ukrainian
Type of government: Republic

Ukraine

Moldova

Romania

BULGARIA

Official name: The Republic of Bulgaria
Capital: Sofia
Area: 42 900 sq miles (111 000 km²)
Population: 8 200 000
Density: 193.4 per sq mile (73.9/km²)
Principal minorities: Turks (9.4%); Romanies (3.4%)
Religions: Orthodox (85.7%); Muslim (13.1%)
Currency: Bulgarian lev
HDI*: 0.758
GNP per head: $1170
Language: Bulgarian
Type of government: Republic with parliament

Bulgaria

MOLDOVA

Official name: The Republic of Moldova
Capital: Chisinau
Area: 13 000 sq miles (33 700 km²)
Population: 4 300 000
Density: 330.7 per sq mile (127.6/km²)
Principal minorities: Ukrainians (13.8%); Russians (13%); Bulgarians (2%); Gagauz (3.5%)
Religion: Orthodox (90%)
Currency: Moldovan leu
HDI*: 0.83
GNP per person: $460
Language: Romanian
Type of government: Republic with parliament

147

Climate, relief and vegetation

Mountains shaped by converging landmasses and plains flattened by retreating glaciers have produced a varied landscape across Eastern Europe. The Carpathians form a sweeping arc to the south, a vast grain-growing belt envelops the north, the Danube snakes its way through nine countries and vineyards occupy the sunny slopes of the Black Sea.

The climate of central and Eastern Europe ranges from the temperate oceanic conditions of Western Europe to the harsh extremes of the Russian interior. Areas such as the Crimea and southern Bulgaria on the Black Sea enjoy the benefits of a Mediterranean climate.

Geographically, the region is defined by northern plains flanked by great mountain chains to the south, creating an area of richly varied landforms and habitats.

AVERAGE TEMPERATURES (°C/°F)		
	January	July
Sofia	–2.2/28.0	20.6/69.1
Minsk	–3.0/26.6	19.0/66.2
Prague	–1.6/29.1	19.4/66.9
Budapest	–2.1/28.2	21.2/70.2
Chisinau	–4.0/24.8	21.0/69.8
Warsaw	–3.1/26.4	18.5/65.3
Bucharest	–3.0/26.6	24.0/75.2
Bratislava	–1.6/29.1	21.1/70.0
Kiev	–3.0/26.6	22.0/71.6

An east-west climatic bridge

Three main air currents dictate the climate of Eastern Europe: subtropical from the south, polar winds from the northern oceans, and even colder streams flowing from Siberia.

Northern Ukraine and eastern Belarus have long, harsh winters with at least 70 days below freezing, while southern Bulgaria and the Black Sea coastal regions enjoy almost Mediterranean conditions. Between these two extremes lie Romania, Hungary, Slovakia and the Czech Republic, with a modified continental climate.

In January, average temperatures in Prague, Budapest and Bucharest hover around freezing. Winter tends to be damp; spring and autumn are relatively dry and pleasant. Summer is usually hot (in Bucharest, the average summer temperature is 24°C/75.2°F), with a tendency for torrential downpours of rain.

Hills and mountains impose considerable regional variations. For example, the temperature range increases in the valleys and mountain-fringed plains of the Czech Republic and Hungary, but decreases in the Bohemian Mountains and the Carpathians.

Snowy heights *The High Tatras, Slovakia's tallest mountain range, has ten peaks measuring more than 8580 ft (2600 m).*

Mountains and lowlands

Eastern Europe divides into four natural regions: the plains that span northern Germany, Poland, Belarus and Ukraine; the ancient forested massifs on the German-Czech border; the younger and higher Alpine mountains such as the Carpathians; and the Black Sea coast.

The entire area was created when the continental plates carrying Africa, Arabia and India collided with the Eurasian landmass 50 million years ago in the so-called Alpine Orogeny.

The process, which incorporated rocks dating from hundreds of millions of years earlier, formed the belt of mountains stretching from southern Europe through the Aegean, Turkey and the Zagros Mountains of Iran to the Himalayas.

Activity continued until the Tertiary Period, about 10 million years ago. Central Europe and the western Mediterranean is now stable, but farther east movement between Africa, Europe, Arabia and Anatolia continues sporadically, giving rise to the earthquake zones of Greece, Turkey and the Caspian region.

The Alpine Orogeny left extensive lowlands, which would later form the Mediterranean, Black Sea and the Caspian. The northern reaches of Eurasia were untouched by the movement.

Relief
height
in metres

	2000
	1000
	400
	200
	0

◀ **RELIEF**

SELECTED PEAKS ▶

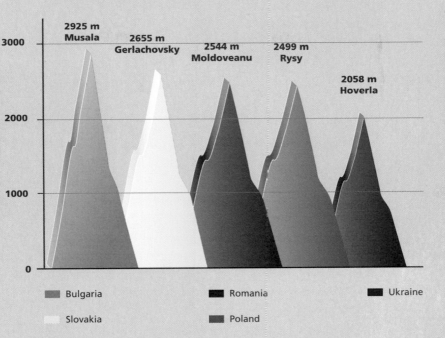

2925 m Musala

2655 m Gerlachovsky

2544 m Moldoveanu

2499 m Rysy

2058 m Hoverla

■ Bulgaria   ■ Romania   ■ Ukraine

□ Slovakia   ■ Poland

The Danube's names

The Danube acquires many different names in the course of its journey from source to delta: Donau (in Germany and Austria), Dunaj (Slovakia), Duna (Hungary), Dunav (Croatia, Yugoslavia and Bulgaria) and Dunarea (Romania).

The northern plains

In the north, the vast plains that extend across Germany, Poland, Belarus and part of the Ukraine owe their existence to the glaciers that spread down from Scandinavia about 10 million years ago, bulldozing the landscapes almost as far south as the Alps. When they retreated about 10000 years ago they deposited a layer of glacial moraine, leaving an immense flat region between the Baltic and the Black Sea lying below 1000 ft (300 m).

On the Baltic coast, the landscape is a mixture of moraine, with wide expanses of sand covered with forests of pines and birches. Poland has more than 9000 post-glacial lakes, the majority of which are clustered in Masuria and Pomerania. Long sandy peninsulas and bays protect the ports of Gdansk and Szczecin.

To the south lies a fertile belt, created when the fierce northerlies of the Ice Age picked up the fine glacial detritus and spread it over what is now southern Poland and Ukraine. The resulting rich agricultural land has made an important contribution to the economies of both countries.

The ancient massifs

A mountain system that dates from well before the Ice Age lies across central Europe. The Bohemian massif and the neighbouring Ore Mountains that define the German-Czech border extend eastwards along the Polish border into the Holy Cross Mountains (Góry Swietokrzyskie). Over the course of time, these mountains were

The Carpathians: a natural paradise

The Carpathians are Europe's least spoiled mountains. Their huge forests are home to 1350 species of flowers and more than 100 species of birds. In Romania – one-third of which is covered in forests and Alpine pasture – more than 500 lynx, 2500 wolves and 5500 brown bears (60 per cent of Europe's population) have been recorded. In winter in Transylvania, it is not unusual to see a bear scavenging through a dustbin.

raised and broken up by immense geological forces, creating a kaleidoscopic fracture zone of uplands and valleys. Heavily eroded over the millennia, the massifs seldom exceed 4900 ft (1500 m). Between them lie sedimentary basins which were laid down by marine incursions.

The plants that covered the area in the Carboniferous period (340-260 million years ago, long before the Alpine Orogeny) decayed to form extensive coal deposits, principally in present-day Silesia, Poland and in the Ore Mountains of the Czech Republic.

On the south-eastern fringes of the ancient massifs, the hills of Moravia slope gently down towards Bratislava, with its rich farmlands and deposits of lignite.

The Carpathian Mountains

Eastern Europe's dominant mountain system, the Carpathians, are an extension of the Alps. They share their most recent origins in the collision between the African and Eurasian continental plates (though the chain contains remnants of much older systems as well). The Carpathians extend for 950 miles (1500 km), reaching a high-point at Mount Gerlachovsky in Slovakia (8711 ft/2655 m).

North of Bratislava, the Little Carpathians mark the beginning of the arc that swings eastwards into a series of eight ranges and blocks, which are subdivided by geologists into eastern and western, and outer and inner regions. The chain as a whole surges across into southern Poland and western Ukraine, sweeping south and east as the Transylvanian Alps to finish in a petrified wave north of Bucharest.

In the south-west, the chain is split by the River Danube as it flows through the Iron Gate between the Banat Mountains of Romania and the Serbian uplands.

Finally, as a sort of pale reflection of the Carpathians proper, Bulgaria's Stara Planina mountains swing eastwards to the Black Sea.

The Black Sea coast and Crimea

The Black Sea laps against the shores of southern Ukraine and the Crimean peninsula. Linked to the mainland by the Perekop Isthmus, Crimea is dominated by the limestone massif of the Crimean Mountains, which rise to 5068 ft (1545 m). The slopes, with their Mediterranean climate, are renowned for their vineyards and for spas such as those in Yalta and its neighbour, Alupka.

Farther east, the Kerch peninsula almost blocks access to the Sea of Azov and its main ports, Mariupol and Beryansk. To the west, access to the shore from the coastal plain is obstructed by off-shore sandbars stretching south to the Danube delta.

The mighty Danube

Whether it is measured by length, volume of flow or surface area, the Danube is Europe's second largest river after the Volga.

Rising in Germany's Black Forest, 2225 ft (678 m) above sea level, the Danube flows for 1770 miles (2850 km), passing through nine countries – Germany, Austria, Slovakia, Hungary, Croatia, Yugoslavia, Bulgaria, Ukraine and Romania. It is fed by 300 tributaries, receiving water from the Alps, Dinaric Alps, Carpathians and Balkan mountains on its route to the Black Sea.

The Danube approaches Eastern Europe from Austria, passing through the Slovakian capital of Bratislava and forming the border between Slovakia and Hungary. At Visegrád in Hungary it twists sharply southwards through a dramatic gorge and flows sedately past Budapest and across the Alföld plain into Croatia and Yugoslavia. Entering southern Romania, the river then squeezes between steep cliffs known as the Iron Gates and out across a wide plain where it forms the Romanian-Bulgarian border. At its delta, the Danube pours into the Black Sea at the rate of 8450 cu yd (6500 m³) per second.

▼ CLIMATE

Climates:
□ Transition zone
■ Continental
■ Mediterranean
■ Mountainous

Population, economy and society

The nations of Eastern Europe have all the thrust of peoples with a strong sense of identity, combined with the complexities imposed by varying cultures and religions. But how can ambition best be realised and identities be fulfilled at a time when the region is suspended between a past that was buoyed up by the former Soviet Union and a future that is defined by the West? This post-communist world is in the throes of adapting to democracy and the market economy. For some, the benefits of capitalism are imminent, for others they are a distant prospect.

The majority of languages spoken in Eastern Europe are Slavonic. In terms of numbers, the East Slavonic branch – Russian, Ukrainian and Belarussian – is the most significant, being spoken by 200 million people. Western Slavonic languages, including Czech, Slovak and Polish, have about 53 million speakers.

Bulgarian is classed as a South Slavonic language, along with Slovenian and Serbo-Croat. Now that Serbia and Croatia are separate nations, the two dialects – Serbian and Croatian – are often treated as separate languages.

The only Romance (Latin-based) language of the region is Romanian, which is spoken by 24 million people.

Hungarian, which is a member of the Finno-Ugric group of languages, has around 13 million speakers. Finnish and Estonian share a few words and an elaborate case system with Hungarian, but these two languages are virtually incomprehensible to speakers of Hungarian.

Nationality: a shifting concept

These broad generalisations hide complex subcultures of minorities that owe their existence to a number of migrations that have taken place over the centuries, sometimes voluntary, sometimes enforced.

Subcultures like these cast a shadow over the whole concept of nationality. For members of such groups, their sense of identity is much better defined by their language or religion or descent than by their country of birth. The nation-state may be seen as conferring 'citizenship', while the idea of 'nationality' is better reserved for whatever defines the subgroup. (Native Americans confront the same issue, which is why many tribes are referred to as 'nations'.) An Eastern European may be a 'Hungarian citizen' of 'German nationality', or a 'Ukrainian citizen' of 'Hungarian nationality'.

Well educated One benefit of communism inherited by Ukraine is the level of education. Ukraine has 750 schools for 750 000 trainees for the professions, and 150 colleges of higher education with 900 000 students.

Historical changes have even made it possible for some individuals to uncouple the notions of language, citizenship and nationality when defining their identity, perhaps to suit the occasion. In 1941, a number of Hungarian citizens of German descent found it convenient to declare that their nationality was German, even though their mother tongue was Hungarian.

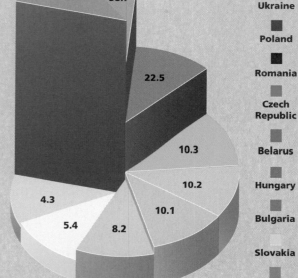

▼ **POPULATIONS**
(millions)

49.9 38.7 22.5 10.3 10.2 10.1 8.2 5.4 4.3

■ Ukraine
■ Poland
■ Romania
■ Czech Republic
■ Belarus
■ Hungary
■ Bulgaria
■ Slovakia
■ Moldova

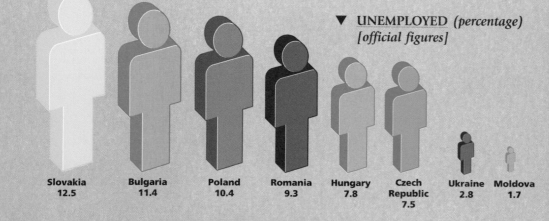

▼ UNEMPLOYED *(percentage)* *[official figures]*

Slovakia	Bulgaria	Poland	Romania	Hungary	Czech Republic	Ukraine	Moldova
12.5	11.4	10.4	9.3	7.8	7.5	2.8	1.7

Ukraine's many rulers

Long-lived inhabitants of the western Ukraine, born before the First World War, would have had five different nationalities. Entering the world in the Habsburg Empire, they soon came under Polish rule. The Soviet Union took control in 1939, was ousted by German-dominated Poland, and then re-took Ukraine in 1944. Independence was finally achieved in 1991. Apart from their mother tongue, Ukrainians had to speak Russian. Now the younger generation are looking to the West and learning English.

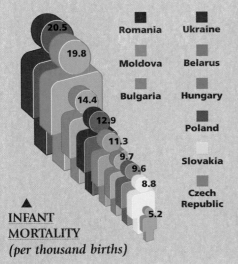

INFANT MORTALITY
(per thousand births)

Romania	20.5
Moldova	19.8
Bulgaria	14.4
	12.9
	11.3
	9.7
	9.6
	8.8
	5.2

Romania Ukraine
Moldova Belarus
Bulgaria Hungary
Poland
Slovakia
Czech Republic

LIFE EXPECTANCY *(in years)*		
	Men	Women
Czech Republic	71	78
Slovakia	69	77
Romania	69	73
Poland	68	77
Hungary	67	75
Bulgaria	67	75
Ukraine	64	74
Moldova	64	71
Belarus	63	74

MORTALITY *(per thousand per year)*	
Bulgaria	14.3
Ukraine	14.2
Hungary	13.9
Belarus	13.5
Romania	12.0
Moldova	11.7
Czech Rep.	10.6
Slovakia	9.9
Poland	9.7

BIRTHRATE *(per thousand per year)*	
Moldova	1.9
Ukraine	1.4
Slovakia	1.4
Poland	1.4
Hungary	1.3
Romania	1.3
Belarus	1.3
Czech Rep.	1.2
Bulgaria	1.1

Today, it would be possible for a resident of Transylvania to be a Romanian of German descent, but with Hungarian as their first language. What nationality he or she might claim would depend as much on feeling as any objective criteria.

From socialism to democracy

The fall of the Berlin Wall in 1989 opened a new era in Eastern Europe. Over the next few years, all the governments of the region collapsed like a house of cards. The regimes that succeeded them were eager to adopt the constitutional trappings familiar in the democratic West.

Poland and Hungary were the first countries to attempt the transition to democracy. In Poland, the trade union Solidarity won almost every seat it contested in the 1989 elections, humiliating the Communist Party, while in Hungary the communists reformed themselves in a change that was so orderly it scarcely seemed like a revolution at all.

Czechoslovakia followed, with its 'Velvet Revolution' – so called because in the days of protest during November 1989 there were no casualties. It installed a democratic government under Vaclav Havel. Bulgaria, having ditched its dictatorial leader Todor Zhivkov, resisted change until 1991, when the painful but non-violent shift to a market economy started in earnest.

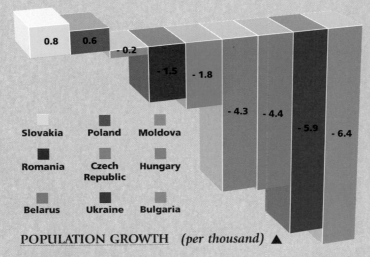

0.8	0.6	- 0.2
	- 1.5	- 1.8
- 4.3	- 4.4	
- 5.9	- 6.4	

Slovakia Poland Moldova
Romania Czech Republic Hungary
Belarus Ukraine Bulgaria

POPULATION GROWTH *(per thousand)* ▲

Only Romania, in the grip of Ceausescu's brutal dictatorship, experienced outright violence, which came to an end with the president's execution on Christmas Day, 1989.

In search of a dream

The euphoria brought on by the end of communism was in part rooted in a dream held by all Eastern European countries: they believed that they would at once share in the blessings of Western-style capitalism. This dream dissipated like morning mist in the harsh light of a new era.

In hindsight, disenchantment was hardly surprising, given that the grim certainties of communism were replaced by the even grimmer consequences of a particularly raw brand of capitalism, unbridled by the checks and balances routine in Western European nations. Though every nation had its own particular problems, each was plunged into crisis. Ruthless businessmen and former *apparatchiks* seized upon state assets.

Systems of social security vanished almost overnight. A decade after the fall of the Berlin Wall, 62 per cent of Hungarians and 67 per cent of Poles proclaimed themselves to be unhappy with their lot.

Stark contrasts

Whichever city is taken as an example, the contrast between the minority of *nouveaux riches* and those left stranded by the tides of transition is a stark one. The housing and shops once reserved for the elite of the Communist Party have given way to luxury estates and chic shops that are entirely out of the reach of ordinary people. Corruption was endemic from the start, along with a steep rise in other social ills, ranging from prostitution and drug trafficking, to the absence of any form of social security.

Communism may have been oppressive and unsustainably inefficient, but it had the

New choices A department store in the Belarussian capital Minsk offers an array of goods, many of them international, that would never have been available under communism. For those who are wealthy enough, capitalism has brought choice.

OWNERSHIP OF CONSUMER GOODS
▼ *(per 1000 inhabitants)*

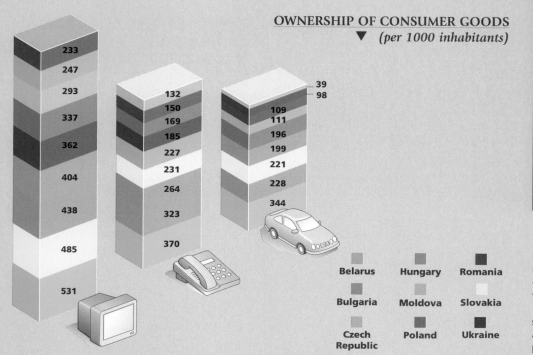

233
247
293
337
362
404
438
485
531

132
150
169
185
227
231
264
323
370

39
98
109
111
196
199
221
228
344

Belarus **Hungary** **Romania**

Bulgaria **Moldova** **Slovakia**

Czech Republic **Poland** **Ukraine**

In just a few years, the region's states pulled back from their traditional roles as providers of education, health, child care and holiday resorts – indeed, everything that had once symbolised the benefits provided by communism.

The rise in the cost of living was in large measure due to the privatisation of government apartment blocks. As a result, the number of people living in poverty increased. The proportion of the population under the poverty line currently stands at 90 per cent in Bulgaria, 65 per cent in Romania (double the 1996 figure) and almost 40 per cent in Hungary (10 per cent in 1989). These reverses took a rapid demographic toll in a corresponding decline in the birthrate and life expectancy.

advantage of providing both stability and jobs. Manufacturers in Eastern European countries had depended on the Soviet Union for their markets. Taxes were low or non-existent. Now, suddenly, the people of Eastern Europe were subjected to the agonies of unemployment, with no benefits to sustain them in their need.

In Slovakia, unemployment rose to an official figure of 12.5 per cent; in Bulgaria to 11.4 per cent. In the Czech Republic, unemployment doubled in less than two years, and a third of the population changed jobs in the 1990s.

Making ends meet   In Sofia, a Bulgarian practises the new science of street-side weighing. Record unemployment in the 1990s forced people to explore any way possible to supplement their meagre and declining incomes.

The shock was the greater because it affected groups that had always enjoyed special protection under communism – groups such as miners, ironworkers, bureaucrats and teachers. The low level of salaries and allowances, especially for those working in the public services, forced many people to take on several jobs. In order to make ends meet, retired people were often obliged to go back to work.

The black economy
These and other consequences of poverty created a 'black' economy that accounted for a high proportion of resources in the domestic economy: 42 per cent in the Czech Republic, 84 per cent in Romania, 85 per cent in Bulgaria. In Ukraine, 82 per cent of the population had a second source of income, while 20 per cent turned to 'economic tourism' – that is, buying goods abroad and then reselling them at home.

Individual and family difficulties have been made worse by the drop in national income and the consequent budgetary restraints caused by the transition from a communist-inspired economy to capitalism.

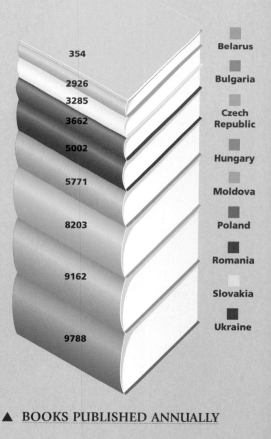

354
2926
3285
3662
5002
5771
8203
9162
9788

Belarus
Bulgaria
Czech Republic
Hungary
Moldova
Poland
Romania
Slovakia
Ukraine

ILLITERACY	
(percentage)	
Romania	2.2
Moldova	1.7
Bulgaria	1.7
Ukraine	1.2
Belarus	1.0
Hungary	0.7
Poland	0.3
Czech Republic	Almost 0
Slovakia	Almost 0

▲ **BOOKS PUBLISHED ANNUALLY**

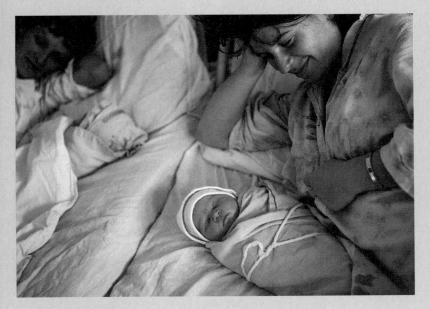

Maternal image One of Eastern Europe's better maternity wards contrasts with the situation in Romania where orphanages overflow with children, a legacy of Ceausescu's ban on contraception and abortion.

▼ GNP PER HEAD IN US DOLLARS

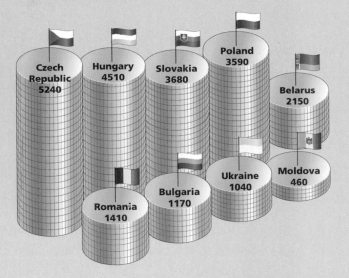

Czech Republic 5240

Hungary 4510

Slovakia 3680

Poland 3590

Belarus 2150

Romania 1410

Bulgaria 1170

Ukraine 1040

Moldova 460

In most of the region's states, population growth is negative – the population is actually shrinking. One measure of the despair felt by many ordinary people is the rise in the number of suicides. To take a Western example, the suicide rate in France was 19.3 per 100 000 in 1995. Hungary's suicide rate is 32.9 per 100 000; in Belarus, the figure is 28 per 100 000.

Agriculture under pressure

Generally across Eastern Europe, agriculture holds a much more important economic place than in Western Europe, whether farming is measured by acreage or by its contribution to the gross domestic product.

But this generalisation disguises the range of differences between economies. In the Czech Republic, for instance, agriculture contributes only 5 per cent to the GDP and employs just 5 per cent of the work force, while in Moldova, the figures are 43 per cent and 45 per cent respectively. In Romania and Bulgaria, the numbers of farm

workers have risen, as town-dwellers have tried to escape privation by seeking subsistence in the countryside.

But comparisons are not always easy, because agricultural economies vary in structure. In Belarus, collective farms and state farms still make up the vast proportion of agricultural land, while in Poland private ownership lasted right through the communist period.

In other states, price liberalisation, privatisation, the end of government grants and the loss of traditional markets have all combined to put agriculture

under intense pressure. Production has dropped markedly, intensifying the inherent disparity between Eastern Europe and Western Europe in terms of productivity: in Eastern and central Europe, the average agricultural worker produces just 11 per cent of his or her counterpart in the European Union.

Transport: from old-fashioned charm to modern efficiency

In its struggle to introduce drastic economic changes, Eastern Europe is hindered by its lack of an efficient means of transporting both goods and people. Rail networks, the pride of former Soviet-style economies, usually supply local needs well. For tourists, trains often offer sleeping berths that are more generous than those in the West. Generally Eastern European networks have an enviable record for good timekeeping.

The problems in the rail industry are twofold: slowness and obsolescence. In Russia – and hence in Ukraine and Belarus – managerial pay was dependent on good timekeeping rather than speed, so schedules were planned with plenty of leeway for delay.

Romania is known for its 'personal' trains, which travel with their doors open, and move so slowly that people can get on and off while they are in motion. As it happens, Romania is likely to become an exception to the rule, because it is

Minorities galore

More than 10 per cent of the population of Eastern Europe belongs to an ethnic minority. From the Middle Ages onwards, German migration eastwards established numerous German communities. In Upper Silesia (Poland), 800 000 people are of German stock. Another 220 000 Germans live in Hungary. After the Ottoman conquest in the 14th century, Turks settled in Bulgaria and now number between 500 000 and 900 000.

Hungary's neighbours have between them 3 million Hungarians. The Roma (Gypsies), once seen as a social problem rather than a minority with rights, make up more than 5 per cent of the population in Slovakia and Romania, between 2 and 5 per cent in Hungary and more than 1 per cent in Bulgaria, Moldova and Ukraine. Despite the flood of Jewish emigration in the 20th century, Hungary remains home to 50 000 Jews.

▼ URBAN POPULATIONS
(percentage of total)

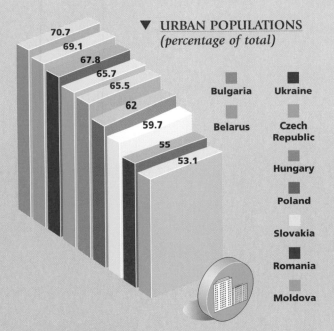

70.7
69.1
67.8
65.7
65.5
62
59.7
55
53.1

Bulgaria

Belarus

Ukraine

Czech Republic

Hungary

Poland

Slovakia

Romania

Moldova

CAPITALS
(inhabitants)

Kiev	2 600 000
Warsaw	2 134 000
Bucharest	2 013 911
Budapest	1 838 000
Minsk	1 725 000
Prague	1 193 000
Sofia	1 116 000
Chisinau	656 000
Bratislava	450 000

CEEC: East looks West

European Union jargon refers to the nations on its eastern borders either as CEEC (Central and Eastern European Countries) or by the French acronym PECO (Pays d'Europe centrale et orientale). These include the republics seen to be in transition from a centralised to a market economy. Seven countries are former Socialist states: Albania, Bulgaria, Hungary, Poland, Romania, the Czech Republic and Slovakia. Two emerged when Yugoslavia collapsed: Croatia and Slovenia. To move from a socialist economic system to a market-based system, all these countries have undertaken profound structural reorganisation, introducing programmes of privatisation, competition, banking and financial reforms and the liberalisation of markets. These reforms are long-term, and have had dire short-term social consequences. Despite this, the CEEC nations all want better links with the global economy as a steppingstone towards integration with Western Europe.

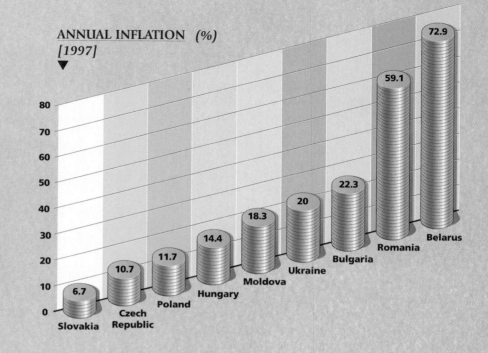

ANNUAL INFLATION *(%)*
[1997]

Country	Inflation
Slovakia	6.7
Czech Republic	10.7
Poland	11.7
Hungary	14.4
Moldova	18.3
Ukraine	20
Bulgaria	22.3
Romania	59.1
Belarus	72.9

currently upgrading its rail infrastructure, thanks to a European Union and EBRD (European Bank for Reconstruction and Development) grant. But most of today's state-run networks lack investment, and are often inadequate for the needs of modern economies. Rolling stock is largely decaying. In Slovakia, only half the rail network is electrified.

On the road

Road systems are underdeveloped by Western standards, with few motorways, and often badly maintained surfaces. The Polish capital of Warsaw is poorly linked to the rest of the country. Motorways in Poland are confined to a couple of places in the south, such as the link between Katowice and Kraków. Road conditions are beginning to suffer from the increase in private car ownership.

In Slovakia, it is easier to get to Bratislava from Vienna or Prague than from the eastern part of

the country. The Czech Republic and Slovakia have only about 625 miles (1000 km) of motorway between them. In Romania, particularly in the north of the country, horse-drawn carts are almost as common a sight as cars.

With the enlargement of the European Union in the next few years, a number of new motorways are planned to speed communications between East and West. But with the East strapped for funds and the West wary of open-ended projects, there is doubt over when, or if, these grand schemes will be fulfilled.

▼ **HEALTH SERVICES**
(per 1000 inhabitants)

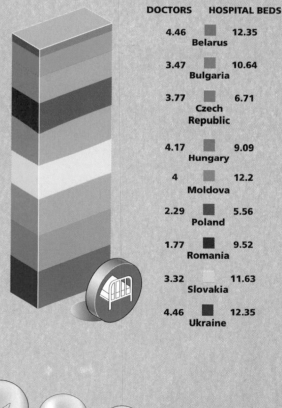

	DOCTORS		HOSPITAL BEDS
Belarus	4.46		12.35
Bulgaria	3.47		10.64
Czech Republic	3.77		6.71
Hungary	4.17		9.09
Moldova	4		12.2
Poland	2.29		5.56
Romania	1.77		9.52
Slovakia	3.32		11.63
Ukraine	4.46		12.35

ELECTRICITY CONSUMPTION

(kilowatt hour per person per year) ▼

Czech Republic	5948
Slovakia	5386
Bulgaria	4991
Hungary	3624
Poland	3540
Ukraine	3482
Belarus	3119
Romania	2744
Moldova	1739

Index

Page numbers in *italics* denote illustrations. The letter and number references in brackets are the co-ordinates for places in the map section, pp 138-45.

Acknowledgments

Abbreviations : t = top, m = middle, b = bottom, l = left, r = right.

FRONT COVER: The Maramures region of Romania HEMISPHERES/B. Gardel
BACK COVER: Children play in Petrín Hill, Prague, Czech Republic, R. HOLZBACHOVA - P. BENET

Pages 4/5: HEMISPHERES/B. Gardel; 6/7: COSMOS/S.P.L/NRSC Lid; 8/9: BIOS/P. Malczewski; 9tr: BIOS/M. Lahe; 9br: BIOS/PANDA PHOTO/G. Marcoaldi; 10: ANA/M. Borchi; 11: BIOS/OKAPIA/F. Magyar; 12t: BIOS/M. Gunther; 12b: WOSTOK PRESS/S. Levigoureux; 12/13: WOSTOK PRESS/G. Giuglio; 14t: HOA QUI/W. Buss; 14/15b: PHOTONONSTOP/B. Morandi; 15t: ANZENBERGER/M. Horvath; 16t: HOA QUI/Ph. Roy; 16/17b: O. GRUNEWALD; 17, 18: BIOS/PANDA PHOTO/A. Nardi; 18/19: BIOS/M. Gunther; 20tl: G. DAGLI ORTI/Museum of History, Bucharest, Romania; 20tr: G. DAGLI ORTI/Archaeological Museum, Plovdiv, Bulgaria; 20bl: © Encyclopaedia Universalis, after Z. Rajewski, *Biskupin*, 1970; 20br: G. DAGLI ORTI/Kazanlak, Bulgaria; 21tr: AKG Paris/E. Lessing; 21m: ANA/P. Cronenberger; 21bl: THE BRIDGEMAN ART LIBRARY/*The baptism of grand duke Vladimir of Kiev*, mural, 1885-1896, by V. Mikhailovitch Vasnetsov (1848-1926), cathedral Vladimir, Kiev, Ukraine; 21br: G. DAGLI ORTI/gallery of 14th century icons, St-Clement Studio, Ohrid, Macedonia; 22tr: HOA QUI/W. Buss; 22ml: G. DAGLI ORTI/*Jan Huss burnt at the stake* Chronicles of Ulrico de Richental, 15th century. National University Library, Prague, Czech Republic; 22b: R. HOLZBACHOVA - P. BENET; 23t: AKG, Paris/E. Lessing/Altarpiece *Scenes from the life and from the Passion of Christ*, 1477-89 Veit Stoss 1140/50-1533 Church of Notre-Dame, Cracow, Poland; 23bl: G. DAGLI ORTI/Nicolas Copernicus, Cracow, Poland; 23mr: G. DAGLI ORTI/*Mathias, king of Hungary*, Lombard school 1485-90, Gallery of Hungarian Art, Budapest, Hungary; 23br: G. DAGLI ORTI/*The Battle of Mohács*, 1526 (detail), Muslim manuscript 'Hunername', Loqman Library at Topkapi, Istanbul, Turkey; 24tl: AKG, Paris/*Defenestration of Prague, 23 May 1618*, 1889, by W. von Brozik (1851-1901); 24tr: AKG, Paris/E. Lessing/*Battle of Mont Blanc*, by P. Snayers (1592-1667)/Musée du Louvre, Paris; 24m: J.-L. CHARMET/Bibliothèque des Arts décoratifs, Paris; 24b: J.L. CHARMET/Bibliothèque nationale, Paris; 25tl: AKG, Paris/T. Kosciuszko, by R. Weibezahl, 1832/Museum of History C. v Rotteck, Pest, Hungary; 25tr: G. DAGLI ORTI/*Marie-Thérèse of Austria*, by M. van Meytens (1695-1770)/Museum of the City, Vienna, Austria; 25bl: G. DAGLI ORTI/Historical Museum of Lorraine, Nancy, France; 25br: PHOTONONSTOP/J. Sierpinski; 26tl: AKG, Paris/*The Polish Prometheus*, 1831, by H. Vernet (1789-1863)/Polish Historical and Literary Society, Paris; 26tr, bl: AKG, Paris; 26br: G. DAGLI ORTI/Museum of the City, Vienna, Austria; 27tl: AKG, Paris/F.C. Wentzel/Private collection, Weissenburg, Germany; 27tr: J. VIGNE/*Le Petit Journal*, 8 December 1912; 27br, 28tl: AKG, Paris; 28tr: J.-L. CHARMET/Photo in *An outlaws diary: Revolution*, 1935-39, by C. de Tormay/Private collection, London; 28m: J.-L. CHARMET/Bibliothèque des Arts décoratifs, Paris; 28br, 29t, bl: AKG, Paris; 29br: HOA QUI/E. Simanor; 30t: AFP/INTERCONTINENTALE; 30ml, mr: AFP; 30b: MAGNUM PHOTOS/J. Koudelka; 31tl: CORBIS SYGMA/P. Habans; 31tr: AFP/L. Kotek - J. Robine; 31m: AFP/J. Robine; 31bl: BOOMERANG/A. P/B.J. Holzner; 31br: AFP/A. Kisbenedek: 32/33: HEMISPHERES/P. Wysocki; 34/35: WOSTOK PRESS/G. Giuglio; 36t: BIOS/M. Gunther; 36bl: COSMOS/P. Boulat; 36br: HOA QUI/D. Noirot; 37t: BIOS/M. Gunther; 37br: BIOS/W.W.F/N. Dickinson; 38/39t: EXPLORER/J.-P. Courau; 38bl: DIAF/F. Soreau; 38br: BIOS/P. Labarbe; 39bl: PHOTONONSTOP/THE PHOTOGRAPHERS CONSORTIUM/C. Bowman; 39br: HOA QUI/P & C. Weisbecker; 40t: HOA QUI/Ph. Roy; 40bl: WOSTOK PRESS/G. Giuglio; 40br: G. DAGLI ORTI/Fishermen on lake Balaton, by M. Geza (1844-87)/National Gallery, Budapest, Hungary; 41t, b: BIOS/R. Rosenthal; 42t: COSMOS/M. Beziat; 42b: BIOS/P. Malczevski; 43tl: HOA QUI/W. Buss; 43tr: BIOS/Klein-Hubert; 43b: O. GRUNEWALD; 44/45t: HEMISPHERES/G. Giulio; 44bl: PHOTONONSTOP/B. Morandi; 44/45b: BIOS/P. Walczeweki; 45tr: BIOS/ M. Gunther; 45m: PHOTONONSTOP/B. Morandi/Architect: L. Cherwol, 1912; 45br: PHOTONONSTOP/T. Waldvski; 46/47: CORBIS SYGMA/S. Attal; 48t: AFP/M. Malinovsky; 48m: REA/F. Levillain; 48bl: WOSTOK PRESS/G. Zarand; 48br: COSMOS/R. Crandall; 49tr: HOA QUI/W. Buss; 49tl: RAPHO/NETWORK/CH. Pilliz; 49br: RAPHO/NETWORK/B. Lewis; 50tr: PHOTONONSTOP/B. Morandi; 50m: WOSTOK PRESS/D. Chouquet; 50b: HOA QUI/W. Buss; 51tl: RAPHO/NETWORK/J. Leighton; 51m: REA/R. Unkel; 51bl: WOSTOK PRESS/I. Benko; 51br: AFP/M. Malinovsky; 52tr: RIA-NOVOSTI/I. Abramotchkine; 52bl: MAGNUM/M. Franck; 52br: AFP/R. Ghement; 53tl, tr: EDITING/P. Schuller; 53mr: REA/SMITH REFLEX/D. Stewart; 53b: HOA QUI/W. Buss; 54tr: CORBIS SYGMA; 54m: ALTITUDE/Y. Arthus-Bertrand; 54b: RAPHO/H. Donnezan; 55t: WOSTOK PRESS/G. Alain; 55bl: AFP/S. Supinsky; 55br: WOSTOK PRESS/F. Zecchin; 56tr, m: HOA QUI/Ph. Roy; 56bl: © Pilsner Urquell; 56b: RAPHO/NETWORK/Ch. Pillitz; 57t: ANA/J.J. Sommeryns; 57ml, b: ANA/P. Cronenberger; 58t: HOA QUI/S Grandadam; 58bl: © Bulgarian Pharmatical Group Ltd; 59tr: CORBIS SYGMA; 59tl: WOSTOK PRESS/D. Chouquet; 59m: HOA QUI/W. Buss; 59b: CORBIS SYGMA/P. Caron; 60/61: HEMISPHERES/B. Gardel; 62t: BOOMERANG/A. P/V. Ghirda; 62m: RIA-NOVOSTI/V. Rodionov; 62bl: WOSTOK PRESS/A. Morkovkin; 62b: RIA-NOVOSTI; 63tl: RIA-NOVOSTI/I. Zenine; 63tr: AFP/V. Drachev; 63bl: AFP/A. Sapronenko; 63br: AFP/S. Supinsky; 64tl: M. LANGROGNET/© Budapester Zeitung; 64tr: M. LANGROGNET/© Pester Lloyd; 64m: EDITING/P. Bard; 64b: GAMMA; 65t: AFP/A. Niedringhaus; 65m: WOSTOK PRESS/Puskas; 65b, 66tr: A. KELER; 66ml: WOSTOK PRESS/I. Benko; 66mr: A. KELER; 66b: WOSTOK PRESS/E. Prinvault; 67tl: WOSTOK PRESS/G. Giuglio; 67m: WOSTOK PRESS/R. Colin; 67b: CORBIS SYGMA/Ph. Caron; 68t: HEMISPHERES/A. Soumillard; 68m: HOA QUI/W. Buss; 68bl: HEMISPHERES/B. Gardel; 68br: WOSTOK PRESS/H. Dez; 69t: COSMOS/ANZENBERGER/R. Haidinger; 69tr: RAPHO/F. Ducasse; 69m: HOA QUI/W. Buss; 69b: RAPHO/F. Ancellet; 70tr: VANDYSTADT/ALLSPORT/R. Cheyne; 70tl: CORBIS SYGMA/TEMPSPORT/Richiardi; 70bl: VANDYSTADT/ALLSPORT/A. Pretty; 70br: PRESSE-SPORT; 71tl: VANDYSTADT/ALLSPORT; 71tr: VANDYSTADT/ALLSPORT/M. Steele; 71bl: VANDYSTADT/ALLSPORT/J. Patronite; 71br: VANDYSTADT/ALLSPORT/T. Duffy; 72tl: AFP/V. Drachev; 72mr: PHOTONONSTOP/J.D. Sudres; 72bl, br: R. HOLZBACHOVA - P. BENET; 73tr: STUDIO X/BILDERBERG/M. Kirchgessner; 73m: HEMISPHERES/M. Borgese; 73bl: CORBIS SYGMA/S. Attal; 73br: RMN/G. Blot/*Gospel of the Meanil monastery*/National Museum, Bucharest, Romania; 74t: HOA QUI/W. Buss; 74m: COSMOS/CONTACT/G. Gordoni; 74bl: CORBIS SYGMA/F. Pagani; 74br: R. HOLZBACHOVA - P. BENET; 75tl: CIRIC/A. Pinoges; 75tr: J. LEON MULLER; 75b: CIRIC/S. Sprague; 76tr: CORBIS SYGMA/P. Turnley; 76ml: PHOTONONSTOP/J. Sierpinski; 76b: WOSTOK PRESS/G. Giuglio; 77t: WOSTOK PRESS/A. Morkovkin; 77bl: HEMISPHERES/B. Gardel; 77br: WOSTOK PRESS; 78t: HOA QUI/ C. Sappa; 78m: WOSTOK PRESS/G. Giuglio; 78b: CORBIS SYGMA/S. Compoint; 79t: EXPLORER/J.M. Steinlein; 79m, b: ANA/R. Charret; 80tr: WOSTOK PRESS/J. Wishnetsky; 80m: PHOTONONSTOP/B. Morandi; 80bl: PHOTONONSTOP/J.D. Sudres; 80bm: HOA QUI/P & C. Weisbecker; 81t: PHOTONONSTOP/J.D. Sudres; 81m: COSMOS/ANZENBERGER/M. Horvath; 81bl: ANA/P. Cronenberger; 81br: M. LANGROGNET/© Zubrowka Pernod S. A; 82tr: WOSTOK PRESS/I. Benko; 82ml: HEMISPHERES/P. Frilet; 82b: HOA QUI/C. Sappa; 83tl: HOA QUI/W. Buss; 83tr: J.-L. CHARMET/Postcard 1906/Private collection; 83bl: PHOTONONSTOP/R. Mazin; 83br: WOSTOK PRESS/G. Giuglio; 84t: PHOTONONSTOP/B. Morandi; 84bl: REA/L. Marin; 84br: ANA/S. Amantini; 85tl: HOA QUI/ICÔNE/Y. Gellie; 85tr: WOSTOK PRESS/R. Colin; 85bl: ANA/G. Cozzi; 85br: HOA QUI/G. Guittard; 86/87: ANA/M. Borchi; 88t: COSMOS/B. Sacha; 88bl: HOA QUI/W. Buss; 88br: COSMOS/B. Sacha; 89tl, tm: ANA/M. Borchi; 89tr: HEMISPHERES/P. Wysocky; 89b: HOA QUI/W. Buss; 90t, m, bl: CORBIS SYGMA/C. Redondo; 91tl: HOA QUI/C. Sappa; 91tr, b: ANA/J.J. Sommeryns; 92t: ANA/P. Cronenberger/Architect: J. Feketehazy, 1894-9; 92/93b: PHOTONONSTOP/SIME/G. Simeone; 93t: COSMOS/ANZENBERGER/M. Horvath; 93b: COSMOS/ANZENBERGER/J. Polleross; 94tl: ANA/P. Cronenberger; 94tr: HOA QUI/C. Sappa; 94b: PHOTONONSTOP/R. Mazin; 95t: ANA/G. Cozzi; 95m: ANA/J. J. Sommeryns; 95b: COSMOS/ANZENBERGER/M. Horvath/Statue of Bela Kun by Varga Imre/Sculpture Park, Budapest, Hungary; 96tr: CORBIS SYGMA/V. Rastelli; 96m: CORBIS SYGMA/P. M. Wilson; 96bl: PHOTONONSTOP/SIME/G. Simeone; 96br: HEMISPHERES/B. Gardel; 97tr, m: HOA QUI/W. Buss; 97b: RAPHO/J.M. Charles; 98/103: R. HOLZBACHOVA - P. BENET; 98t: HOA QUI/Ph. Renault; 98bl: HOA QUI/W. Buss; 98br: WOSTOK PRESS/G. Giuglio; 99t, m, bl: R. HOLZBACHOVA - P. BENET; 99mr: HOA QUI/S. Grandadam; 99br: WOSTOK PRESS/G. Giuglio; 100tr: R. HOLZBACHOVA - P. BENET; 100bl: HOA QUI/C. Sappa; 100bm, 100/101b: R. HOLZBACHOVA - P. BENET; 101tl: WOSTOK PRESS/P. Zupnik; 101tr: WOSTOK PRESS/C. Shyman; 101br: HOA QUI/Ph. Renault; 102tl: PHOTONONSTOP/R. Mazin; 102tm: ANA/S. Cellai; 102ml: HOA QUI/Ph. Renault; 102mm: EXPLORER/P. Wysocki; 102mr: WOSTOK PRESS/G. Giuglio; 102bl: R. HOLZBACHOVA - P. BENET; 102bm: PHOTONONSTOP/J. Sierpinski; 102br: HOA QUI/C. Sappa; 103t: ANA/S. Cellai; 103bl: HOA QUI/Ph. Renault; 103br: R. HOLZBACHOVA - P. BENET; 104tm: HOA QUI/P. Escudero; 104tr: ANA/S. Cellai; 104b: PHOTONONSTOP/F. Soreau; 105tl: PHOTONONSTOP/J.D. Sudres; 105mr: PHOTONONSTOP/J.-D. Sudres/Sculptor: Natan Rapaport -Architect: M. Suzin, 1948; 105b: ANA/S. Amantini; 106t: HOA QUI/W. Buss; 106bl: ANA/G. Cozzi; 106br, 107tl, m: HOA QUI/W. Buss; 107b: RAPHO/M. Baret; 108tr, m: HOA QUI/W. Buss; 108bl: RIA-NOVOSTI/I. Somov - E. Koktyche; 108br: RIA-NOVOSTI/S. Samokhine/Architect: Y. Ginka, Y. Linevitch, A. Gorbatchev, 1965; 109t: RIA-NOVOSTI/B. Manouchine; 109m: RIA-NOVOSTI/B. Babanov; 109b: RIA-NOVOSTI/Y. Somov; 110tl: NATIONAL GEOGRAPHIC/D. Conger; 110tr: AFP/S. Supinsky; 110b: HOA QUI/B. Perousse; 111t: CORBIS SYGMA/Ch. O'Rear; 111m: CORBIS SYGMA/D. Conger; 111br: HOA QUI/W. Buss; 111b: HOA QUI/P. Perousse; 112tr, m: PHOTONONSTOP/B. Morandi; 112b: RAPHO/G. Nutan; 113t: PHOTONONSTOP/D. Thierry; 113bl: CORBIS SYGMA/P. Turnley; 113br: CORBIS SYGMA/D. & P. Turnley; 114t, m: CORBIS SYGMA/Ph. Caron; 114b: COSMOS/N. Jallot; 115t: EXPLORER/L. Fleury; 115bl: REALSOFT/V. Corcimari/*Nezavisimaya Moldova*, with thanks to Dimitrii Lozan; 115br: HOA QUI/W. Buss; 116t: COSMOS/J. Wishnetsky; 116bl: REA/LAIF/R. Bermes; 116br: COSMOS/R. Crandall; 117tl: G. DAGLI ORTI/Museum of History, Sofia, Bulgaria; 117tr: CORBIS SYGMA/S. Attal; 117m: CORBIS SYGMA/S. Vannini; 117bl: G. DAGLI ORTI; 117br: WOSTOK PRESS/J. Wishnetsky; 118/119: RAPHO/G. Sioen; 120tr: J. VIGNE; 120m: THE BRIDGEMAN ART LIBRARY/*Franz Kafka*, 1992/I. Hughes, The Feming-Wyfold Art Foundation; 120bl: L. MONNIER; 120br: W. Oschatz © Suhrkamp Verlag, Frankfurt; 121tl: J.-L. CHARMET; 121tr: CORBIS SYGMA/S. Bassouls; 121m: L. MONNIER; 121bl: CORBIS SYGMA/E. Grochowiak; 121br: R. HOLZBACHOVA - P. BENET; 122t: AGENCE ENGUERAND/BERNAND/T. Valès ; 122m: AGENCE ENGUERAND/BERNAND/B. Enguerand/*Love in the Crimea*, S. Mzorek/production by: J. Lavelli, 1994 – Théâtre de la Colline, Paris; 122bl: R. HOLZBACHOVA - P. BENET/Archives of the National Theatre, Prague; 122br: AGENCE ENGUERAND/BERNAND/M. Enguerand/*Let the Artists Die*, T. Kantor, 1985, Avignon, France; 123tr: THE BRIDGEMAN ART LIBRARY/*The Samaritan*, 1897, by Alfons Mucha (1860-1939)/Ferrers Gallery, London © ADAGP, Paris, 2001; 123bl: BIBLIOTHÈQUE FORNEY/*The Rite of Spring, circa* 1967, Jan Lenica Wielki Theatre, Warsaw, Pologne © ADAGP, Paris, 2001; 123br: CIRIP/A. Gesgon/*Amnesty International*, 1975 – Roman Cieslewicz (1930-96) © ADAGP, Paris, 2001; 124tr: RUE DES ARCHIVES; 124ml: CORBIS SYGMA/Ch. Simonpietri; 124b: CORBIS SYGMA/E. Grochowiak; 125t: RUE DES ARCHIVES/*The Shout*, 1978, J. Skolimowski; 125bl: RUE DES ARCHIVES/*Wygasle Czasy*, 1987, K. Zanussi; 125br: CORBIS SYGMA/COLL. KIPA/*Three Colours – Red*, 1996, K. Kieslowski; 126t: RUE DES ARCHIVES/*One Flew Over the Cuckoo's Nest*, 1975, M. Forman; 126m: COLL. CHRISTOPHE L/*Ubu*, J. Lenica, 1979/© ADAGP, Paris, 2001 ; 126bl: RUE DES ARCHIVES; 126br: collection of the International Institute of Puppetry, Charleville-Mézières; 127tr: Ex-Libris/J. Skupa (1892-1957), UNIMA, Prague, with the kind permission of Mrs Malikova; 127m: collection of the International Institute of Puppetry, Charleville-Mezières; 127bl: R. HOLZBACHOVA - P. BENET; 127br: collection of the International Institute of Puppetry, Charleville-Mezières ; 128tr: *Brassaï in his laboratory*, 1931-2, Brassaï (1899-1984)/© Gilberte Brassaï; 128m: MAGNUM PHOTOS/*Ukraine, ferme collective*, 1947, R. Capa (1913-1954); 128b: PATRIMOINE PHOTOGRAPHIQUE/*Wandering Musician*, 1921, Abony, Hungary/Photo A. Kertesz (1894-1985)/© Ministrt of Culture, France; 129tl: THE BRIDGEMAN ART LIBRARY/*The Cock*, 1924, C. Brancusi/Musée national d'art moderne, Paris © ADAGP, Paris, 2001; 129mt: ANA/J. J. Sommeryns; 129bl: THE BRIDGEMAN ART LIBRARY/*Self-portrait*, L. Moholy-Naguy (1895-1946)/Hungarian Gallery Nemzeti, Budapest, Hungary © ADAGP, Paris, 2001; 129br: G. DAGLI ORTI/*Lines, Surfaces, Depths*, 1913-14/F. Kupka (1871-1957)/Naitonal Gallery, Prague © ADAGP, Paris, 2001; 130tr: CORBIS SYGMA/ Hulton-Deutsch Collection; 130m: THE BRIDGEMAN ART LIBRARY/*Moravska Lidora Poésie*, L. Janacek illustrated by K. Svolinsky, 1896/British Library, London; 130bl: THE BRIDGEMAN ART LIBRARY/*B. Smetana (1824-84) and his friends in 1865*, 1923/F. Dvorak, 1862/Private Collection Philips, The International Fine Art Auctioneers; 130br: G. DAGLI ORTI/Archives of A. Dvorak, Prague; 131tl: PHOTONONSTOP/J. Sierpinski; 131mr: G. DAGLI ORTI/House of Bela Bartok, Budapest, Hungary; 131bl: COSMOS/M. Hilgert/Sculptor: V. Szymanouwoki, 1926; 131br: MUZSIKAS FEAT. MARTA SEBESTYEN/Béla Kasa; 132tr: WOSTOK PRESS/Atila; 132ml: RAPHO/J.-M. Charles; 132br: EXPLORER/A. Philippon; 133tr: HOA QUI/W. Buss; 133m: R. HOLZBACHOVA - P. BENET; 133b: EXPLORER/GEOPRESS; 134tr: EXPLORER/R. Mattes; 134m: WOSTOK PRESS/I. Lugossy; 134b: ANA/P. Cronenberger; 134br, 135t: HEMISPHERES/B. Gardel; 135m: PHOTONONSTOP/J.-P. Garcin; 135bl: HEMISPHERES/B. Gardel; 135br: WOSTOK PRESS/J. Wishnetsky; 136/137: HOA QUI/W. Buss; 148: ANZENBERGER/T. Anzenberger; 150: AZIMUTT/F. Levillain; 152: CORBIS SYGMA/S. Attal; 153: RAPHO/W. Winckler.

Printing and binding: Printer Industria Gráfica S.A., Barcelona
Colour separations: Station Graphique, Ivry-sur-Seine

617-013-02